IBRAHIM ANDERSON

Optimized Computer Programming With C#10 And .NET 6

Dive into Advanced Strategies for Crafting Lightning-Fast, Resilient Applications with C# 10.0 and .NET 6

Copyright © 2024 by Ibrahim Anderson

All rights reserved. No part of this publication may be reproduced, stored or transmitted in any form or by any means, electronic, mechanical, photocopying, recording, scanning, or otherwise without written permission from the publisher. It is illegal to copy this book, post it to a website, or distribute it by any other means without permission.

First edition

This book was professionally typeset on Reedsy.
Find out more at reedsy.com

Contents

The Case for High Performance Computing in .NET	1
Understanding the Fundamentals of Performance Optimization	29
Advanced Multithreading with C#10	56
Memory Management and Optimization in .NET 6	86
SIMD Programming and High-Performance Math Operations	116
P/Invoke and Native Interoperability for Performance Gains	146
Low-Level Programming with Unsafe Code	176
Data Structures and Algorithms for High Performance	199
High-Performance Networking in .NET 6	219
Efficient File and I/O Handling	244
Real-World Case Studies and Challenges	265
Performance Testing and Benchmarking	281
High-Performance Data Analytics with .NET	319
High-Performance Cross-Platform Development	341
Future-Proofing High-Performance Applications	367

The Case for High Performance Computing in .NET

Defining High-Performance Computing (HPC)

High-Performance Computing (HPC) is a field dedicated to solving complex computational problems that exceed the capabilities of standard computing systems. At its core, HPC revolves around the utilization of powerful hardware and sophisticated software paradigms to process and analyze large datasets, perform massive computations, and simulate intricate models quickly and efficiently. This makes HPC indispensable in fields such as scientific research, financial modeling, medical analysis, artificial intelligence, weather forecasting, and many others where processing vast amounts of data or running intensive computations is critical.

Understanding the Concept of High-Performance Computing

HPC is fundamentally about maximizing the efficiency and speed of computational tasks by leveraging parallelism, distributed computing, and efficient algorithmic designs. Essentially, the aim of HPC is to bring greater computing power to bear on problems that would take significantly longer with traditional computing approaches.

In the context of .NET and C#, HPC is not just a theoretical concept but a practical approach to designing and building applications that need to handle high volumes of data or perform resource-intensive operations. With recent advancements in C#10 and .NET 6, developers now have access to a robust set of tools and libraries that enable them to achieve high levels of performance without sacrificing productivity or ease of development.

Key Elements of HPC

High-Performance Computing is characterized by a few key elements:

1. **Parallel Processing:** One of the core aspects of HPC is the use of parallel processing, where tasks are divided into smaller sub-tasks that can be executed simultaneously across multiple processing units (CPUs or GPUs). This is often achieved through multithreading, multiprocessing, or using specialized frameworks for parallel computing.
2. **Distributed Computing:** HPC applications often leverage distributed computing techniques to spread computations across multiple machines or nodes in a network. This allows for handling significantly larger datasets and performing computations at scales that would be impossible on a single machine.
3. **Optimized Algorithms:** HPC applications rely on highly optimized algorithms that are tailored to extract maximum performance from the underlying hardware. These algorithms are designed to minimize complexity and utilize advanced data structures for efficiency.
4. **Efficient Memory Management:** In HPC, memory usage plays a crucial role. Efficient management of memory resources, such as minimizing memory fragmentation, reducing garbage collection impact, and leveraging low-level optimizations, is critical to achieving high performance.

The Need for HPC

Why does the world need High-Performance Computing? The answer lies in the ever-increasing demand for processing power. As technology advances, the scope and complexity of problems that need to be solved are growing exponentially. Whether it's in the realm of real-time data analysis for stock markets, simulation of nuclear reactions, or training sophisticated machine learning models, traditional computing resources often fall short.

HPC solutions are designed to fill this gap by providing a framework to harness greater computational power, either through scaling up (adding more powerful processors) or scaling out (using more machines). The development of sophisticated algorithms and parallel processing techniques allows HPC to push the boundaries of what is computationally feasible.

Applications of High-Performance Computing

1. **Scientific Research and Simulations:**
2. One of the most well-known applications of HPC is in the field of scientific research. From simulating molecular interactions in drug discovery to modeling climate change patterns and astrophysical phenomena, HPC has revolutionized how scientists conduct research. The power to run simulations and analyze results quickly has enabled researchers to make groundbreaking discoveries at an unprecedented rate.
3. **Financial Modeling and Risk Analysis:**
4. In the financial sector, HPC is used to run complex algorithms for risk assessment, market predictions, and real-time analytics. Financial institutions rely heavily on high-performance computing for tasks such as algorithmic trading, portfolio optimization, and fraud detection.
5. **Machine Learning and Artificial Intelligence:**
6. HPC plays a vital role in the development and training of machine learning models. Training neural networks, especially deep learning models, requires substantial computational power, and HPC clusters with powerful GPUs are commonly used to speed up this process.
7. **Weather Forecasting and Climate Studies:**
8. Accurate weather forecasting depends on the processing and analysis of massive datasets, which include satellite data, historical weather patterns, and real-time sensor information. HPC systems enable meteorologists to run simulations and predictive models that would be impossible with traditional computing systems.
9. **Medical Imaging and Genomics:**
10. In the field of healthcare, HPC is used to analyze medical images and

genetic data. It aids in tasks such as cancer detection through image recognition algorithms, genome sequencing for personalized medicine, and simulating the effects of drugs on the human body.

Performance Metrics in HPC

High-Performance Computing focuses on improving specific performance metrics. These metrics determine the efficiency and effectiveness of a high-performance solution:

1. **Throughput:** This refers to the number of operations or tasks that can be completed within a given time frame. In HPC, increasing throughput is often achieved by parallelizing tasks and utilizing distributed systems.
2. **Latency:** Latency measures the time delay between an input or request and the corresponding output or response. HPC aims to minimize latency by optimizing code execution paths and efficiently managing I/O operations.
3. **Scalability:** Scalability refers to the ability of a system to handle increased workload by adding resources such as more processors, memory, or nodes. An HPC solution must be designed to scale efficiently without significant performance degradation.
4. **Efficiency:** Efficiency is defined as the ratio of useful work done by a system to the total energy consumed. Optimized algorithms and hardware-aware programming techniques in HPC are employed to improve efficiency and reduce unnecessary energy usage.
5. **Resource Utilization:** In HPC, the goal is to make optimal use of the available computational resources. This means maximizing CPU and memory utilization while minimizing idle time or bottlenecks.

High-Performance Computing in .NET and C#10

With the release of C#10 and .NET 6, Microsoft has introduced several features and enhancements that align closely with the principles of High-Performance Computing. These include:

1. **Improved Asynchronous Programming Capabilities:**
2. C#10 continues to refine asynchronous programming with enhanced language features and APIs. Asynchronous code execution is fundamental in many HPC scenarios to ensure that I/O-bound tasks do not become bottlenecks.
3. **Memory Efficiency with Span<T> and Memory<T>:**
4. Managing memory efficiently is crucial in HPC. .NET 6 provides several constructs like *Span<T>*, *Memory<T>*, and ref structs that allow developers to perform memory operations without unnecessary copying or allocations. These types offer a way to work with arrays and memory buffers in a highly performant manner.
5. **Parallel Programming with the Task Parallel Library (TPL):**
6. TPL in .NET 6 offers developers a simple yet powerful way to write multithreaded applications. It abstracts the complexities of managing threads, enabling developers to focus on designing high-performance solutions that take full advantage of multicore processors.
7. **SIMD Support for Vectorized Operations:**
8. SIMD (Single Instruction, Multiple Data) allows the execution of the same operation on multiple data points simultaneously. .NET 6 has improved support for SIMD instructions, enabling developers to write code that takes advantage of vectorized computations to boost performance.
9. **Native Interoperability:**
10. Sometimes, achieving high performance requires leveraging low-level optimizations or calling into native code. .NET 6 provides robust interop capabilities that allow seamless integration with C or C++ code. This can be useful in scenarios where native code libraries offer specialized optimizations or hardware-specific advantages.

High-Performance Computing Beyond Hardware

HPC is not solely about hardware improvements; it also focuses on the efficient use of existing resources through better software design, algorithm optimization, and leveraging modern programming paradigms. While high-performance hardware such as multicore processors and GPUs are essential, efficient software is what enables these hardware resources to be utilized effectively.

The combination of .NET 6's optimizations and C#10's new features provides developers with a versatile platform for tackling high-performance tasks. By adopting best practices in parallel programming, memory management, and leveraging the latest advancements in the .NET ecosystem, developers can build applications capable of processing vast datasets, running complex simulations, and delivering results faster than ever before.

The Future of HPC in .NET Development

As technology evolves, so does the need for more computational power. The ongoing improvements in .NET and C# are paving the way for future developments in High-Performance Computing. Looking ahead, we can expect the following trends to shape the future of HPC in .NET development:

1. **Improved Support for GPU Computing:**
2. While .NET currently has some support for GPU-based computations through libraries like *DirectCompute* or interop with CUDA, we can anticipate more seamless integration of GPU-based programming models in future versions of .NET.
3. **Integration with AI and Machine Learning:**
4. As AI and machine learning continue to grow in prominence, .NET's ecosystem is expanding to support these workloads more effectively. This includes optimized libraries and frameworks designed to run AI models efficiently on .NET platforms.
5. **Advancements in Quantum Computing:**
6. While still in its early stages, quantum computing has the potential to revolutionize HPC. .NET developers are already exploring quantum computing through Microsoft's *Quantum Development Kit (QDK)*, which provides tools to experiment with quantum algorithms.
7. **Cloud-Based HPC Solutions:**
8. The rise of cloud computing has made HPC resources more accessible than ever. Azure and other cloud providers offer powerful HPC clusters

on-demand, allowing developers to scale their applications without investing in on-premises infrastructure. The .NET ecosystem is well-positioned to leverage these cloud-based solutions, enabling developers to build high-performance applications in a cost-effective and scalable manner.

High-Performance Computing is a critical discipline that enables developers to push the boundaries of what is computationally possible. By leveraging parallelism, optimized algorithms, and efficient memory management, HPC applications can handle immense workloads and deliver results faster than traditional computing solutions.

For developers working in the .NET ecosystem, understanding and implementing HPC principles is essential. With C#10 and .NET 6, Microsoft has provided a powerful set of tools and features that make it easier than ever to build high-performance applications. By mastering these capabilities, developers can tackle even the most demanding computational challenges with confidence and efficiency.

HPC in .NET isn't just about improving performance; it's about reimagining what's possible in software development. From scientific research to financial modeling, from AI to real-time analytics, the future of High-Performance Computing in .NET promises to be an exciting journey of innovation and discovery.

Why Choose C#10 and .NET 6 for HPC?

Choosing the right tools and platform is critical when developing high-performance applications. Traditionally, C++ has been the go-to language for high-performance computing due to its low-level capabilities and fine-grained control over system resources. However, with the advancements in C#10 and .NET 6, developers now have a viable and often more productive alternative that delivers robust performance without sacrificing modern language features or ease of development.

1. Modern Language Features with Performance Focus

C#10 continues to push the boundaries of what a modern programming language can offer. Microsoft has consistently aimed to introduce language features that not only enhance developer productivity but also contribute to better performance. Key improvements and features in C#10 make it a strong candidate for High-Performance Computing:

- **Enhanced Pattern Matching:** The improvements in pattern matching allow for more expressive and concise code. It enables developers to write cleaner conditional logic, which indirectly aids in code maintenance and optimization.
- **Record Types and Value-Based Equality:** C#10 introduces further refinements in record types, which offer developers a way to model immutable data structures with value-based equality. For high-performance applications, immutability can help avoid unnecessary copying of data and improve thread safety in concurrent environments.
- **Source Generators:** Source Generators, introduced in .NET 5 and refined in .NET 6, allow developers to generate code at compile-time. This reduces the runtime overhead and can be used to optimize performance-critical sections of code by automating repetitive patterns or injecting boilerplate code.
- **Minimal APIs:** Although primarily aimed at simplifying web development, the minimal API structure in .NET 6 can be leveraged to build lightweight, high-performance services and microservices, which are often integral to HPC scenarios.

2. Significant Performance Enhancements in .NET 6

.NET 6 brings a host of performance optimizations that make it a compelling choice for HPC applications. These optimizations cover various areas such as just-in-time (JIT) compilation, garbage collection, memory management, and runtime improvements:

- **Improved JIT Compiler:** The new Tiered Compilation approach optimizes the startup and runtime performance of applications. The JIT compiler progressively compiles the code in multiple passes, applying more aggressive optimizations as the application runs longer. This leads to faster execution for long-running applications, a common scenario in HPC.
- **Garbage Collection (GC) Enhancements:** .NET 6 offers numerous improvements in garbage collection, reducing GC pause times and improving overall throughput. For high-performance computing, where large datasets and frequent memory allocations are the norms, minimizing GC pauses is critical to achieving consistent performance.
- **Profile-Guided Optimization (PGO):** PGO is an advanced optimization technique that uses runtime profile information to optimize code paths that are frequently executed. In HPC, this can lead to significant performance gains in scenarios where certain computational routines are repeatedly invoked.
- **Native Interoperability Improvements:** .NET 6 enhances interoperability with native code, allowing developers to call into unmanaged libraries or APIs without significant overhead. This opens up possibilities for integrating high-performance native libraries or leveraging specialized hardware optimizations.

3. Comprehensive Parallel and Asynchronous Programming Model

One of the pillars of High-Performance Computing is the ability to parallelize workloads and perform asynchronous operations efficiently. C#10 and .NET 6 provide a rich set of libraries and constructs that make this possible:

- **Task Parallel Library (TPL):** TPL abstracts away the complexity of managing threads and thread pools, allowing developers to focus

on writing parallelized code. It provides constructs like Parallel.For, Parallel.ForEach, and Task.WhenAll, which enable easy scaling of compute-bound operations across multiple cores.
- **Asynchronous Programming with Async/Await:** C#10's async/await syntax is a powerful tool for managing asynchronous operations without blocking threads. This is essential for I/O-bound HPC tasks, where reading or writing large datasets to disk or network can be a significant bottleneck.
- **Parallel LINQ (PLINQ):** PLINQ extends the capabilities of LINQ (Language Integrated Query) by introducing parallel execution. This allows developers to query collections concurrently, which can lead to substantial performance improvements when processing large datasets.

4. SIMD Support and Hardware Acceleration

.NET 6 has continued to improve support for SIMD (Single Instruction Multiple Data) operations. SIMD enables the execution of a single instruction on multiple data points simultaneously, leveraging modern CPU architectures. This is especially beneficial for high-performance computing scenarios involving numerical computations, image processing, or vector calculations:

- **Vector<T> Types:** .NET's System.Numerics namespace includes the Vector<T> types that allow developers to write vectorized code using familiar C# constructs. These types automatically map to the underlying SIMD instructions supported by the CPU, boosting the performance of data-parallel computations.
- **Hardware Acceleration through Intrinsics:** For developers needing even more control over hardware, .NET 6 offers the ability to write low-level, hardware-specific instructions through intrinsics. This allows direct access to processor-specific features like AVX (Advanced Vector Extensions) or SSE (Streaming SIMD Extensions).

5. Memory Efficiency and Low-Level Programming Capabilities

HPC applications are often memory-intensive, requiring careful management of memory allocations and deallocations to avoid bottlenecks. C#10 and .NET 6 provide several features to help developers write memory-efficient code:

- **Span<T> and Memory<T>:** The introduction of *Span<T>* and *Memory<T>* types in .NET provides developers with the ability to perform safe, low-overhead slicing of arrays and buffers without incurring the costs of copying. This is invaluable for scenarios where large arrays or memory blocks need to be processed in a high-performance context.
- **Ref Structs and ByRef Returns:** The concept of ref struct in C# enables stack-only allocations, avoiding heap allocations and minimizing garbage collection pressure. When combined with by-ref returns, it provides a way to write performant code that accesses memory directly without unnecessary indirection.
- **Unsafe Code and Pointers:** C#10 offers the flexibility of using unsafe code for situations where low-level memory manipulation is required. While unsafe code should be used with caution, it allows developers to access pointers and manipulate memory directly, which can be critical for squeezing out extra performance in memory-bound applications.

6. High-Performance I/O Operations

I/O is a major performance bottleneck in many applications, especially in scenarios involving large datasets. C#10 and .NET 6 introduce several features to improve the efficiency of I/O-bound operations:

- **Asynchronous Streams:** Asynchronous streams allow developers to consume data asynchronously, minimizing blocking and improving throughput. This is particularly useful in HPC scenarios where data from files, databases, or network streams must be processed efficiently.
- **FileStream Enhancements:** .NET 6 offers optimizations in file I/O operations by reducing allocations and improving buffer management within the FileStream class. This leads to faster file read and write

operations, which are crucial for data-intensive HPC tasks.

7. Cross-Platform Support and Scalability

.NET 6 is a truly cross-platform framework, allowing developers to build and deploy high-performance applications on Windows, Linux, and macOS. This broad support offers several key advantages:

- **Cross-Platform Consistency:** The ability to write high-performance code that runs consistently across different operating systems is a significant advantage for organizations with diverse infrastructure requirements. This also opens up the possibility of using Linux-based HPC clusters or cloud-based solutions.
- **Docker and Kubernetes Integration:** The cross-platform nature of .NET 6, combined with containerization technologies like Docker, makes it easier to deploy HPC workloads in containerized environments. This is particularly beneficial for scaling applications in distributed systems and managing large-scale deployments on platforms like Kubernetes.

8. Native Support for Cloud-Based HPC Solutions

The integration between .NET and Azure enables developers to leverage powerful cloud-based HPC solutions. Azure provides a range of HPC services, including scalable compute resources, parallel file systems, and specialized machine learning infrastructure. With .NET 6, developers can build applications that seamlessly integrate with Azure's HPC offerings:

- **Azure Batch for HPC Workloads:** Azure Batch is a cloud-based service that allows developers to scale large parallel and batch workloads efficiently. By using .NET 6, developers can create batch processing applications that automatically scale based on demand, reducing the overhead of managing on-premises infrastructure.
- **Integration with Azure Kubernetes Service (AKS):** .NET 6's support for Kubernetes and containerized deployments enables HPC applications to be orchestrated and managed using industry-standard platforms.

This ensures that large-scale applications can run efficiently in cloud environments.

9. Robust Ecosystem and Community Support

One of the key strengths of .NET 6 and C#10 is the vibrant ecosystem and strong community support. The .NET community is active in contributing libraries, tools, and best practices, all of which enhance the productivity and effectiveness of developers working on high-performance applications:

- **Powerful Third-Party Libraries:** Libraries such as *Math.NET Numerics*, *Accord.NET*, and *Microsoft ML.NET* offer specialized functionality for mathematical computations, numerical analysis, and machine learning. These libraries, combined with .NET's native capabilities, allow developers to build sophisticated HPC applications more efficiently.
- **Open-Source and Transparent Development:** The open-source nature of .NET means that developers have complete visibility into the runtime's implementation. This transparency allows for a deeper understanding of performance-critical areas and fosters innovation in building high-performance solutions.

10. Productivity and Developer Experience

While performance is the primary goal of HPC, developer productivity remains an essential factor. C#10 and .NET 6 strike a balance between providing low-level control and maintaining a high level of productivity through modern language features and a powerful IDE (Integrated Development Environment):

- **Visual Studio and Code Profiling Tools:** Visual Studio's integrated profiling tools, along with third-party tools like *dotTrace* and *PerfView*, provide a seamless developer experience for diagnosing performance issues and fine-tuning code. These tools are essential in HPC scenarios, where identifying bottlenecks can be a complex task.
- **Language and IDE Features:** C#10's improved syntax, combined with Vi-

sual Studio's intelligent code suggestions, refactoring capabilities, and debugging tools, makes it easier to write high-performance code. This results in a shorter development cycle and fewer errors in performance-critical code paths.

C#10 and .NET 6 offer a comprehensive and powerful platform for High-Performance Computing, combining modern language features, robust runtime optimizations, and a rich set of libraries and tools. The advancements in parallel and asynchronous programming, memory efficiency, SIMD support, and cross-platform capabilities make it an excellent choice for building HPC applications in a productive and scalable manner.

By choosing C#10 and .NET 6 for HPC, developers gain the ability to leverage modern software engineering paradigms without compromising on performance. Whether it's running large-scale simulations, processing massive datasets, or building high-frequency trading systems, C#10 and .NET 6 provide the foundation and flexibility needed to achieve high levels of performance in a broad range of applications.

.NET 6 Performance Improvements: A Snapshot

One of the primary goals of .NET 6 was to enhance performance across the entire platform. The updates and changes in .NET 6 have resulted in a faster, more efficient runtime that is capable of meeting the demands of modern, high-performance applications. From just-in-time (JIT) compilation to garbage collection optimizations, .NET 6 introduces improvements that collectively provide a significant performance boost compared to its predecessors.

1. JIT Compilation and Tiered Compilation Enhancements

The JIT (Just-In-Time) compiler in .NET 6 received substantial updates, focusing on improving both startup performance and long-term execution efficiency. One of the core techniques that enable these improvements is **Tiered Compilation**. Introduced in .NET Core 3.0 and refined in .NET 6, Tiered Compilation allows the runtime to dynamically decide which parts of the code to optimize based on the frequency and criticality of execution paths.

- **Tier 0 Compilation:** This level provides a lightweight and fast compilation that prioritizes startup performance. In Tier 0, the JIT compiler quickly generates code with minimal optimization, allowing the application to begin executing almost immediately.
- **Tier 1 Compilation:** As the application runs and the runtime collects profiling information, critical or frequently executed methods are promoted to Tier 1. At this stage, the JIT compiler applies more aggressive optimizations based on the collected data, leading to improved runtime performance without requiring a complete recompilation.

This dual approach to compilation results in better startup times for short-lived applications, while longer-running applications benefit from progressively enhanced performance as they execute. For high-performance computing (HPC) applications, where long-running processes are common, Tiered Compilation offers an efficient balance between initial responsiveness and long-term performance.

2. Garbage Collection (GC) Optimizations

Garbage Collection plays a vital role in managing memory in managed environments like .NET. In high-performance scenarios, even minor GC pauses can disrupt processing, especially when dealing with large datasets or memory-intensive workloads. .NET 6 introduces several key enhancements to the GC that help mitigate these issues:

- **Improved Concurrent Garbage Collection:** .NET 6 refines the behavior of concurrent garbage collection, allowing it to work more effectively

alongside application threads. This reduces the impact of GC pauses on application performance, leading to smoother and more predictable behavior in memory-intensive applications.
- **Better Heap Fragmentation Handling:** Heap fragmentation can lead to inefficient memory usage and increased GC activity. .NET 6 includes improvements to address heap fragmentation, optimizing how the runtime allocates and deallocates memory. This results in a more compact memory layout and reduced GC overhead.
- **GC Configurability:** In .NET 6, developers have more control over GC settings, allowing them to fine-tune garbage collection behavior based on the specific requirements of their application. This is particularly useful in HPC scenarios where predictable memory behavior is crucial for performance consistency.

3. Profile-Guided Optimization (PGO)

Profile-Guided Optimization (PGO) is a sophisticated optimization technique that uses runtime-generated profiles to inform code compilation. In .NET 6, PGO plays a significant role in boosting performance by enabling the JIT compiler to make informed decisions about which code paths to optimize more aggressively.

- **Dynamic PGO:** Unlike traditional static PGO, which requires developers to provide pre-collected profiles, dynamic PGO in .NET 6 collects profile data during the actual execution of the application. This allows the runtime to adapt optimizations based on real-world usage patterns, resulting in higher efficiency and responsiveness.
- **Impact of PGO on Performance:** Dynamic PGO leads to more focused optimizations, such as inlining hot methods, better register allocation, and eliminating redundant code paths. This can lead to substantial performance gains in scenarios where certain functions or loops are heavily utilized, as is often the case in HPC applications.

4. Native Interoperability and P/Invoke Improvements

For many high-performance applications, achieving optimal results involves calling native code through mechanisms like P/Invoke (Platform Invocation). In .NET 6, improvements to native interoperability reduce the overhead associated with calling unmanaged code and interacting with native libraries:

- **Reduced Marshaling Costs:** The marshaling process, which involves converting data between managed and unmanaged formats, has been optimized in .NET 6 to reduce overhead. This is critical in HPC scenarios where frequent calls to native code can become a bottleneck.
- **DirectAccess for P/Invoke:** DirectAccess is a technique in .NET 6 that optimizes the way managed code interacts with unmanaged memory, reducing unnecessary copies and improving the efficiency of memory-bound operations. This is particularly beneficial for applications that rely on large datasets or low-level memory manipulation.

5. System.Text.Json Performance Enhancements

Serialization and deserialization are common tasks in many high-performance applications, especially those dealing with data exchange or distributed computing. .NET 6 introduces improvements to the System.Text.Json library that make it faster and more memory-efficient:

- **Faster Serialization and Deserialization:** .NET 6 includes optimizations in the System.Text.Json library that significantly improve the speed of JSON serialization and deserialization. This is achieved through improved code paths and reduced memory allocations during parsing and writing.
- **Source Generation for JSON Serialization:** .NET 6 introduces source generators for JSON serialization, allowing developers to generate serialization code at compile time. This eliminates the need for runtime reflection and reduces the overhead of dynamically building serialization logic, leading to more efficient data handling.

6. File I/O and Networking Enhancements

File I/O and network operations can become bottlenecks in HPC applications, especially when handling large datasets or communicating between distributed nodes. .NET 6 introduces several key improvements in these areas:

- **FileStream Performance Improvements:** FileStream in .NET 6 has been restructured to reduce internal allocations and improve buffer management, leading to faster file read and write operations. This results in significant performance gains in scenarios where high-throughput file access is essential.
- **Improved Sockets Performance:** .NET 6 optimizes the performance of socket operations by reducing contention in asynchronous networking code paths. This is crucial for high-performance network applications where low-latency communication is a priority.
- **HTTP/3 Support:** With the introduction of HTTP/3 in .NET 6, applications can take advantage of the latest advancements in web protocols to achieve lower latency and higher throughput in network communications. This is particularly beneficial for applications that rely on efficient data transfer across distributed systems.

7. Span<T> and Memory<T> Optimizations

Efficient memory management is crucial for achieving high performance in applications that handle large amounts of data or require frequent memory operations. .NET 6 refines the use of Span<T> and Memory<T>, providing developers with tools to perform low-overhead memory manipulations:

- **Faster Span<T> Operations:** Improvements in .NET 6 enhance the performance of common Span<T> operations, such as slicing, copying, and indexing. This allows developers to manipulate in-memory buffers more efficiently, reducing the need for unnecessary memory allocations.
- **Refined Memory Safety Features:** .NET 6 continues to provide enhanced

memory safety features, such as read-only spans and memory-mapped files. These features enable developers to perform high-performance operations without sacrificing safety or stability.

8. SIMD and Vector<T> Enhancements

SIMD (Single Instruction, Multiple Data) capabilities are essential for performing vectorized operations, which can significantly boost the performance of mathematical and numerical computations. .NET 6 continues to expand support for SIMD through enhancements to the System.Numerics namespace and Vector<T> types:

- **Expanded SIMD Operations:** .NET 6 includes optimizations and expanded support for SIMD instructions, enabling developers to write vectorized code that takes full advantage of modern CPU architectures. This is particularly beneficial for applications involving matrix calculations, image processing, or scientific simulations.
- **New Hardware Intrinsics:** In addition to existing SIMD support, .NET 6 introduces new hardware intrinsics that allow developers to directly access specialized CPU instructions. This provides greater control over low-level optimizations, enabling developers to fine-tune their applications for maximum performance.

9. Performance Improvements in Reflection and Linq

Reflection and LINQ are widely used features in many applications, but they can often introduce performance overhead. .NET 6 includes improvements that mitigate these costs:

- **Optimized Reflection:** Reflection operations in .NET 6 have been optimized to reduce their impact on performance. This is achieved through caching and improved code paths, allowing reflection-based code to execute more efficiently.
- **Improved LINQ Performance:** LINQ queries benefit from a variety of optimizations in .NET 6, including better handling of enumerables

and reduced memory allocations. These improvements lead to faster execution of LINQ-based operations, which are commonly used in data processing and transformation tasks.

10. Runtime and Library Enhancements for Performance Consistency

Finally, .NET 6 includes a range of smaller but impactful improvements across the runtime and standard libraries, all of which contribute to a more consistent and efficient performance profile:

- **Reduced Memory Allocations Across Libraries:** Many core libraries in .NET 6 have been refactored to reduce unnecessary memory allocations. This leads to lower GC pressure and improves the overall throughput of memory-bound applications.
- **Faster String Operations:** Common string operations, such as concatenation, formatting, and comparisons, have been optimized in .NET 6. This results in faster execution of string-intensive code, which is especially useful in text-heavy applications.
- **Performance Consistency Across Platforms:** One of the key goals of .NET 6 is to provide consistent performance across different operating systems. This has been achieved through improvements in cross-platform runtimes, ensuring that applications perform equally well on Windows, Linux, and macOS.

.NET 6 represents a significant leap forward in terms of performance, offering a wide range of optimizations and enhancements that make it an excellent choice for High-Performance Computing applications. From improvements in JIT compilation and garbage collection to enhanced memory management and SIMD support, .NET 6 provides developers with a comprehensive set of tools to build fast and efficient applications.

By adopting these performance improvements, developers can leverage the power of .NET 6 to tackle demanding computational workloads, process large datasets, and achieve consistent performance across platforms. As the demand for high-performance solutions continues to grow, .NET 6 positions itself as a powerful and versatile framework capable of meeting the challenges of modern computing.

Case Studies in Industry Applications

High-Performance Computing (HPC) is not just an abstract concept; it plays a crucial role across various industries, driving advancements, enabling innovations, and optimizing critical processes. From scientific research and financial modeling to machine learning and real-time analytics, HPC applications built on C#10 and .NET 6 demonstrate the versatility and power of this technology stack. This section delves into several case studies that illustrate the real-world impact of HPC solutions developed using C#10 and .NET 6.

1. Financial Services: Real-Time Risk Analysis and High-Frequency Trading

Problem Statement:

In the financial services industry, risk management and high-frequency trading (HFT) are two critical areas where performance is paramount. Financial institutions must process vast amounts of market data in real time to make informed trading decisions and assess risks accurately. Delays in processing or insufficient scalability can lead to significant financial losses.

Solution Approach:

A major investment firm decided to build a real-time risk analysis and HFT system using C#10 and .NET 6. The objective was to create an application that could:

- Ingest large volumes of market data with minimal latency.
- Execute complex algorithms for risk assessment and decision-making.

- Scale horizontally to handle increasing market fluctuations.

Implementation:

The development team utilized several features of C#10 and .NET 6 to achieve their goals:

- **Parallel Programming with TPL:** The team used the Task Parallel Library (TPL) to parallelize data processing tasks, taking advantage of multi-core CPUs to perform computations concurrently. This enabled the system to ingest and analyze vast amounts of market data without bottlenecks.
- **Memory Management with Span<T> and Ref Structs:** To handle large datasets efficiently, the developers leveraged *Span<T>* and ref structs to minimize memory allocations and avoid unnecessary copying of data. This reduced garbage collection overhead, leading to more predictable and consistent performance.
- **Low-Latency Networking with Sockets:** The application's communication layer used optimized sockets in .NET 6 to achieve low-latency data transmission between trading algorithms and market data sources. The team also implemented custom protocols to further reduce network overhead.

Outcome:

The new system achieved significantly lower latency in processing market data, resulting in faster decision-making and improved trading performance. The firm reported a 40% increase in trading execution speed and a substantial reduction in operational risk due to the real-time risk assessment capabilities. The use of C#10 and .NET 6 provided the flexibility to iterate on algorithms quickly while maintaining high performance.

2. Healthcare: Genomic Data Analysis and Personalized Medicine

Problem Statement:

In the healthcare sector, genomic data analysis is a cornerstone of personalized medicine. Analyzing large-scale genomic datasets to identify specific markers and correlations requires substantial computational power. A leading genomics research organization aimed to develop an HPC solution to speed up the analysis of patient genetic data and improve diagnosis accuracy.

Solution Approach:

The research organization chose to implement their genomic analysis pipeline using C#10 and .NET 6, focusing on creating a solution that could:

- Process terabytes of genomic data efficiently.
- Apply machine learning models to identify genetic markers.
- Scale to handle increasing volumes of data without performance degradation.

Implementation:

The development team utilized the following strategies:

- **Data Processing with PLINQ:** The organization leveraged Parallel LINQ (PLINQ) to parallelize data queries and transformations, enabling fast processing of large datasets stored in relational databases. This approach reduced the time needed to filter and aggregate data significantly.
- **Machine Learning with ML.NET:** The team employed ML.NET to build and deploy machine learning models directly within the .NET ecosystem. These models were used to classify genetic sequences and predict patient outcomes based on historical data. The ability to integrate ML.NET seamlessly with .NET 6 allowed for a streamlined workflow.
- **Efficient I/O with FileStream and Asynchronous Operations:** The team optimized file I/O operations by using asynchronous streams and the improved *FileStream* implementation in .NET 6. This allowed them to read and write large genomic datasets without causing I/O bottlenecks.

Outcome:

The HPC solution significantly reduced the time required to analyze genomic data, from several hours to under 30 minutes per patient. This enabled the research organization to provide faster diagnoses and more accurate treatment recommendations, ultimately improving patient outcomes. By leveraging .NET 6, the team was able to build a highly performant and scalable solution with a relatively small development effort.

3. Energy Sector: Real-Time Monitoring and Predictive Maintenance
Problem Statement:

In the energy sector, monitoring the health of equipment in power plants and predicting potential failures is critical to maintaining efficiency and preventing costly downtime. A global energy company needed a high-performance solution to analyze sensor data in real-time and provide predictive maintenance insights.

Solution Approach:

The company decided to build a real-time monitoring and analytics system using C#10 and .NET 6. The system needed to:

- Ingest and process real-time sensor data streams from hundreds of equipment units.
- Detect anomalies and predict equipment failures using machine learning models.
- Scale horizontally to accommodate additional power plants and equipment.

Implementation:

The development team leveraged the following capabilities:

- **Real-Time Data Ingestion with Asynchronous Streams:** The team utilized asynchronous streams in .NET 6 to efficiently process real-time sensor data without blocking threads. This allowed them to handle thousands of data points per second with minimal latency.
- **SIMD Optimizations for Anomaly Detection:** The developers used SIMD

instructions in .NET 6 to accelerate numerical calculations in anomaly detection algorithms. This reduced the time needed to analyze sensor readings and identify potential issues.
- **Cloud-Based Scaling with Azure Kubernetes Service (AKS):** The company deployed their solution on Azure Kubernetes Service (AKS), taking advantage of .NET 6's cross-platform capabilities and integration with Docker. This enabled them to scale the application dynamically based on workload demand.

Outcome:

The real-time monitoring system improved the accuracy of anomaly detection by 30%, reducing unplanned downtime by 25%. The predictive maintenance capabilities allowed the company to take proactive measures and avoid equipment failures, leading to significant cost savings. By adopting .NET 6, the development team achieved a scalable and reliable solution that could be deployed across multiple power plants with ease.

4. Gaming Industry: Real-Time Multiplayer Game Engine

Problem Statement:

In the gaming industry, real-time multiplayer games require a highly performant backend to handle game state synchronization, player interactions, and complex game logic. A gaming studio aimed to develop a new multiplayer game engine that could support thousands of concurrent players while maintaining a smooth gameplay experience.

Solution Approach:

The studio chose C#10 and .NET 6 to build their multiplayer game engine, focusing on creating a solution that could:

- Process real-time player inputs and synchronize game state efficiently.
- Handle network communications with minimal latency.
- Scale horizontally to support increasing numbers of concurrent players.

Implementation:

The development team leveraged the following features:

- **High-Performance Networking with Kestrel and Sockets:** The team utilized the Kestrel web server for HTTP-based communications and raw sockets for low-latency interactions between game clients and the server. This combination allowed them to achieve high throughput and low latency for real-time player interactions.
- **Task Parallel Library for Game Logic Execution:** Game logic, such as physics calculations and AI behavior, was parallelized using the Task Parallel Library (TPL). This allowed the engine to fully utilize multi-core processors and maintain high frame rates.
- **Memory-Efficient Data Structures with Span<T> and Memory<T>:** To manage the game state efficiently, the developers used *Span<T>* and *Memory<T>* for in-memory data handling. This reduced the impact of garbage collection and ensured a smooth gaming experience.

Outcome:

The multiplayer game engine achieved excellent performance, with the ability to support over 10,000 concurrent players per server instance. The use of .NET 6 enabled the studio to develop and iterate on game features quickly while maintaining a high level of performance. The game received positive reviews for its smooth and responsive gameplay, and the studio was able to scale their infrastructure efficiently to accommodate a growing player base.

5. Scientific Research: Climate Modeling and Weather Simulation

Problem Statement:

Climate modeling and weather prediction require massive computational resources to simulate atmospheric conditions and predict future weather patterns. A climate research organization needed to develop a high-performance solution to run large-scale simulations and analyze the results efficiently.

Solution Approach:

The research organization chose C#10 and .NET 6 to build their simulation software, focusing on creating a solution that could:

- Run large-scale simulations of climate models using parallel and distributed computing techniques.
- Perform numerical calculations and matrix operations efficiently.
- Visualize and analyze the simulation results in real-time.

Implementation:
The development team implemented the following strategies:

- **Distributed Computing with .NET 6:** The team used .NET 6's cross-platform capabilities to deploy their solution across a cluster of Linux-based servers. They utilized Azure Batch for scaling the simulations dynamically based on workload requirements.
- **Vectorized Operations with SIMD:** The numerical calculations in the climate models, such as solving differential equations and performing matrix multiplications, were optimized using SIMD instructions in .NET 6. This resulted in a substantial performance boost for mathematical operations.
- **Real-Time Visualization with Blazor and SignalR:** The team used Blazor and SignalR to create a web-based dashboard for visualizing simulation results in real-time. This allowed researchers to monitor and interact with the simulations from any location.

Outcome:
The climate modeling solution achieved a 3x improvement in simulation speed compared to the previous implementation. Researchers were able to run more detailed simulations and analyze the impact of various climate scenarios with greater accuracy. The use of .NET 6 provided the team with a flexible and scalable platform to support their research initiatives.

These case studies demonstrate the versatility and power of C#10 and .NET 6 in building high-performance applications across a wide range of industries. By leveraging modern language features, advanced parallelism, efficient memory management, and powerful runtime optimizations, developers can achieve impressive results in even the most demanding scenarios.

Whether it's real-time financial analysis, genomic data processing, multiplayer gaming, or climate modeling, .NET 6 provides the tools and capabilities to meet the challenges of High-Performance Computing. The combination of performance, scalability, and developer productivity makes C#10 and .NET 6 a compelling choice for organizations seeking to push the boundaries of what's possible in their respective domains.

Understanding the Fundamentals of Performance Optimization

Core Principles of Performance and Efficiency

Optimizing the performance of an application requires a deep understanding of fundamental principles and best practices. High-Performance Computing (HPC) applications often demand that software makes full use of available resources while minimizing bottlenecks and unnecessary overhead. To achieve this, developers must be well-versed in the core principles of performance and efficiency, which act as the foundation for building fast, scalable, and reliable software solutions.

This section explores these core principles, offering insights and practical strategies to help you develop applications that maximize both performance and efficiency.

1. The Principle of Optimized Resource Utilization

At its core, performance optimization revolves around making the most efficient use of the available hardware resources such as CPU, memory, disk, and network bandwidth. Achieving this requires an understanding of the specific workloads your application needs to handle and optimizing accordingly.

Key Considerations:

- **CPU Utilization:** Maximize the use of available CPU cores by leveraging parallel processing, multithreading, and SIMD (Single Instruction Multiple Data) capabilities.
- **Memory Management:** Minimize memory usage and fragmentation by using efficient data structures, avoiding unnecessary allocations, and implementing custom memory management techniques when needed.
- **Disk I/O Efficiency:** Optimize disk access patterns by using asynchronous I/O operations and proper caching mechanisms to reduce read and write latency.
- **Network Bandwidth Optimization:** For distributed systems or applications reliant on remote data, minimize data transmission overhead through compression, efficient data encoding, and optimizing request-response cycles.

2. The Principle of Minimizing Latency and Response Time

Reducing latency is essential for applications that rely on real-time processing or have strict timing constraints. Whether it's the response time of a web application or the latency in real-time communication between distributed nodes, latency is a crucial performance metric.

Strategies to Minimize Latency:

- **Non-Blocking Operations:** Use asynchronous programming models like async/await in C# to ensure that operations such as network I/O, file access, and database queries do not block the main processing thread.
- **Caching Mechanisms:** Implement caching to reduce the frequency of expensive data retrieval operations. Utilize in-memory caches like MemoryCache in .NET or distributed caches like Redis to store frequently accessed data.
- **Efficient Serialization and Deserialization:** Minimize the overhead of data transfer by using optimized serialization formats and avoiding unnecessary conversions. JSON and binary serialization techniques like Protocol Buffers can be used to reduce serialization overhead.

3. The Principle of Reducing Complexity

Reducing algorithmic and code complexity plays a key role in boosting performance. This involves selecting efficient algorithms and data structures, simplifying logic, and avoiding unnecessary abstractions.

Key Techniques:

- **Algorithmic Optimization:** Understand the time complexity (O-notation) of algorithms and choose the most appropriate ones based on the application's workload. For example, use hash-based collections for frequent lookups instead of iterating through lists.
- **Data Structure Optimization:** Use appropriate data structures that are optimized for your workload. If you need fast insertion and deletion, consider using linked lists. For searching and retrieval, balanced trees or hash tables may be a better fit.
- **Code Refactoring:** Remove redundant logic and refactor complex code blocks into simpler, more maintainable routines. Code that is easier to understand is also easier to optimize.

4. The Principle of Leveraging Parallelism

Modern computer systems are equipped with multi-core processors capable of executing multiple instructions simultaneously. Leveraging parallelism effectively is key to achieving high performance in compute-bound applications.

Approaches to Parallelism:

- **Multithreading and TPL:** Use the Task Parallel Library (TPL) in .NET to parallelize independent tasks and computations. This allows you to split workloads across multiple cores and achieve better CPU utilization.
- **Data Parallelism with PLINQ:** Parallel LINQ (PLINQ) enables data parallelism by automatically distributing query operations across multiple threads. This is ideal for applications that process large datasets and perform independent computations on each element.
- **SIMD and Vectorization:** For numerically intensive operations, utilize

SIMD (Single Instruction Multiple Data) features available in .NET to execute vectorized instructions. This enables the CPU to perform the same operation on multiple pieces of data simultaneously, greatly enhancing throughput.

5. The Principle of Efficient Memory Management

Memory management can have a significant impact on an application's performance. Efficiently allocating, using, and deallocating memory reduces the overhead of garbage collection and prevents memory leaks.

Best Practices:

- **Minimize Allocations:** Avoid unnecessary allocations by using value types (structs) when appropriate and leveraging memory-friendly constructs like *Span<T>* and *Memory<T>*. These types reduce the overhead of memory copying and allocation.
- **Pooling and Object Reuse:** Use object pooling to reduce the overhead of frequent object instantiation. The .NET ObjectPool class allows developers to maintain a pool of reusable objects, reducing garbage collection pressure.
- **Efficient String Manipulation:** Strings are immutable in .NET, which can lead to excessive allocations when performing extensive string operations. Consider using *StringBuilder* for concatenation and employing efficient substring extraction techniques.

6. The Principle of Scalability

Scalability is about ensuring that your application can handle increased workloads gracefully by utilizing additional resources, either by scaling up (adding more power to existing hardware) or scaling out (adding more instances or nodes). Scalability is a critical aspect of building high-performance applications.

Scalability Approaches:

- **Horizontal Scaling with Distributed Systems:** Use distributed comput-

ing models and microservices architecture to scale horizontally. This enables applications to handle higher loads by distributing workloads across multiple servers or nodes.
- **Vertical Scaling with Multithreading:** Within a single server, scale vertically by optimizing the use of CPU cores through multithreading and parallel execution of tasks.
- **Load Balancing and Fault Tolerance:** Implement load balancing strategies to distribute workloads evenly and handle failures gracefully. Use cloud services like Azure Kubernetes Service (AKS) to automatically scale based on demand.

7. The Principle of Profiling and Measuring

"You can't improve what you can't measure." Accurate performance optimization relies on measuring the application's current performance and identifying bottlenecks. Profiling tools and benchmarking techniques play a crucial role in guiding optimization efforts.

Profiling Techniques:

- **Code Profiling:** Use profiling tools like Visual Studio Profiler, PerfView, or JetBrains dotTrace to identify hot paths and code sections with high CPU usage. Profilers can help you discover inefficient algorithms, excessive memory allocations, or blocking calls that impact performance.
- **Performance Benchmarking:** Establish baseline performance metrics using benchmarking tools like BenchmarkDotNet. Run benchmarks on critical methods and compare the results before and after applying optimizations.
- **Heap Analysis:** Analyze memory usage and heap allocation patterns using memory profilers. Look for signs of memory leaks, excessive fragmentation, or unnecessary large object allocations that impact garbage collection.

8. The Principle of Asynchronous and Non-Blocking I/O

Applications that depend heavily on I/O operations, such as reading or writing large files, interacting with databases, or communicating over networks, can benefit from asynchronous programming. Non-blocking I/O ensures that the main thread remains responsive, even during intensive I/O tasks.

Asynchronous Programming Strategies:

- **Async/Await in C#:** Take advantage of async/await in C# to perform asynchronous I/O operations efficiently. This allows the application to continue processing other tasks while waiting for I/O-bound tasks to complete.
- **Asynchronous Streams:** Use asynchronous streams to consume large data streams without blocking. This is useful in scenarios where data must be processed incrementally as it arrives, such as reading large files or receiving data from a network socket.
- **Task-Based Asynchronous Pattern (TAP):** Adhere to the TAP model when designing asynchronous APIs, ensuring that all I/O-bound methods return Task objects and are easily composable.

9. The Principle of Profiling and Testing for Real-World Conditions

Optimizing an application for theoretical scenarios is not enough. Real-world usage conditions can differ significantly from development and testing environments, leading to unforeseen bottlenecks or inefficiencies.

Best Practices for Real-World Profiling:

- **Load Testing:** Conduct load tests that simulate real-world usage patterns and peak loads. Tools like Apache JMeter, Locust, or Azure Load Testing can be used to create realistic scenarios.
- **Stress Testing:** Push your application to its limits to understand how it behaves under extreme conditions. Stress testing helps identify points of failure and performance degradation under heavy load.
- **Monitoring and Alerts:** Deploy monitoring solutions such as Prometheus, Grafana, or Azure Monitor to track key performance metrics in production. Set up alerts to notify you of unusual spikes in

resource usage or degradation in response times.

10. The Principle of Minimizing Contention and Synchronization Overhead

In multi-threaded applications, resource contention and synchronization overhead can negatively impact performance. Minimizing contention ensures that parallel tasks can proceed without unnecessary delays.

Techniques to Reduce Contention:

- **Avoid Shared State:** Design your application to minimize shared mutable state between threads. Whenever possible, use immutable data structures or local copies of data to avoid contention.
- **Use Lock-Free Data Structures:** Where shared state is unavoidable, use lock-free data structures like *ConcurrentQueue*, *ConcurrentDictionary*, or thread-safe collections provided by the .NET framework. These collections minimize locking and allow for more efficient access by multiple threads.
- **Granular Locking:** If locks are necessary, use fine-grained locking techniques to limit the scope and duration of locks. This reduces the likelihood of thread contention and deadlocks.

Understanding and applying the core principles of performance and efficiency is essential for developing high-performance applications in C#10 and .NET 6. By focusing on optimized resource utilization, minimizing latency, leveraging parallelism, and employing effective memory management, developers can create scalable and responsive applications that meet demanding workloads.

Furthermore, embracing a culture of profiling and testing under real-world conditions ensures that optimizations are grounded in reality and that applications are resilient to unexpected challenges. High-Performance Computing is not just about faster code but smarter code—code that balances speed with stability, scalability, and maintainability.

With these core principles in mind, you are equipped to build and optimize applications that not only perform well under ideal conditions but excel under real-world demands.

Benchmarking Techniques and Tools

Benchmarking is a critical part of performance optimization. It involves systematically measuring the performance of different parts of an application to establish a baseline, identify bottlenecks, and evaluate the effectiveness of optimizations. In the context of high-performance computing with C#10 and .NET 6, benchmarking provides insights into how code behaves under different conditions, allowing developers to make data-driven decisions about where to focus their optimization efforts.

This section will delve into key benchmarking techniques and tools that developers can use to measure, analyze, and optimize the performance of their applications.

1. The Purpose of Benchmarking

Benchmarking is essential for several reasons:

- **Identify Bottlenecks:** It helps in identifying parts of the code that consume the most resources or take the longest time to execute.
- **Measure Optimization Impact:** Benchmarking allows developers to measure the impact of optimizations and validate improvements against baseline metrics.
- **Guide Development Priorities:** By revealing performance hotspots, benchmarking helps developers prioritize their efforts on areas that will yield the greatest performance gains.
- **Provide Evidence for Decisions:** Data gathered from benchmarking provides evidence-based insights that guide architectural or design decisions, ensuring that trade-offs are informed and purposeful.

2. Establishing Baseline Performance Metrics

Before applying optimizations, it is essential to establish a baseline by measuring the current state of the application. This involves running benchmarks on critical sections of code and collecting key performance metrics such as execution time, memory usage, CPU usage, and I/O throughput.

Best Practices for Establishing Baselines:

- **Use Realistic Data Sets:** Run benchmarks with representative data sets that mimic real-world usage. Avoid using artificially small or contrived examples that don't reflect actual application scenarios.
- **Run Benchmarks Multiple Times:** To account for variability, run each benchmark multiple times and take the average. This reduces the impact of outliers and gives a more accurate picture of typical performance.
- **Monitor System Resources:** Use monitoring tools to track CPU, memory, disk, and network utilization during benchmarks. This helps in understanding the broader impact of code changes on the entire system.

3. Benchmarking Techniques

There are several techniques that can be employed to perform effective benchmarking:

- **Micro-Benchmarking:** This involves isolating and measuring the performance of small units of code, such as individual methods or classes. Micro-benchmarking provides fine-grained insights into the behavior of specific algorithms or operations.
- **Macro-Benchmarking:** In contrast, macro-benchmarking measures the performance of the entire application or large subsystems. It focuses on overall throughput, latency, and responsiveness under realistic workloads.
- **Comparative Benchmarking:** In this technique, two or more implementations of a feature are compared to identify the most efficient one. Comparative benchmarking is useful when experimenting with alternative algorithms or refactored code.

- **Stress Benchmarking:** This technique involves pushing the application to its limits by increasing the workload or running it under extreme conditions. Stress benchmarking helps uncover hidden bottlenecks or resource constraints that might not be apparent under normal loads.

4. **Tools for Benchmarking in .NET 6**

.NET 6 offers several powerful tools for benchmarking, each suited to different use cases. Below are the most widely used tools for developers working in the .NET ecosystem:

1. **BenchmarkDotNet:**
2. **Overview:** BenchmarkDotNet is the most popular benchmarking library in the .NET ecosystem. It provides a simple and intuitive way to write and run benchmarks, offering comprehensive reports with detailed performance metrics.
3. **Key Features:**

- Supports benchmarking individual methods or code blocks with high precision.
- Automatically manages warm-up runs to reduce the impact of JIT compilation on measurements.
- Provides comprehensive reporting, including execution time, memory allocations, and hardware details.
- Supports parameterized benchmarks, enabling the measurement of code behavior under different input conditions.
- **Usage Example:**

```csharp
using BenchmarkDotNet.Attributes;
using BenchmarkDotNet.Running;
```

```
public class MyBenchmarks
{
    private readonly int[] numbers = Enumerable.Range(1,
    1000).ToArray();

    [Benchmark]
    public int SumLinq() => numbers.Sum();

    [Benchmark]
    public int SumForLoop()
    {
        int sum = 0;
        for (int i = 0; i < numbers.Length; i++)
        {
            sum += numbers[i];
        }
        return sum;
    }
}

public static class Program
{
    public static void Main(string[] args)
    {
        var summary = BenchmarkRunner.Run<MyBenchmarks>();
    }
}
```

dotTrace:

Overview: JetBrains dotTrace is a powerful profiler for .NET applications, providing detailed insights into code execution and performance bottlenecks. While it is primarily a profiler, dotTrace can be used in combination with benchmarks to gather in-depth performance data.

Key Features:

- Offers various profiling modes, including CPU sampling, tracing, and

timeline profiling.
- Provides visualizations of execution paths, call stacks, and resource usage.
- Allows comparison of performance snapshots to track the impact of code changes.
- **Use Case:** Profiling an application to identify CPU-heavy methods or functions with high call frequency.

PerfView:

Overview: PerfView is a lightweight, open-source performance analysis tool developed by Microsoft. It focuses on analyzing CPU usage and memory consumption, making it a useful complement to BenchmarkDotNet.

Key Features:

- Captures detailed performance traces and supports event-based analysis using ETW (Event Tracing for Windows).
- Provides flame graphs and call tree visualizations to help pinpoint bottlenecks.
- Supports real-time monitoring and post-mortem analysis of performance traces.
- **Use Case:** Analyzing long-running applications or identifying hotspots in complex multi-threaded scenarios.

Visual Studio Performance Profiler:

Overview: The built-in Performance Profiler in Visual Studio is a convenient tool for developers who want to quickly profile and analyze their .NET applications.

Key Features:

UNDERSTANDING THE FUNDAMENTALS OF PERFORMANCE OPTIMIZATION

- Supports CPU usage, memory allocation, and I/O profiling.
- Provides integrated reports and visualizations within the Visual Studio environment.
- Allows developers to profile applications without additional setup or configuration.
- **Use Case:** Quick profiling sessions during development to identify immediate bottlenecks or inefficiencies.

5. Practical Guidelines for Effective Benchmarking

To get accurate and meaningful results from benchmarking, it's essential to follow certain best practices:

- **Warm Up Your Code:** Ensure that the code is fully warmed up before taking measurements. This helps to eliminate the impact of JIT compilation, lazy initialization, or other factors that affect initial performance.
- **Isolate Code Under Test:** Minimize external factors that might impact the results. For example, ensure that no background processes or unrelated tasks are running during the benchmark.
- **Use Release Builds:** Always benchmark the application in Release mode with optimizations enabled. Debug builds often include additional checks and debugging information that can skew results.
- **Control Environmental Variables:** Run benchmarks in a controlled environment with consistent hardware, OS settings, and network conditions. Even slight changes in system load or network latency can impact results.
- **Measure Memory Allocations:** In addition to execution time, consider measuring memory allocations to identify inefficient memory usage. BenchmarkDotNet and other tools can provide detailed memory allocation reports.

6. Interpreting Benchmark Results

Interpreting benchmarking results requires a keen understanding of what the metrics represent and how they relate to the broader goals of performance optimization. Here are some common metrics to consider and what they indicate:

- **Execution Time:** Measures the time taken for a piece of code to execute. Lower execution times are generally desirable, but always consider the context—reducing execution time at the cost of memory or scalability might not be ideal.
- **Throughput:** Represents the number of operations completed per unit of time. High throughput is essential for applications that need to process large volumes of data or handle a high number of transactions.
- **Memory Allocations:** Tracks the amount of memory allocated by the code. High allocations can lead to increased garbage collection pressure, which in turn can impact overall application responsiveness.
- **CPU Utilization:** Indicates how effectively the application utilizes available CPU cores. Look for excessively high CPU usage in situations where it should be idle or low utilization when heavy processing is expected.
- **Latency:** Measures the time delay between a request and its response. This is particularly important in networked or real-time systems where responsiveness is crucial.

7. Evaluating the Effectiveness of Optimizations

After establishing a baseline and making changes to optimize code, it's crucial to run benchmarks again to evaluate the effectiveness of the changes. This involves comparing the new benchmark results to the baseline metrics to see if the optimizations had the intended impact.

Steps to Evaluate Effectiveness:

1. **Compare Metrics:** Look for improvements in key metrics like execution time, throughput, and memory usage. Ideally, the optimized code should show consistent improvements across multiple benchmark runs.
2. **Analyze Trade-Offs:** Sometimes, optimizing for one metric can

negatively impact another. For example, reducing execution time might increase memory usage. Carefully consider these trade-offs and decide based on the broader goals of the application.
3. **Validate with Real-World Workloads:** Ensure that optimizations translate to real-world scenarios by running benchmarks with realistic workloads and usage patterns. This helps confirm that the improvements are not limited to contrived benchmarks.

Benchmarking is a vital part of building and maintaining high-performance applications. By establishing baseline metrics, employing effective techniques, and using the right tools, developers can gain valuable insights into how their code performs and where it needs improvement. In the context of C#10 and .NET 6, tools like BenchmarkDotNet, dotTrace, and PerfView provide powerful capabilities to measure, analyze, and optimize performance at various levels.

Effective benchmarking is more than just measuring execution time—it involves a holistic approach to evaluating memory usage, CPU efficiency, latency, and scalability. With these techniques and tools at your disposal, you can build applications that are not only fast but also efficient, scalable, and resilient under real-world conditions.

Identifying and Addressing Common Bottlenecks

Bottlenecks are sections of code or system resources that limit the overall performance of an application. They often manifest as slow execution times, high memory consumption, or excessive CPU usage. Identifying and addressing these bottlenecks is a critical aspect of optimizing high-performance applications built with C#10 and .NET 6.

In this section, we'll explore common bottlenecks, discuss techniques to identify them, and provide strategies to effectively address them.

1. Common Types of Bottlenecks

Bottlenecks can arise in various forms, depending on the nature of the application and the workload it handles. Below are some of the most common types of bottlenecks:

- **CPU Bottlenecks:** Occur when the application is CPU-bound, meaning it is using all available CPU resources, leaving other hardware components underutilized. This often results in slow execution times for CPU-intensive tasks such as mathematical computations, image processing, or data encryption.
- **Memory Bottlenecks:** Happen when an application consumes an excessive amount of memory, leading to frequent garbage collection or even out-of-memory errors. Memory bottlenecks are common in applications that process large datasets, retain too many objects in memory, or create memory leaks.
- **I/O Bottlenecks:** Arise from slow disk or network operations. These are common in applications that involve frequent file reads and writes, database interactions, or network communications. I/O bottlenecks often cause high latency and low throughput.
- **Network Bottlenecks:** Occur when the application depends on network resources for data exchange, such as web requests or remote API calls. High latency or low bandwidth can limit an application's responsiveness and performance.
- **Lock Contention Bottlenecks:** Occur when multiple threads or processes compete for access to shared resources. This results in delays as threads wait for locks to be released. Lock contention is common in multi-threaded applications that use synchronization mechanisms like lock statements, Mutex, or Semaphore.

2. Techniques for Identifying Bottlenecks

Identifying bottlenecks requires a systematic approach and the use of appropriate tools to gather performance data. Here are key techniques to help you identify bottlenecks effectively:

Code Profiling:

Profiling tools like JetBrains dotTrace, Visual Studio Profiler, and PerfView can provide insights into which methods or code paths are consuming the most CPU, memory, or I/O resources. Profiling tools typically allow you to:

- View a breakdown of CPU usage by method or function.
- Analyze call stacks to understand which methods are invoking bottle-necked code.
- Measure memory allocations and garbage collection activity to detect memory-related bottlenecks.

Performance Counters and System Monitoring:

System monitoring tools, such as Windows Performance Monitor or Azure Monitor, can track system-level metrics like CPU usage, disk I/O, memory utilization, and network throughput. Performance counters provide a high-level view of resource consumption and help pinpoint whether bottlenecks are related to hardware constraints or software inefficiencies.

Event Tracing for Windows (ETW) and PerfView:

ETW is a powerful mechanism for tracing low-level system and application events in Windows. PerfView leverages ETW data to visualize CPU activity, garbage collection events, and I/O operations, making it easier to identify resource-intensive code paths.

Benchmarking with Baselines:

Establish baseline performance metrics using benchmarking tools like BenchmarkDotNet. Once you have a baseline, you can measure deviations from the baseline after applying changes. Significant deviations indicate potential bottlenecks.

Heap Analysis and Memory Profiling:

Memory profilers allow you to analyze the managed heap and detect objects that consume a large amount of memory or aren't being released.

Tools like dotMemory and Visual Studio's Memory Profiler provide detailed insights into memory usage, helping you find memory leaks or inefficient object allocations.

3. Addressing CPU Bottlenecks

When CPU bottlenecks are identified, the goal is to reduce the computational load on the CPU or distribute the workload more effectively. Here are strategies to address CPU bottlenecks:

- **Optimize Algorithms and Data Structures:**
- Choose efficient algorithms and data structures that minimize CPU cycles. For instance, replace an $O(n^2)$ algorithm with an $O(n \log n)$ alternative when sorting large collections or performing frequent searches.
- **Parallelize Workloads:**
- Distribute CPU-intensive tasks across multiple cores using parallel programming constructs like TPL (Task Parallel Library) or PLINQ. Identify opportunities to use SIMD instructions to accelerate vectorizable operations.
- **Use Asynchronous Programming:**
- Offload I/O-bound operations from CPU-bound threads using asynchronous methods. This frees up CPU resources for tasks that require processing power.
- **Profile and Refactor Hot Paths:**
- Focus on optimizing hot paths, which are sections of code that execute frequently or consume a large amount of CPU resources. Refactor or re-implement these paths to reduce their execution time.

4. Addressing Memory Bottlenecks

Memory bottlenecks can be caused by excessive memory allocations, memory leaks, or inefficient object management. Here are strategies to address memory bottlenecks:

- **Minimize Allocations and Reduce GC Pressure:**
- Use value types (structs) instead of reference types where possible to reduce heap allocations. Leverage *Span<T>* and *Memory<T>* to work with in-memory data efficiently without creating unnecessary copies. Object pooling techniques can also help minimize garbage collection pressure by reusing frequently created objects.
- **Detect and Fix Memory Leaks:**
- Use memory profilers to identify objects that remain in memory longer than necessary. Look for retained objects that are no longer needed or event handlers that hold references to objects unintentionally. Fix memory leaks by explicitly releasing resources or removing unnecessary references.
- **Optimize Large Object Heap (LOH) Usage:**
- Allocate large objects carefully to avoid frequent LOH allocations and deallocations. When possible, reduce the size of objects or use array pooling to manage large data structures.
- **Use Lightweight Data Structures:**
- Choose memory-efficient data structures that fit the workload. For example, use linked lists or hash tables if they are more appropriate for your use case than arrays or lists.

5. Addressing I/O Bottlenecks

I/O bottlenecks can significantly impact performance, especially in applications that involve frequent file access, database queries, or network communication. Here are strategies to address I/O bottlenecks:

- **Asynchronous I/O Operations:**
- Use asynchronous methods for file and network I/O to prevent blocking the main thread. The async/await pattern in C# makes it easy to write non-blocking I/O code, improving throughput and responsiveness.
- **Implement Caching Mechanisms:**
- Cache frequently accessed data to reduce the number of disk reads or database queries. In-memory caches like MemoryCache in .NET or

distributed caches like Redis can be effective in reducing I/O overhead.

- **Batch and Optimize I/O Operations:**
- Where feasible, batch I/O operations to minimize the number of disk or network accesses. For example, read or write data in larger chunks rather than making multiple small requests.
- **Use Optimized File Streams:**
- Take advantage of the improvements in FileStream in .NET 6, which offers more efficient buffer management and reduced internal allocations. Use FileOptions like SequentialScan or RandomAccess to hint at the access pattern, enabling the OS to optimize disk caching.

6. Addressing Network Bottlenecks

Network bottlenecks arise due to high latency or insufficient bandwidth, especially in distributed systems or applications that communicate over the internet. Here are strategies to address network bottlenecks:

- **Minimize the Number of Network Requests:**
- Reduce the frequency and volume of network requests by batching multiple operations into a single request or using message queues for communication between distributed services.
- **Optimize Data Transmission:**
- Compress data before transmitting it over the network to reduce bandwidth usage. Choose efficient serialization formats like Protocol Buffers or MessagePack to encode data compactly.
- **Use Efficient Network Protocols:**
- When possible, use low-latency protocols such as HTTP/2 or gRPC instead of traditional HTTP/1.1. These protocols reduce the overhead of establishing and managing connections.
- **Implement Caching and Load Balancing:**
- Use caching to avoid redundant network requests, and load balancing to distribute network traffic evenly across servers or service instances.

7. Addressing Lock Contention Bottlenecks

Lock contention occurs when multiple threads compete for access to shared resources, leading to delays as threads wait for locks to be released. Here are strategies to address lock contention bottlenecks:

- **Minimize Shared State:**
- Reduce or eliminate shared mutable state by using immutable data structures or thread-local storage. This reduces the need for synchronization and prevents lock contention.
- **Use Concurrent Collections:**
- Leverage thread-safe collections like ConcurrentDictionary, ConcurrentQueue, or ConcurrentBag to manage shared resources efficiently. These collections use fine-grained locking or lock-free algorithms to reduce contention.
- **Refactor Critical Sections:**
- Minimize the amount of code within critical sections. Reduce the duration of locks by isolating only the necessary code, allowing other threads to proceed without waiting unnecessarily.
- **Implement Reader-Writer Locks:**
- When read-heavy access patterns are expected, use reader-writer locks like ReaderWriterLockSlim to allow multiple readers to access shared resources concurrently while still preventing data corruption during writes.

Identifying and addressing bottlenecks is a vital aspect of building and maintaining high-performance applications. By understanding common bottlenecks and applying targeted strategies, you can significantly improve the efficiency, responsiveness, and scalability of your application. Whether dealing with CPU, memory, I/O, network, or lock contention bottlenecks, the key is to approach optimization systematically—using profiling tools, benchmarking techniques, and best practices to make informed decisions.

With a clear understanding of these principles and strategies, you are equipped to tackle performance challenges confidently and deliver robust, high-performing applications in C#10 and .NET 6.

Practical "Performance Tip" Boxes

When developing high-performance applications, small changes can make a big difference. This section presents a series of concise and actionable performance tips designed to guide developers in optimizing their C# and .NET 6 applications. These "Performance Tip" boxes aim to highlight best practices, common pitfalls, and effective techniques for improving the performance of various application components.

Performance Tip #1: Optimize LINQ Queries

Use Case: When working with large collections and frequent data processing operations using LINQ.

Tip: Prefer methods that avoid deferred execution when you only need the results once. Use methods like ToList(), ToArray(), or .Count() at the end of LINQ chains to prevent multiple evaluations of the same query. Additionally, where possible, replace LINQ with simple loops for critical paths.

```csharp
// Inefficient LINQ Query - Executes twice
var expensiveQuery = myCollection.Where(x => x.IsActive && x.Score > 50);
var count = expensiveQuery.Count();
var average = expensiveQuery.Average(x => x.Score);

// Optimized Approach - Execute the query once
var filteredResults = myCollection.Where(x => x.IsActive && x.Score > 50).ToList();
var count = filteredResults.Count;
var average = filteredResults.Average(x => x.Score);
```

Performance Tip #2: Use StringBuilder for Concatenation

Use Case: When performing multiple string concatenations in loops or

UNDERSTANDING THE FUNDAMENTALS OF PERFORMANCE OPTIMIZATION

processing large strings.

Tip: Since strings are immutable, using StringBuilder is significantly more efficient for repeated concatenations. Avoid using the + or += operators in loops, as each operation creates a new string instance.

```csharp
// Inefficient String Concatenation
string result = "";
for (int i = 0; i < 1000; i++)
{
    result += i.ToString();
}

// Optimized Approach
var stringBuilder = new StringBuilder();
for (int i = 0; i < 1000; i++)
{
    stringBuilder.Append(i.ToString());
}
string result = stringBuilder.ToString();
```

Performance Tip #3: Leverage Span<T> for Memory Efficiency

Use Case: When processing large data arrays or manipulating memory blocks.

Tip: Use Span<T> or Memory<T> to efficiently slice and manipulate arrays without creating additional allocations. This reduces memory pressure and speeds up processing.

```csharp
// Inefficient Array Slicing
byte[] data = new byte[1000];
byte[] slice = new byte[500];
Array.Copy(data, 100, slice, 0, 500);
```

```
// Optimized Approach using Span<T>
Span<byte> dataSpan = new byte[1000];
Span<byte> slice = dataSpan.Slice(100, 500);
```

Performance Tip #4: Avoid Premature Parallelization

Use Case: When considering parallelizing tasks for performance gains.

Tip: Not all workloads benefit from parallelism. Overhead from creating and managing tasks can degrade performance, especially for small workloads or I/O-bound tasks. Use parallel processing only for CPU-bound, large, or highly independent tasks.

```csharp
// Example of unnecessary parallelism for small tasks
Parallel.For(0, 10, i =>
{
    Console.WriteLine("Processing small task: " + i);
});

// Sequential execution is more efficient for small or I/O-bound tasks
for (int i = 0; i < 10; i++)
{
    Console.WriteLine("Processing small task: " + i);
}
```

Performance Tip #5: Use ConfigureAwait(false) in Library Code

Use Case: When working with asynchronous code in libraries.

Tip: By default, await captures the current synchronization context, which can cause unnecessary overhead in library code. Use ConfigureAwait(false) to avoid capturing the context and reduce thread switching costs.

```csharp
// Inefficient: Captures synchronization context unnecessarily
await DoSomeAsyncOperation();
```

UNDERSTANDING THE FUNDAMENTALS OF PERFORMANCE OPTIMIZATION

```
// Optimized Approach
await DoSomeAsyncOperation().ConfigureAwait(false);
```

Performance Tip #6: Optimize Collections for Frequent Access Patterns

Use Case: When frequently accessing or modifying collections like dictionaries, lists, or arrays.

Tip: Choose the right collection for the task. For frequent lookups, prefer Dictionary<K, V> or HashSet<T>. For sequential access, List<T> is efficient. If order and quick insertions are needed, consider using a LinkedList<T>.

csharp

```
// Inefficient: Using a List for frequent lookups
List<int> numbers = new List<int> { 1, 2, 3, 4, 5 };
bool containsNumber = numbers.Contains(3);

// Optimized Approach: Using a HashSet for O(1) lookups
HashSet<int> numbersSet = new HashSet<int> { 1, 2, 3, 4, 5 };
bool containsNumber = numbersSet.Contains(3);
```

Performance Tip #7: Use ReadOnlySpan<T> for Immutable Data

Use Case: When dealing with large read-only data or performing read-only operations on buffers or strings.

Tip: Use ReadOnlySpan<T> to indicate that the data should not be modified. This provides both performance benefits and clarity of intent.

csharp

```
// Example using ReadOnlySpan<T>
ReadOnlySpan<char> readOnlyData = "ReadOnlyData".AsSpan();
char firstChar = readOnlyData[0]; // Access data without modification
```

Performance Tip #8: Optimize JSON Serialization with Source Generators

Use Case: When serializing or deserializing JSON frequently.

Tip: Use System.Text.Json with source generators to pre-generate serialization logic at compile time, reducing runtime overhead and improving performance.

```csharp
// Use source generators to pre-compile JSON serialization code
[JsonSerializable(typeof(MyClass))]
public partial class MyJsonContext : JsonSerializerContext { }

// Optimized serialization using source-generated context
MyClass myObject = new MyClass();
string json = JsonSerializer.Serialize(myObject,
MyJsonContext.Default.MyClass);
```

Performance Tip #9: Prefer ValueTask Over Task for High-Performance Scenarios

Use Case: When working with high-frequency, low-latency asynchronous operations.

Tip: If the asynchronous result is often already available, consider using ValueTask instead of Task to reduce the overhead of heap allocations.

```csharp
// Using Task for frequently completed operations
public Task<int> GetValueAsync() => Task.FromResult(42);

// Optimized Approach using ValueTask
public ValueTask<int> GetValueAsync() => new ValueTask<int>(42);
```

Performance Tip #10: Profile Before You Optimize

Use Case: When considering performance optimizations in any area of your application.

Tip: Always use profiling tools like BenchmarkDotNet, Visual Studio Profiler, or PerfView to measure performance before applying optimizations. Avoid speculative changes based solely on assumptions.

UNDERSTANDING THE FUNDAMENTALS OF PERFORMANCE OPTIMIZATION

These practical "Performance Tip" boxes provide targeted advice for improving the performance of C#10 and .NET 6 applications. By implementing these tips and following the principles of efficient resource management, developers can build more responsive, scalable, and optimized applications. Remember, effective performance optimization is about making incremental, data-driven improvements that collectively lead to significant gains.

Advanced Multithreading with C#10

Introduction to Multithreading and Task Parallel Library (TPL)

Multithreading is a programming technique that allows multiple threads to execute concurrently within a single application. This parallel execution enables software to perform multiple operations simultaneously, leading to increased responsiveness and improved performance, especially on multi-core processors. Multithreading is essential for high-performance applications, particularly when handling tasks that can be divided into smaller, independent units of work.

With the advancement of modern processors, which often come equipped with multiple cores, leveraging multithreading effectively has become crucial. In C#10 and .NET 6, the **Task Parallel Library (TPL)** is the primary framework for implementing multithreaded and parallelized code, making it easier for developers to write scalable and efficient applications.

1. What is Multithreading?

Multithreading refers to the execution of multiple threads concurrently within the same process. A thread is essentially a lightweight process that shares memory space with other threads in the same application. By running multiple threads concurrently, applications can efficiently utilize the CPU's processing power to perform several tasks simultaneously.

Key Concepts:

- **Thread:** The smallest unit of execution within a process. Each thread

runs independently and can perform specific tasks simultaneously.
- **Concurrency vs. Parallelism:** While concurrency refers to the ability of an application to handle multiple tasks at once, parallelism involves executing multiple tasks simultaneously. Multithreading can achieve both concurrency and parallelism, depending on how the threads are scheduled and executed.
- **Context Switching:** The act of switching between threads by the operating system to give each thread a chance to execute. This process introduces some overhead, which needs to be minimized for optimal performance.

2. Challenges of Manual Multithreading

Before the introduction of TPL, developers had to create and manage threads manually using the Thread class. While this provided flexibility, it also introduced complexity and risks, such as:

- **Thread Management:** Manually creating and managing threads, synchronizing shared data, and handling exceptions can lead to complex and error-prone code.
- **Thread Pool Limitations:** Manual multithreading often did not leverage the thread pool effectively, leading to potential overuse or underuse of system resources.
- **Synchronization Issues:** Developers had to use low-level synchronization primitives like locks, mutexes, and semaphores, which could easily introduce deadlocks or performance bottlenecks if not handled carefully.

3. Overview of Task Parallel Library (TPL)

The Task Parallel Library (TPL) was introduced to simplify and enhance multithreaded programming in .NET. It abstracts the low-level details of thread management, enabling developers to focus on the logic of concurrent operations rather than the complexities of thread synchronization and lifecycle management.

Key Features of TPL:

- **Tasks over Threads:** TPL encourages the use of *Tasks* instead of manually creating and managing threads. A *Task* represents an asynchronous operation, which the TPL schedules on available threads in the thread pool.
- **Efficient Thread Pool Management:** TPL automatically manages the thread pool, dynamically creating and adjusting the number of threads based on the workload.
- **Built-in Support for Parallelism:** TPL provides high-level constructs like Parallel.For, Parallel.ForEach, and PLINQ (Parallel LINQ) for easily implementing data parallelism.
- **Exception Handling and Cancellation:** TPL includes mechanisms for handling exceptions and supports task cancellation via *CancellationToken*, making it easier to write robust and responsive code.

4. Basics of Working with TPL

In TPL, a *Task* is the core unit of work. It represents a single asynchronous operation that runs independently. The most common way to create a task is to use the Task class or the Task.Run method, which queues the task to the default task scheduler for execution.

Example: Creating and Running a Basic Task

```csharp
Task myTask = Task.Run(() =>
{
    // Simulate some work
    Console.WriteLine("Task is running");
    Thread.Sleep(1000);
});
myTask.Wait(); // Wait for the task to complete
```

The above example demonstrates a basic usage of a task. The task runs asynchronously and independently of the main thread. The Wait() method is used to block the calling thread until the task completes.

Creating and Running Tasks

There are multiple ways to create and run tasks in TPL. Here are some of the common approaches:

- **Using Task Factory (Task.Factory.StartNew)**

```csharp
Task task1 = Task.Factory.StartNew(() =>
{
    Console.WriteLine("Task 1 is executing");
});
task1.Wait();
```

- **Using Task.Run (Recommended)**

```csharp
Task task2 = Task.Run(() =>
{
    Console.WriteLine("Task 2 is executing");
});
task2.Wait();
```

Best Practice: Use Task.Run for CPU-bound operations that can be offloaded to a background thread. For I/O-bound operations, consider using asynchronous methods (async and await) to prevent blocking threads.

5. Using Task-based Asynchronous Pattern (TAP)

The Task-based Asynchronous Pattern (TAP) is a pattern in .NET that allows developers to write asynchronous code using tasks. It is recommended to use async and await keywords for creating asynchronous methods.

Example: Asynchronous Method with TAP

csharp

```
public async Task<int> CalculateSumAsync(int a, int b)
{
    await Task.Delay(500); // Simulate some asynchronous work
    return a + b;
}

// Calling the async method
int result = await CalculateSumAsync(5, 10);
Console.WriteLine($"Sum: {result}");
```

In the example above, the CalculateSumAsync method performs a simulated asynchronous operation using await. The await keyword ensures that the calling thread does not block while waiting for the task to complete, enhancing responsiveness.

6. Leveraging Parallelism with Parallel Class

The TPL provides a Parallel class to perform parallelized operations over collections or ranges. This is particularly useful for data parallelism scenarios, where the same operation needs to be applied to multiple data items independently.

Example: Using Parallel.For

csharp

```
int[] numbers = new int[1000000];
Parallel.For(0, numbers.Length, i =>
{
    numbers[i] = i * i;
});
```

Example: Using Parallel.ForEach

csharp

```csharp
List<string> names = new List<string> { "Alice", "Bob", "Charlie" };
Parallel.ForEach(names, name =>
{
    Console.WriteLine($"Processing {name}");
});
```

In both examples, the Parallel.For and Parallel.ForEach methods automatically distribute the workload across multiple threads, taking full advantage of multi-core processors.

7. Task Continuations

TPL allows tasks to be chained together using continuations, enabling developers to specify a follow-up action that runs after a task completes. This feature is useful for organizing asynchronous workflows where the result of one task feeds into the next.

Example: Chaining Tasks with Continuations

```csharp
Task firstTask = Task.Run(() =>
{
    Console.WriteLine("First task is executing");
    Thread.Sleep(1000);
});

Task continuationTask = firstTask.ContinueWith(prevTask =>
{
    Console.WriteLine("Continuation task is executing");
});
continuationTask.Wait();
```

In this example, continuationTask starts only after firstTask completes. This chaining can help create complex asynchronous workflows with clear and manageable code.\

8. Handling Exceptions in TPL

When tasks encounter exceptions, TPL provides a mechanism to capture and handle them gracefully. Exceptions in tasks are aggregated and wrapped in an AggregateException.

Example: Handling Task Exceptions

```csharp
try
{
    Task failingTask = Task.Run(() =>
    {
        throw new InvalidOperationException("An error occurred");
    });
    failingTask.Wait();
}
catch (AggregateException ex)
{
    foreach (var innerException in ex.InnerExceptions)
    {
        Console.WriteLine($"Caught exception: {innerException.Message}");
    }
}
```

In this example, the AggregateException is caught and processed, ensuring that multiple exceptions from nested tasks are not lost.

9. Cancelling Tasks with CancellationToken

TPL supports task cancellation using the CancellationToken structure. This allows developers to gracefully stop tasks when a cancellation request is received.

Example: Cancelling a Task

```csharp
CancellationTokenSource cts = new CancellationTokenSource();
CancellationToken token = cts.Token;

Task cancellableTask = Task.Run(() =>
```

```
    {
        for (int i = 0; i < 10; i++)
        {
            if (token.IsCancellationRequested)
            {
                Console.WriteLine("Task was cancelled");
                return;
            }
            Console.WriteLine($"Processing {i}");
            Thread.Sleep(500);
        }
    }, token);

    // Request cancellation
    cts.Cancel();
    cancellableTask.Wait();
```

In this example, the task periodically checks for the cancellation token status. When the cancellation is requested, the task exits gracefully.

10. Best Practices for Multithreading with TPL

To leverage multithreading effectively, consider the following best practices:

- **Use Asynchronous Programming for I/O-Bound Tasks:** For I/O-bound operations such as file reads, network requests, or database calls, prefer asynchronous methods with async and await instead of creating tasks manually.
- **Avoid Blocking Calls in Tasks:** Minimize the use of blocking calls like Wait() or Result inside tasks, as they can lead to deadlocks or degrade responsiveness. Use await instead for better task scheduling.
- **Prefer Task-based Patterns:** Follow the Task-based Asynchronous Pattern (TAP) for writing asynchronous code. Avoid directly managing threads unless absolutely necessary.
- **Use the Thread Pool Wisely:** Tasks created using TPL are executed on the thread pool. However, overloading the thread pool with CPU-bound

tasks can starve other critical tasks. Understand the difference between CPU-bound and I/O-bound tasks and use the appropriate pattern.

Multithreading and the Task Parallel Library (TPL) in C#10 and .NET 6 provide developers with powerful tools to write concurrent and parallel code efficiently. TPL abstracts the complexities of thread management, synchronization, and exception handling, allowing developers to focus on the core logic of their applications.

By leveraging tasks, parallel constructs, and best practices in multithreading, developers can create scalable, responsive, and high-performance applications. As hardware continues to evolve with more cores and advanced processing capabilities, mastering multithreading with TPL is an essential skill for building the software of the future.

Deep Dive into Parallel LINQ (PLINQ)

Parallel LINQ (PLINQ) is an extension of LINQ (Language Integrated Query) in .NET that provides a powerful mechanism for performing parallelized data processing over collections. PLINQ enables developers to take advantage of multicore processors by automatically parallelizing LINQ queries, which can significantly enhance performance in scenarios that involve large data sets or intensive processing.

PLINQ is built on top of the Task Parallel Library (TPL), providing an easy way to write parallelized code with a declarative style similar to traditional LINQ. This combination of simplicity and power makes PLINQ a valuable tool for developers aiming to optimize the performance of data-intensive applications.

1. What is PLINQ?

PLINQ stands for Parallel Language Integrated Query. It extends LINQ by allowing queries to run in parallel, leveraging multiple processor cores. PLINQ essentially breaks down LINQ queries into smaller tasks, distributes them across multiple threads, and then aggregates the results to produce a final output.

PLINQ is ideal for scenarios where the same operation needs to be performed independently on multiple elements in a collection. By executing these operations in parallel, PLINQ reduces the total processing time, especially for CPU-bound tasks.

2. Benefits of PLINQ

- **Automatic Parallelization:** PLINQ automatically distributes the workload across available processor cores without requiring developers to manually create and manage threads.
- **Declarative Syntax:** It retains the familiar LINQ syntax, making it easier for developers to adopt and understand.
- **Dynamic Load Balancing:** PLINQ dynamically adjusts the degree of parallelism based on the current system workload, optimizing resource utilization.
- **Fault Tolerance:** It automatically handles exceptions and cancellation, simplifying the development of robust parallelized applications.

3. Basic Usage of PLINQ

PLINQ is simple to use. To convert a LINQ query into a PLINQ query, all you need to do is call the .AsParallel() method on a collection. This instructs PLINQ to execute subsequent query operations in parallel.

Example: Converting LINQ to PLINQ

```csharp
var numbers = Enumerable.Range(1, 1000000);

// LINQ query
```

```csharp
var evenNumbers = numbers.Where(n => n % 2 == 0);

// PLINQ query
var parallelEvenNumbers = numbers.AsParallel().Where(n => n % 2
== 0);
```

In the above example, the .AsParallel() method converts the traditional LINQ query into a parallelized query. By doing this, the filtering operation (Where) will be distributed across multiple threads.

4. Controlling the Degree of Parallelism

PLINQ allows you to control the number of threads it uses by specifying the degree of parallelism. This can be useful when you want to limit or increase the number of threads based on your system's capabilities.

Example: Specifying Degree of Parallelism

```csharp
var parallelQuery = numbers.AsParallel()
                    .WithDegreeOfParallelism(4) // Limit
                    to 4 threads
                    .Where(n => n % 2 == 0);
```

Best Practice: It's usually best to let PLINQ determine the optimal degree of parallelism. However, if you have specific knowledge of your system or workload, you can fine-tune this value to achieve the desired balance between concurrency and system load.

5. Ordering with PLINQ

By default, PLINQ does not guarantee the order of elements in the output, as parallel execution can process elements in a non-sequential manner. However, if maintaining the order of elements is essential, you can use the AsOrdered() method.

Example: Preserving Order in PLINQ

```csharp
var orderedResults = numbers.AsParallel()
                    .AsOrdered() // Ensure the output
                    maintains the original order
                    .Where(n => n % 2 == 0);
```

Using AsOrdered() introduces some overhead, as PLINQ must take extra steps to maintain the order. Therefore, use this method only when ordering is necessary.

6. Merging Results with PLINQ

When PLINQ processes data in parallel, it needs to merge the results from multiple threads into a single output. The merging strategy can significantly impact performance, especially in cases involving large data sets or complex operations.

PLINQ provides the following merge options:

- **Default:** Uses an adaptive algorithm to determine the best merge strategy.
- **NotBuffered:** Processes and returns elements as soon as they are ready. This is useful for streaming large results.
- **FullyBuffered:** Waits for all threads to complete and then processes all elements together. This is efficient for small to medium-sized results.

Example: Using Merge Options

```csharp
var parallelQuery = numbers.AsParallel()
.WithMergeOptions(ParallelMergeOptions.NotBuffered)
.Where(n => n % 2 == 0);
```

7. Handling Exceptions in PLINQ

When executing queries in parallel, exceptions can occur on one or more threads. PLINQ aggregates these exceptions into an AggregateException, which can be caught and handled accordingly.

Example: Handling Exceptions in PLINQ

```csharp
try
{
    var results = numbers.AsParallel()
                    .Where(n =>
                    {
                        if (n == 500)
                            throw new
                            InvalidOperationException("An
                            error occurred");
                        return n % 2 == 0;
                    })
                    .ToList();
}
catch (AggregateException ex)
{
    foreach (var innerException in ex.InnerExceptions)
    {
        Console.WriteLine($"Caught exception:
        {innerException.Message}");
    }
}
```

In the above example, if an exception occurs during the parallel execution of the query, it is caught as an AggregateException, and each individual exception can be processed separately.

8. Query Cancellation in PLINQ

PLINQ supports query cancellation through the use of a CancellationToken. This feature is useful when you need to stop a long-running query in response to user input or other conditions.

Example: Cancelling a PLINQ Query

```csharp
CancellationTokenSource cts = new CancellationTokenSource();

try
{
    var results = numbers.AsParallel()
                         .WithCancellation(cts.Token)
                         .Where(n => n % 2 == 0)
                         .ToList();
}
catch (OperationCanceledException)
{
    Console.WriteLine("Query was cancelled.");
}

// Trigger cancellation
cts.Cancel();
```

In this example, the WithCancellation method specifies a CancellationToken for the query. When the cancellation is requested, the query stops processing and throws an OperationCanceledException.

9. Combining PLINQ with LINQ

PLINQ can be combined with traditional LINQ operations to create complex query pipelines. This allows you to leverage the best of both worlds—using parallelism for data-intensive tasks and LINQ for simpler sequential operations.

Example: Combining PLINQ with LINQ

```csharp
var results = numbers.AsParallel()
                     .Where(n => n % 2 == 0) // Parallelized operation
```

```
.AsSequential() // Switch back to
sequential mode
.OrderBy(n => n); // Sequential sorting
operation
```

In this example, the query uses PLINQ for filtering but switches back to sequential LINQ for sorting. This is because parallelized sorting can introduce significant overhead, especially if ordering is critical.

10. Best Practices for Using PLINQ

To maximize the effectiveness of PLINQ, consider the following best practices:

- **Use PLINQ for CPU-bound Tasks:** PLINQ is most effective for CPU-bound tasks where each element in the collection requires independent computation. Avoid using PLINQ for I/O-bound operations or small workloads where the overhead of parallelization outweighs the benefits.
- **Avoid Complex Operations in PLINQ:** Simple operations like filtering, mapping, and reducing work well with PLINQ. However, avoid using it for complex tasks that involve heavy synchronization, state management, or non-deterministic results.
- **Use the Default Parallelism:** Let PLINQ manage the degree of parallelism unless you have specific performance considerations. Manual adjustments can sometimes lead to suboptimal results if not carefully tuned.
- **Handle Exceptions Gracefully:** Always be prepared to handle exceptions in PLINQ, as they can occur on multiple threads. Use AggregateException to capture and process exceptions effectively.
- **Measure and Benchmark:** Before introducing PLINQ, measure the baseline performance and run benchmarks after applying PLINQ to ensure it results in a measurable improvement. Parallelism is not always beneficial, especially for small datasets.

PLINQ is a powerful extension to LINQ that allows developers to parallelize data processing tasks easily and efficiently. By leveraging multiple cores, PLINQ can significantly improve the performance of applications that involve large datasets or CPU-bound computations. Its declarative syntax, combined with dynamic load balancing, automatic parallelization, and built-in exception handling, makes it a valuable tool for high-performance computing in C#10 and .NET 6.

However, as with all parallel programming constructs, careful consideration is needed to determine when and how to use PLINQ effectively. By following best practices and understanding the nuances of parallel execution, developers can harness the full power of PLINQ to build scalable and responsive applications.

Leveraging Asynchronous Programming in C#10

Asynchronous programming has become a cornerstone of modern software development, enabling developers to write responsive, scalable, and efficient applications. In C#10 and .NET 6, asynchronous programming is primarily achieved through the use of the async and await keywords, which allow for non-blocking operations in a clean and intuitive manner. This style of programming is crucial in scenarios where applications need to perform I/O-bound tasks or manage concurrency without tying up system resources unnecessarily.

1. Why Asynchronous Programming Matters

Asynchronous programming allows an application to perform tasks concurrently, which means it can continue executing other operations while waiting for long-running tasks to complete. This approach is essential for improving application responsiveness and scalability, particularly in situations like:

- **I/O-bound tasks:** Reading from files, making HTTP requests, accessing databases, or interacting with APIs.
- **Real-time applications:** Handling real-time notifications, live updates, or streaming data.
- **User interfaces:** Keeping UIs responsive by offloading background work from the main thread.

In traditional synchronous programming, tasks are executed one after the other, which can lead to blocked threads, unresponsive interfaces, and inefficient resource utilization. Asynchronous programming addresses these challenges by offloading long-running tasks to the background while allowing other parts of the application to continue executing.

2. Understanding async and await

The async and await keywords are the foundation of asynchronous programming in C#. They allow developers to define asynchronous methods and consume asynchronous tasks without complex callbacks or manual thread management.

- **async:** The async keyword is used to declare an asynchronous method. It indicates that the method contains one or more await expressions.
- **await:** The await keyword suspends the execution of the method until the awaited task completes. During this suspension, control returns to the caller, which can continue executing other tasks.

Example: Basic Asynchronous Method

```csharp
csharp

public async Task<string> GetDataAsync()
{
    await Task.Delay(1000); // Simulate a delay or I/O operation
    return "Data retrieved";
}
```

```
public async Task MainAsync()
{
    string data = await GetDataAsync();
    Console.WriteLine(data);
}
```

In this example, GetDataAsync is an asynchronous method that simulates a delay. The await keyword allows the main method to continue executing other operations while waiting for GetDataAsync to complete.

3. Best Practices for Asynchronous Programming

Asynchronous programming can introduce complexities, so it's essential to follow best practices to ensure the code is efficient and maintainable:

- **Use async All the Way:** Asynchronous methods should call other asynchronous methods rather than mixing synchronous and asynchronous code. This approach, known as "async all the way," prevents potential deadlocks and improves readability.
- **Avoid Blocking Calls:** Avoid using .Wait() or .Result on asynchronous tasks, as these blocking calls can lead to deadlocks or degrade performance. Always use await instead.
- **Return Task or ValueTask:** Return Task or ValueTask instead of void for asynchronous methods, except for top-level event handlers. This allows the caller to await the method and handle exceptions effectively.

4. Task-based Asynchronous Pattern (TAP)

The Task-based Asynchronous Pattern (TAP) is the recommended model for writing asynchronous code in .NET. It uses tasks (Task or Task<T>) to represent asynchronous operations. TAP provides several advantages:

- **Consistency:** Methods that follow TAP have a consistent naming convention (Async suffix) and return a Task or Task<T>.
- **Exception Handling:** Tasks allow for clean exception handling with try/catch blocks and await.

Example: Using TAP

```csharp
public async Task<int> ComputeSumAsync(int a, int b)
{
    await Task.Delay(100); // Simulate a delay
    return a + b;
}

public async Task MainAsync()
{
    try
    {
        int sum = await ComputeSumAsync(5, 10);
        Console.WriteLine($"Sum: {sum}");
    }
    catch (Exception ex)
    {
        Console.WriteLine($"An error occurred: {ex.Message}");
    }
}
```

5. ValueTask for Optimized Asynchronous Code

C# introduced the ValueTask structure to optimize scenarios where asynchronous results are often already available. Unlike Task, ValueTask avoids unnecessary allocations by reusing results or directly returning a completed task.

When to Use ValueTask:

- Use ValueTask in high-performance scenarios where allocations need to be minimized.
- Avoid using ValueTask for public APIs or complex workflows where tasks may be awaited multiple times.

Example: Using ValueTask

csharp

```csharp
public ValueTask<int> GetCachedValueAsync(bool isCached)
{
    return isCached ? new ValueTask<int>(42) : new
    ValueTask<int>(ComputeValueAsync());

    async Task<int> ComputeValueAsync()
    {
        await Task.Delay(100); // Simulate a delay
        return 42;
    }
}
```

6. Asynchronous Streams with IAsyncEnumerable<T>

.NET provides asynchronous streams using the IAsyncEnumerable<T> interface and the await foreach loop. This feature allows developers to iterate over asynchronous data streams efficiently, making it ideal for scenarios like reading large datasets or streaming real-time data.

Example: Asynchronous Stream

csharp

```csharp
public async IAsyncEnumerable<int> GenerateNumbersAsync()
{
    for (int i = 1; i <= 5; i++)
    {
        await Task.Delay(500); // Simulate an asynchronous operation
        yield return i;
    }
}

public async Task ProcessNumbersAsync()
{
    await foreach (var number in GenerateNumbersAsync())
    {
```

```
        Console.WriteLine($"Received number: {number}");
    }
}
```

In this example, the GenerateNumbersAsync method yields numbers asynchronously. The await foreach loop allows for consuming the stream efficiently without blocking.

7. Handling Exceptions in Asynchronous Code

Exception handling is a critical aspect of writing robust asynchronous code. When an exception occurs in an asynchronous method, it is propagated to the caller and can be caught using a try/catch block around the await expression.

Example: Exception Handling in Asynchronous Methods

```csharp

public async Task<int> DivideAsync(int numerator, int denominator)
{
    if (denominator == 0)
        throw new DivideByZeroException("Denominator cannot be zero");

    await Task.Delay(100); // Simulate a delay
    return numerator / denominator;
}

public async Task MainAsync()
{
    try
    {
        int result = await DivideAsync(10, 0);
        Console.WriteLine($"Result: {result}");
    }
    catch (DivideByZeroException ex)
    {
        Console.WriteLine($"Caught exception: {ex.Message}");
```

        }
}

8. Cancellation in Asynchronous Operations

Asynchronous operations can be canceled using a CancellationToken. This allows developers to gracefully stop long-running tasks in response to user actions or system events.

Example: Using CancellationToken

```csharp
public async Task PerformLongOperationAsync(CancellationToken cancellationToken)
{
    for (int i = 0; i < 10; i++)
    {
        // Check for cancellation
        if (cancellationToken.IsCancellationRequested)
        {
            Console.WriteLine("Operation canceled.");
            return;
        }

        await Task.Delay(500, cancellationToken); // Support cancellation in async operation
        Console.WriteLine($"Processing {i}");
    }
}

public async Task MainAsync()
{
    CancellationTokenSource cts = new CancellationTokenSource();
    Task task = PerformLongOperationAsync(cts.Token);

    // Cancel the task after 2 seconds
    await Task.Delay(2000);
    cts.Cancel();
```

```
    await task;
}
```

9. Asynchronous Design Patterns

When designing asynchronous applications, consider the following patterns and practices:

- **Fire-and-Forget:** This pattern involves launching an asynchronous task without awaiting it. Use this pattern cautiously, as unhandled exceptions can lead to application instability. It's suitable for logging or telemetry tasks that should not block the main flow.
- **Fan-out/Fan-in:** This pattern involves launching multiple asynchronous tasks (fan-out) and then waiting for all of them to complete (fan-in). It's ideal for processing multiple independent operations concurrently.
- **Producer-Consumer:** This pattern is commonly used in multithreaded scenarios where one part of the application produces data and another part consumes it. Use asynchronous streams (IAsyncEnumerable<T>) for implementing this pattern efficiently.

10. Best Practices for Asynchronous Programming

To fully leverage the power of asynchronous programming in C#10 and .NET 6, consider these best practices:

- **Prefer Asynchronous I/O over Parallel I/O:** Use asynchronous methods for I/O-bound operations, as they are more efficient than creating multiple threads to handle I/O tasks concurrently.
- **Handle Timeouts and Cancellations:** Implement timeouts and support cancellation tokens to improve resilience and responsiveness, especially in long-running operations.
- **Use ConfigureAwait(false) in Libraries:** For library code, use ConfigureAwait(false) to avoid capturing the synchronization context, reducing unnecessary context switches and improving performance.

- **Avoid async void:** Except for top-level event handlers, avoid using async void methods. Instead, return a Task or Task<T> to allow proper exception handling and awaiting.

Asynchronous programming in C#10 and .NET 6 is an essential tool for building scalable and responsive applications. By leveraging the async and await keywords, tasks, and modern features like asynchronous streams, developers can write efficient, non-blocking code that improves the user experience and system throughput.

Understanding and following best practices in asynchronous programming, including effective exception handling, cancellation support, and optimized resource management, allows developers to create robust and maintainable solutions. By adopting these techniques and patterns, you can build applications that are well-suited to handle the complexities of modern software development, including real-time updates, high concurrency, and distributed architectures.

Case Studies: Real-World High-Performance Applications

High-performance applications are a necessity in today's fast-paced, data-driven environment. Businesses and industries demand solutions that can efficiently handle large-scale computations, process vast amounts of data, or support real-time decision-making. In this chapter, we will explore real-world case studies that demonstrate how C#10 and .NET 6 have been successfully leveraged to build high-performance applications. These case studies highlight the challenges faced, solutions implemented, and the key takeaways for developers.

1. **Financial Services: Real-Time Market Data Processing**
   Problem Statement:

A leading financial services firm needed to build a real-time market data processing system capable of ingesting and analyzing data feeds from multiple financial markets. The existing system was slow, faced latency issues, and was unable to scale efficiently with increasing data volumes.

Solution Approach:

The development team decided to use C#10 and .NET 6 to build a new system that could process market data with low latency and high throughput. The system's requirements included real-time ingestion, data filtering, analytics, and delivery of trading insights to downstream systems.

Implementation:

- **Asynchronous I/O with Task-based Asynchronous Pattern (TAP):** The team utilized asynchronous programming to handle real-time market feeds, enabling the application to ingest data continuously without blocking I/O threads. This approach reduced data ingestion latency significantly.
- **Parallel Data Processing with PLINQ:** Parallel LINQ (PLINQ) was used to parallelize data filtering and transformation operations. PLINQ automatically distributed the workload across multiple cores, allowing the system to process large amounts of market data concurrently.
- **Low-Latency Networking with Sockets:** The team leveraged the improved networking features in .NET 6 to establish low-latency connections with market data sources. They used efficient serialization techniques to minimize the size of data packets being transmitted.

Outcome:

The new system achieved a 50% reduction in data processing latency and a 3x increase in data throughput. The adoption of C#10 and .NET 6's asynchronous and parallel programming features enabled the firm to handle increasing market volumes without sacrificing performance. Real-time analytics improved trading decision accuracy, resulting in increased profits.

Key Takeaway:

Effective use of asynchronous I/O and parallelism can significantly enhance the performance of real-time applications, particularly in data-intensive industries like finance.

2. Healthcare: Genomic Data Analysis for Personalized Medicine
Problem Statement:

A healthcare research organization aimed to develop a high-performance application to analyze genomic data for personalized medicine. The goal was to identify genetic markers linked to various diseases and recommend personalized treatment plans based on genomic profiles. The existing solution struggled with processing terabytes of genomic data efficiently.

Solution Approach:

The development team chose C#10 and .NET 6 to build a scalable genomic analysis pipeline. Key challenges included processing large datasets, performing complex mathematical computations, and ensuring efficient memory management.

Implementation:

- **Efficient Memory Management with Span<T> and Memory<T>:** The team leveraged Span<T> and Memory<T> to efficiently handle large in-memory datasets without excessive allocations or memory copying. This approach reduced memory overhead and improved processing speed.
- **Parallel Execution with Task Parallel Library (TPL):** The pipeline was designed using TPL to parallelize computational tasks, such as DNA sequence alignment and statistical analysis. This enabled the application to distribute workload evenly across all available cores.
- **Asynchronous Data Loading with IAsyncEnumerable<T>:** To handle large data files, the team used asynchronous streams (IAsyncEnumerable<T>) for incremental data loading and processing. This reduced I/O bottlenecks and memory consumption.

Outcome:

The new genomic analysis pipeline reduced data processing time from hours to minutes, enabling researchers to quickly identify genetic markers and recommend personalized treatments. The combination of efficient memory handling and parallel processing significantly improved the overall throughput and scalability of the system.

Key Takeaway:

Leveraging advanced data structures and parallel processing techniques in C#10 and .NET 6 can lead to substantial improvements in the performance of scientific and healthcare applications.

3. Logistics: Real-Time Route Optimization for Fleet Management

Problem Statement:

A logistics company required a real-time fleet management system capable of dynamically optimizing delivery routes based on traffic conditions, order priority, and driver availability. The existing solution struggled to provide timely updates and lacked the scalability to support a growing fleet.

Solution Approach:

The development team built a high-performance fleet management system using C#10 and .NET 6, focusing on optimizing real-time route calculations and system responsiveness.

Implementation:

- **Asynchronous Programming for Real-Time Data Ingestion:** The system used asynchronous programming with async and await to continuously ingest traffic data and driver location updates from multiple sources. This allowed for non-blocking processing of real-time events.
- **Parallel Algorithms for Route Optimization:** The team implemented parallel algorithms to dynamically calculate and update delivery routes based on real-time data. They used TPL to distribute the route calculations across multiple cores, reducing processing time for large fleets.
- **Caching with Distributed Systems:** The system employed caching mechanisms to store frequently accessed route information, reducing redundant computations and improving response times.

Outcome:

The new fleet management system achieved a 30% reduction in delivery times and a 20% increase in fleet efficiency. The combination of asynchronous data ingestion and parallel route optimization enabled the company to provide real-time route updates and respond quickly to changing traffic conditions.

Key Takeaway:

Combining asynchronous data ingestion with parallel algorithms can lead to significant performance gains in real-time logistics and routing applications.

4. Manufacturing: Predictive Maintenance with IoT Data Streams

Problem Statement:

A manufacturing company needed a solution to predict equipment failures in their production lines based on real-time IoT sensor data. The existing monitoring system struggled with latency issues and frequent data loss, affecting production efficiency.

Solution Approach:

The development team chose C#10 and .NET 6 to build a high-performance predictive maintenance system capable of processing IoT data streams and predicting equipment failures in real-time.

Implementation:

- **Asynchronous Streams with IAsyncEnumerable<T>:** The team used asynchronous streams to process sensor data in real-time, enabling the system to handle large data streams without blocking threads. This approach improved data ingestion and reduced latency.
- **Machine Learning Integration with ML.NET:** The system employed ML.NET to train and deploy machine learning models that predicted equipment failures based on historical sensor data. The team optimized the inference process to run efficiently on multiple cores.
- **Parallel Data Processing with PLINQ:** The team used PLINQ to parallelize data filtering and preprocessing tasks, such as outlier detection

and data normalization, before feeding the data into machine learning models.

Outcome:

The predictive maintenance system reduced equipment downtime by 40% and improved overall production efficiency. The use of asynchronous streams and parallel processing enabled the system to handle large volumes of IoT data in real-time and provide timely maintenance alerts.

Key Takeaway:

Asynchronous streams and parallel processing are essential for handling real-time IoT data streams and enabling predictive analytics in manufacturing environments.

5. Gaming Industry: Real-Time Multiplayer Game Server

Problem Statement:

A game development studio needed to build a real-time multiplayer game server capable of handling thousands of concurrent players. The existing server architecture suffered from performance issues, leading to high latency and frequent disconnects.

Solution Approach:

The development team built a high-performance multiplayer game server using C#10 and .NET 6, focusing on optimizing network communication, player state synchronization, and server scalability.

Implementation:

- **Task Parallel Library for Game State Updates:** The server used TPL to parallelize game state updates, distributing player actions and physics calculations across multiple cores. This reduced the time required to update the game world for all players.
- **Low-Latency Networking with Kestrel and Sockets:** The team leveraged Kestrel's low-latency capabilities for HTTP-based communications and raw sockets for direct player-to-server connections. This combination enabled fast and reliable data exchange between the server

and game clients.
- **Efficient Memory Management with Object Pools:** To handle high player counts, the server used object pools to recycle frequently used game objects, reducing memory allocations and garbage collection overhead.

Outcome:

The multiplayer game server achieved a 50% reduction in player latency and a significant increase in player concurrency. The use of parallel processing, low-latency networking, and efficient memory management enabled the game to provide a smooth and responsive multiplayer experience.

Key Takeaway:

Combining parallel processing with low-latency networking is critical for building real-time multiplayer game servers capable of supporting large player bases.

These case studies demonstrate the versatility and power of C#10 and .NET 6 in building high-performance applications across various industries. Whether it's real-time financial analysis, healthcare data processing, logistics optimization, manufacturing predictive maintenance, or gaming, the features and capabilities of .NET 6 provide the necessary foundation for scalable, responsive, and efficient solutions.

By leveraging asynchronous programming, parallel processing, efficient memory management, and modern networking features, developers can tackle the challenges of real-world high-performance applications and deliver solutions that meet the demands of today's data-driven world.

Memory Management and Optimization in .NET 6

Advanced Memory Profiling and Optimization

Effective memory management is crucial for building high-performance applications. In .NET 6, memory profiling and optimization involve a deep understanding of how memory is allocated, used, and released within an application. Advanced memory profiling techniques can help identify memory leaks, excessive allocations, inefficient use of data structures, and other issues that impact application performance.

This chapter explores the advanced concepts and best practices for memory profiling and optimization in .NET 6, focusing on the tools and techniques available to developers to build memory-efficient applications.

1. Why Memory Profiling Matters

Memory profiling is the process of analyzing an application's memory usage to identify potential issues such as excessive allocations, memory leaks, high garbage collection (GC) pressure, and inefficient data structures. Efficient memory usage is critical for applications that handle large datasets, perform real-time processing, or run in environments with limited resources.

Key reasons for memory profiling include:

- **Reducing Memory Leaks:** Memory leaks can cause applications to consume more memory over time, leading to poor performance and even system crashes.
- **Minimizing GC Pressure:** High memory allocations result in frequent garbage collection cycles, which can degrade application responsiveness.
- **Improving Scalability:** Memory-optimized applications can handle larger workloads and support more concurrent users without degrading performance.
- **Optimizing Resource-Constrained Environments:** Efficient memory management is essential for applications running in low-resource environments like mobile devices, embedded systems, or cloud services with memory limitations.

2. The Managed Heap and Garbage Collection in .NET 6

In .NET 6, all memory allocated for reference types and certain value types resides in the *managed heap*. The .NET runtime includes a garbage collector (GC) that automatically manages memory by releasing unused objects and reclaiming space. Understanding the managed heap and GC behavior is fundamental to effective memory management.

Key Concepts:

- **Generations:** The .NET garbage collector divides objects into three generations: Gen 0, Gen 1, and Gen 2. New objects are allocated in Gen 0, and surviving objects are promoted to higher generations.
- **Large Object Heap (LOH):** Objects larger than 85,000 bytes are allocated in the LOH, which is managed separately. Frequent large allocations can lead to memory fragmentation and increased GC pressure.
- **Garbage Collection Modes:** .NET supports different GC modes, including workstation GC (optimized for client applications) and server GC (optimized for high-throughput server applications).

3. Memory Profiling Tools for .NET 6

Several tools are available for profiling memory in .NET 6, each offering unique features and insights. The choice of tool depends on the specific profiling requirements and the type of application being analyzed.

1. Visual Studio Profiler:

Visual Studio's built-in memory profiler provides an intuitive interface for analyzing memory usage. It includes features such as heap snapshots, instance counting, and object allocation tracking.

Key Features:

- Take heap snapshots at different points in time to compare memory usage.
- Identify large objects or objects that remain in memory longer than expected.
- View details about allocated objects, including their types, sizes, and lifetimes.

2. dotMemory:

JetBrains dotMemory is a comprehensive memory profiling tool for .NET applications. It offers detailed insights into memory usage, including heap analysis, object retention graphs, and memory allocation patterns.

Key Features:

- Analyze memory leaks by tracking object retention and identifying root objects.
- View memory traffic to identify excessive memory allocations and deallocations.
- Compare memory snapshots to detect changes in memory usage over time.

3. PerfView:

PerfView is an open-source profiling tool developed by Microsoft. While it is primarily used for CPU profiling, it also includes powerful memory

analysis capabilities.
Key Features:

- Analyze .NET GC events to understand memory allocation patterns and GC behavior.
- View detailed allocation call stacks to identify the source of memory allocations.
- Generate heap dumps for further analysis with external tools.

4. Windows Performance Recorder (WPR) and Windows Performance Analyzer (WPA):
WPR and WPA are advanced profiling tools from Microsoft that can capture low-level memory events, including kernel-mode and user-mode memory allocations.
Key Features:

- Capture detailed ETW (Event Tracing for Windows) events related to memory allocations.
- Visualize memory usage over time and identify high-memory-consumption phases.
- Correlate memory events with other system metrics such as CPU usage and I/O activity.

4. Analyzing and Interpreting Memory Profiler Results
Memory profiling tools provide a wealth of information about an application's memory usage, but interpreting this data effectively is key to identifying optimization opportunities. Here are some common memory-related issues to watch for and how to interpret profiler results:

- **High Allocation Rate:** Indicates that the application is creating objects at a rapid pace. High allocation rates can lead to frequent garbage collection cycles and impact application performance. Profiler tools can help identify the code paths responsible for excessive allocations.

- **Retained Objects:** Objects that remain in memory even after they are no longer needed can cause memory leaks. Profilers can track retained objects and identify their root references, allowing developers to address the source of the memory leak.
- **Large Object Heap (LOH) Fragmentation:** Frequent allocations in the LOH can lead to memory fragmentation, which reduces the efficiency of memory usage. Profilers can provide insights into large object allocations and suggest opportunities to optimize data structures or reduce allocation sizes.
- **High GC Frequency:** Frequent garbage collection cycles can indicate that the application is under high memory pressure. Profilers can analyze GC events and show which objects are being collected repeatedly.

Example Analysis Workflow:

1. **Start with a Baseline:** Take an initial memory snapshot to establish a baseline memory usage profile.
2. **Identify High Allocation Methods:** Use allocation views or call stacks to find methods that are allocating large amounts of memory.
3. **Check for Memory Leaks:** Look for objects that are not being released or are growing in size over time. Examine their root references and analyze how they are being held in memory.
4. **Review LOH Usage:** Check the LOH usage and look for large objects that could be fragmented or inefficiently allocated.
5. **Compare Snapshots:** Take additional memory snapshots after changes or specific actions in the application to compare and track memory usage over time.

5. Advanced Memory Optimization Techniques

After identifying memory-related issues, the next step is to apply advanced memory optimization techniques to improve application performance. Below are some key strategies:

1. Optimize Data Structures:

- **Use Span<T> and Memory<T>:** These stack-based memory constructs reduce heap allocations and avoid unnecessary copying of large data structures. They are particularly useful for handling large arrays or buffers efficiently.
- **Choose the Right Collection:** Use collections that are optimized for specific operations. For example, use List<T> for sequential access and Dictionary<TKey, TValue> for frequent lookups.
- **Use Immutable Data Structures:** Immutable collections prevent accidental data modifications and reduce the risk of shared state issues in multi-threaded applications.

2. Reduce Large Object Heap (LOH) Allocations:

- **Avoid Allocating Large Arrays or Strings:** If possible, break large objects into smaller segments to reduce LOH usage. Use array pooling or segmented data structures to manage large datasets more efficiently.
- **Use Array Pools:** Leverage the ArrayPool<T> class in .NET to recycle and reuse large arrays instead of creating new ones each time. This reduces both memory fragmentation and allocation overhead.

3. Implement Object Pooling: Object pooling is a technique that allows the reuse of frequently created objects instead of repeatedly allocating and deallocating them. In .NET, you can use the ObjectPool<T> class or implement custom pooling logic for commonly used objects.

Example of Using Object Pooling:

```csharp
public class MyPooledObject
{
    public int Id { get; set; }
}

var pool = new DefaultObjectPool<MyPooledObject>(new
```

```
DefaultPooledObjectPolicy<MyPooledObject>());

var pooledObject = pool.Get();
pooledObject.Id = 42;
pool.Return(pooledObject);
```

4. Optimize String Handling: Strings are immutable in .NET, which means that every modification creates a new string instance. To reduce memory allocations:

- Use StringBuilder for concatenating multiple strings.
- Intern frequently used strings using String.Intern.
- Avoid unnecessary string conversions, especially in tight loops or large datasets.

5. Minimize Boxing and Unboxing: Boxing and unboxing occur when value types are converted to reference types and vice versa. This operation incurs performance and memory costs. To avoid boxing:

- Use generics to create type-safe collections and methods.
- Explicitly convert between value types and reference types only when necessary.

6. Reducing Garbage Collection Pressure

Reducing garbage collection pressure involves minimizing unnecessary memory allocations and optimizing the lifetime of objects. Here are some strategies to achieve this:

- **Use Value Types Instead of Reference Types:** Value types (structs) are allocated on the stack, reducing heap pressure. However, use value types judiciously to avoid copying large structs, which can lead to performance degradation.
- **Minimize Temporary Allocations:** Avoid creating temporary objects

in performance-critical code paths. Use caching mechanisms or reuse existing objects where possible.
- **Control Object Lifetimes:** Reduce the scope of objects and variables to ensure they are collected promptly. Use weak references for objects that are not critical but should be retained if possible.

Using Span<T>, Memory<T>, and Ref Returns

Efficient memory management is crucial for high-performance applications, particularly those that process large amounts of data or require real-time responsiveness. In .NET 6, Span<T>, Memory<T>, and ref returns provide developers with tools to handle memory in a more efficient and low-overhead manner. These features enable fine-grained control over memory usage, helping to minimize allocations, reduce copying, and avoid unnecessary heap pressure.

1. Overview of Span<T> and Memory<T>

Span<T> and Memory<T> are stack-allocated memory abstractions introduced in .NET Core and enhanced in later versions. They allow developers to work with slices of memory efficiently, without the overhead of heap allocations and unnecessary data copying.

- **Span<T>:** Represents a contiguous region of arbitrary memory on the stack. It can point to arrays, slices of arrays, strings, or native memory. Span<T> is allocated on the stack, providing better performance and lower allocation costs.
- **Memory<T>:** Represents a span-like structure that can be allocated on either the stack or the heap. Memory<T> is more versatile than Span<T> and can be used in asynchronous methods where the stack might not be available.

Key Advantages of Span<T> and Memory<T>:

- **Low Allocation Overhead:** Both Span<T> and Memory<T> minimize heap allocations, reducing garbage collection pressure.
- **Efficient Slicing:** They provide an easy way to work with slices of data without copying the underlying array or buffer.
- **Interoperability:** They allow interop scenarios with native code or unmanaged memory, making them ideal for high-performance applications.

2. Working with Span<T>

Span<T> is a lightweight memory view that allows developers to work with a contiguous block of memory. It can be used to reference an array, slice an existing array, or interact with memory blocks.

Example: Slicing an Array with Span<T>

```csharp
int[] numbers = new int[] { 1, 2, 3, 4, 5, 6, 7, 8, 9 };
Span<int> middleSection = numbers.AsSpan(2, 4); // Slices the array [3, 4, 5, 6]

for (int i = 0; i < middleSection.Length; i++)
{
    Console.WriteLine(middleSection[i]); // Output: 3, 4, 5, 6
}
```

Example: Modifying a Slice

```csharp
Span<int> firstHalf = numbers.AsSpan(0, 4);
firstHalf[0] = 42;
Console.WriteLine(numbers[0]); // Output: 42
```

In this example, Span<T> provides a way to view and modify a segment of the original array without creating additional memory allocations. Any modifications made to the Span<T> are reflected in the underlying array.

3. Working with Memory<T>

While Span<T> is stack-only and cannot be used in asynchronous methods, Memory<T> offers the flexibility of heap-based storage. It retains the slicing capabilities of Span<T>, but it can be passed around and used in scenarios where the stack might not be accessible.

Example: Passing Memory in Asynchronous Methods

```csharp
public async Task ProcessDataAsync(Memory<byte> buffer)
{
    // Perform asynchronous I/O operations on the buffer
    await Task.Delay(1000); // Simulate async work
    Span<byte> span = buffer.Span;
    span[0] = 42; // Modify data in the span
}
```

In this example, the buffer is passed as Memory<byte>, allowing it to be used asynchronously. Inside the method, the memory is accessed using the Span property to modify the data.

4. Performance Considerations with Span<T> and Memory<T>

Span<T> and Memory<T> provide several performance benefits, but there are a few considerations to keep in mind:

- **Stack Allocation and Size:** Span<T> relies on stack allocation, which is limited in size. Large allocations should use Memory<T> or other heap-based structures to avoid stack overflow.
- **Bounds Checking:** Span<T> performs bounds checking to prevent out-of-bounds access, which provides safety at a slight performance cost. However, this is usually negligible compared to the cost of heap allocations.

5. Ref Returns in C#

Ref returns allow methods to return a reference to a variable, enabling direct modifications of the returned value. This can significantly reduce memory allocations and improve performance by avoiding unnecessary copying of large data structures.

Syntax for Ref Returns:

- ref Keyword in Method Signature: Indicates that the method returns a reference.
- ref Keyword in Return Statement: Specifies the return of a reference to a variable.

Example: Returning a Reference from an Array

```csharp
public ref int GetElementRef(int[] array, int index)
{
    if (index < 0 || index >= array.Length)
        throw new IndexOutOfRangeException();

    return ref array[index]; // Return a reference to the
    element at the specified index
}

// Usage example
int[] numbers = { 10, 20, 30 };
ref int element = ref GetElementRef(numbers, 1); // Get a
reference to the second element
element = 42; // Modify the element directly
Console.WriteLine(numbers[1]); // Output: 42
```

In this example, the method GetElementRef returns a reference to an element in an array. The caller can then modify the element directly through the reference, avoiding the need to copy the value.

6. Combining Span<T>, Memory<T>, and Ref Returns for Performance

Span<T>, Memory<T>, and ref returns can be combined to build high-performance code that minimizes allocations and maximizes efficiency. Here are some practical scenarios where these features shine:

1. Efficient Data Processing in Buffers:

When working with large buffers or data streams, Span<T> can be used to create lightweight views of the data, while Memory<T> ensures compatibility with asynchronous methods. Ref returns can be employed to provide efficient access to specific elements in the buffer.

Example: Using Span<T>, Memory<T>, and Ref Returns in a Data Processing Pipeline

```csharp
public ref byte GetByteRef(Memory<byte> buffer, int index)
{
    if (index < 0 || index >= buffer.Length)
        throw new IndexOutOfRangeException();

    return ref buffer.Span[index]; // Return a reference to the
    byte at the specified index
}

public void ProcessBuffer(Memory<byte> buffer)
{
    ref byte firstByte = ref GetByteRef(buffer, 0);
    firstByte = 255; // Modify the first byte directly

    Span<byte> slice = buffer.Span.Slice(1, 4); // Create a
    slice of the buffer
    for (int i = 0; i < slice.Length; i++)
    {
        slice[i] = (byte)(slice[i] + 1); // Increment each byte
        in the slice
    }
}
```

In this example, GetByteRef returns a reference to a byte in the buffer, allowing direct modifications. The ProcessBuffer method then creates a Span<T> slice of the buffer and performs in-place modifications efficiently.

2. Optimizing String Manipulation:

String manipulation can be expensive due to the immutability of strings. Span<char> and ReadOnlySpan<char> allow efficient manipulation of substrings without allocating new strings, making them ideal for parsing or formatting scenarios.

Example: Efficient String Parsing with ReadOnlySpan<char>

```csharp
public static int ParseFirstNumber(ReadOnlySpan<char> input)
{
    int result = 0;
    foreach (char c in input)
    {
        if (char.IsDigit(c))
        {
            result = result * 10 + (c - '0');
        }
        else
        {
            break; // Stop parsing on the first non-digit character
        }
    }
    return result;
}

string data = "12345,67890";
int firstNumber = ParseFirstNumber(data.AsSpan()); // Parse the first number efficiently
Console.WriteLine(firstNumber); // Output: 12345
```

7. Best Practices for Using Span<T>, Memory<T>, and Ref Returns

- **Use Span<T> for Performance-Critical Code:** When you need high

performance and low memory overhead, consider using Span<T> for operations that can be safely performed on the stack.
- **Prefer Memory<T> for Asynchronous Code:** Use Memory<T> when working with large data sets or in scenarios where stack-based allocation is not feasible, such as asynchronous methods or long-lived objects.
- **Use Ref Returns for Large or Frequently Accessed Data:** Ref returns are ideal for providing efficient access to large data structures, such as arrays or complex objects, without copying.
- **Minimize Stack Size with Large Data:** Be cautious when using large data sets with Span<T> to avoid stack overflows. Switch to Memory<T> or other heap-based storage if the size exceeds stack limits.

Span<T>, Memory<T>, and ref returns provide developers with powerful tools for efficient memory management in .NET 6. These features enable fine-grained control over memory usage, reduce unnecessary heap allocations, and enhance the performance of data-intensive applications. By leveraging these constructs, developers can build high-performance applications that are both responsive and scalable, without sacrificing code clarity or maintainability.

Garbage Collection Optimization Techniques

Garbage Collection (GC) in .NET is a managed memory feature that automatically releases unused memory, freeing developers from manually managing allocations and deallocations. However, inefficient GC behavior can lead to application performance degradation, with issues such as increased latency, frequent pauses, and excessive memory usage. Optimizing GC is crucial for high-performance applications, especially those that require low latency or deal with large datasets.

This section explores advanced garbage collection optimization techniques in .NET 6, helping developers understand and control GC behavior to maximize application efficiency.

1. Understanding .NET's Garbage Collection

The .NET runtime uses a generational garbage collection algorithm that categorizes objects into three generations based on their lifespan:

- **Generation 0 (Gen 0):** Contains short-lived objects. These are typically objects that are allocated and quickly become unreachable.
- **Generation 1 (Gen 1):** Acts as a buffer between short-lived (Gen 0) and long-lived (Gen 2) objects. Objects that survive a Gen 0 collection are promoted to Gen 1.
- **Generation 2 (Gen 2):** Contains long-lived objects, such as static objects or objects that persist for the lifetime of the application.

Large Object Heap (LOH): The LOH stores objects larger than 85,000 bytes. Unlike smaller objects, large objects are allocated directly into Gen 2. Excessive LOH allocations can lead to memory fragmentation and increased GC pressure.

GC Modes in .NET 6:

- **Workstation GC:** Optimized for desktop and client applications. Provides a low-latency experience by running GC on a single core.
- **Server GC:** Optimized for high-throughput applications, like web servers and cloud services. Utilizes multiple threads for garbage collection, improving scalability.

2. Optimizing Garbage Collection Behavior

Optimizing GC behavior involves understanding how memory is allocated and collected and applying techniques to reduce the frequency and duration of garbage collection cycles. Here are some strategies for optimizing garbage collection:

1. Minimize Allocations in High-Frequency Code Paths

One of the most effective ways to optimize GC is to reduce the number of allocations in performance-critical code paths. Each allocation contributes to GC pressure, so minimizing unnecessary allocations can significantly reduce GC frequency and improve performance.

Techniques to Minimize Allocations:

- **Use Value Types (struct) Instead of Reference Types:** Value types are allocated on the stack, avoiding heap allocations. However, avoid using large structs as they can lead to high copying costs.
- **Reuse Objects:** Implement object pooling using the ObjectPool<T> class or custom pooling logic to reuse frequently created objects, reducing allocation costs.
- **Avoid Boxing and Unboxing:** Avoid operations that convert value types to reference types and vice versa, as these cause heap allocations and increase GC pressure.

Example: Reducing Allocations in a Loop

```csharp
// Inefficient: Allocates a new string in each iteration
for (int i = 0; i < 1000; i++)
{
    string message = "Processing item " + i; // Allocates a new string
}

// Optimized: Uses StringBuilder to minimize allocations
var sb = new StringBuilder();
for (int i = 0; i < 1000; i++)
{
    sb.Clear();
    sb.Append("Processing item ").Append(i);
    string message = sb.ToString();
}
```

2. Optimize Large Object Heap (LOH) Allocations

The LOH is managed separately from other objects and is not compacted during garbage collection, leading to potential fragmentation. Excessive LOH allocations can cause frequent Gen 2 collections, which are more expensive in terms of time and resources.

Techniques to Optimize LOH:

- **Use Array Pooling for Large Arrays:** Use ArrayPool<T> to recycle large arrays instead of frequently allocating new ones. This reduces LOH fragmentation and the frequency of Gen 2 collections.
- **Break Large Objects into Smaller Segments:** If possible, split large objects into smaller chunks that can be allocated in Gen 0 or Gen 1. This reduces LOH pressure and improves memory efficiency.

Example: Using Array Pooling

```csharp
var arrayPool = ArrayPool<byte>.Shared;
byte[] buffer = arrayPool.Rent(100000); // Rent a large array from the pool

// Perform operations on the buffer

arrayPool.Return(buffer); // Return the array to the pool
```

3. Control Object Lifetimes

Optimizing object lifetimes involves reducing the amount of time objects spend in higher generations (Gen 1 and Gen 2). The longer an object stays in memory, the more expensive it becomes to collect.

Techniques to Control Object Lifetimes:

- **Reduce the Scope of Objects:** Limit the scope of objects to prevent them from being promoted to higher generations. Declare objects within the narrowest possible scope and avoid storing them in long-lived data structures unnecessarily.

- **Use Weak References:** When appropriate, use WeakReference<T> for objects that are optional or can be recreated if needed. Weak references do not prevent objects from being collected by GC.

Example: Using Weak References for Caching

```csharp
var cache = new Dictionary<int, WeakReference<object>>();

void AddToCache(int key, object value)
{
    cache[key] = new WeakReference<object>(value);
}

bool TryGetFromCache(int key, out object value)
{
    if (cache.TryGetValue(key, out WeakReference<object> weakRef) && weakRef.TryGetTarget(out value))
    {
        return true;
    }

    value = null;
    return false;
}
```

4. Optimize Garbage Collection Settings
Use Server GC for High-Throughput Applications:

If your application is a web server, cloud service, or high-throughput application, enable Server GC to utilize multiple threads for garbage collection. This improves scalability and throughput in multi-core environments.

Configure GC Settings in runtimeconfig.json:

```json
{
  "runtimeOptions": {
    "configProperties": {
      "System.GC.Server": true, // Enable Server GC
      "System.GC.RetainVM": false // Control VM memory release
      behavior
    }
  }
}
```

5. Profile and Monitor GC Events

Use memory profiling tools like Visual Studio Profiler, dotMemory, and PerfView to analyze GC behavior in your application. These tools provide insights into the number of Gen 0, Gen 1, and Gen 2 collections, the duration of each collection, and the allocation patterns.

Key Metrics to Monitor:

- **Gen 0, Gen 1, and Gen 2 Collection Counts:** Frequent collections indicate high allocation rates or memory leaks.
- **LOH Allocations:** Monitor large object allocations and fragmentation levels.
- **GC Pause Times:** Measure the duration of GC pauses to understand their impact on application responsiveness.

Example: Analyzing GC Events with PerfView

1. **Capture a GC trace** using PerfView to collect detailed information about GC events.
2. **Analyze the trace** to identify the number and duration of Gen 0, Gen 1, and Gen 2 collections.
3. **Identify high-allocation methods** using the allocation view, which shows the methods responsible for the most memory allocations.

3. Using Span<T> and Memory<T> to Reduce Allocations

As discussed earlier, Span<T> and Memory<T> provide a way to work with slices of data without allocating additional memory. By using these constructs, developers can avoid copying large arrays or buffers, reducing memory pressure and improving GC performance.

4. Managing Finalizers and IDisposable

Finalizers (~ClassName) and IDisposable are mechanisms for releasing unmanaged resources. However, improper use of finalizers can lead to increased GC pressure and memory retention.

Best Practices for Finalizers and IDisposable:

- **Implement IDisposable and Use using Statements:** For classes that manage unmanaged resources, implement the IDisposable interface and use using statements to ensure timely resource cleanup.
- **Avoid Finalizers if Possible:** Finalizers delay garbage collection and can increase memory usage. Use them only when necessary, and implement IDisposable for deterministic cleanup.

Example: Implementing IDisposable for Resource Cleanup

```csharp
csharp

public class ResourceHolder : IDisposable
{
    private bool disposed = false;

    public void Dispose()
    {
        Dispose(true);
        GC.SuppressFinalize(this); // Prevent finalizer from
        running
    }

    protected virtual void Dispose(bool disposing)
    {
```

```csharp
            if (!disposed)
            {
                if (disposing)
                {
                    // Release managed resources
                }
                // Release unmanaged resources

                disposed = true;
            }
        }

        ~ResourceHolder()
        {
            Dispose(false);
        }
    }
```

5. Asynchronous and Lazy Initialization

Lazy initialization and asynchronous initialization are techniques that can help improve memory efficiency by deferring the creation of objects until they are needed.

- **Lazy<T>:** Use the Lazy<T> class to create objects only when they are accessed for the first time. This reduces unnecessary allocations during startup or when the object is not always needed.
- **Asynchronous Initialization:** When initializing objects that depend on asynchronous operations, use asynchronous methods and avoid blocking calls to reduce memory consumption during initialization.

Example: Lazy Initialization

```csharp
public class ExpensiveResource
{
```

```
    private readonly Lazy<ExpensiveResource> _instance = new
    Lazy<ExpensiveResource>(() => new ExpensiveResource());

    public static ExpensiveResource Instance => _instance.Value;
}
```

Garbage collection optimization in .NET 6 involves a combination of reducing allocations, controlling object lifetimes, optimizing LOH usage, and leveraging advanced memory management features. By understanding how the garbage collector operates and employing strategies to reduce its workload, developers can build efficient and scalable applications that perform well under varying conditions.

Using memory profiling tools to monitor GC events and analyze memory usage patterns is essential for identifying optimization opportunities. By following best practices and implementing techniques like object pooling, weak references, array pooling, and Lazy initialization, developers can minimize GC overhead and achieve optimal application performance.

Practical Examples and Code Snippets

In this section, we will explore practical examples and code snippets that illustrate the garbage collection optimization techniques discussed in the previous sections. These examples demonstrate real-world scenarios and how specific strategies can be applied to improve memory management and garbage collection performance in .NET 6.

1. Reducing Allocations with Object Pooling

Object pooling is a technique used to minimize memory allocations by reusing objects instead of creating new ones. This is especially useful for frequently created objects that are expensive to initialize or contribute significantly to memory pressure.

Example: Implementing an Object Pool for Reusable Objects

```csharp
using Microsoft.Extensions.ObjectPool;

public class ReusableObject
{
    public int Id { get; set; }
    public string Name { get; set; }
}

public class ReusableObjectPolicy : PooledObjectPolicy<ReusableObject>
{
    public override ReusableObject Create() => new ReusableObject();

    public override bool Return(ReusableObject obj)
    {
        // Reset object state before returning to pool
        obj.Id = 0;
        obj.Name = string.Empty;
        return true;
    }
}

public class ObjectPoolDemo
{
    public void DemonstrateObjectPooling()
    {
        var pool = new DefaultObjectPool<ReusableObject>(new ReusableObjectPolicy());

        // Rent an object from the pool
        var obj = pool.Get();
        obj.Id = 42;
```

```
            obj.Name = "ReusableObject";

            // Return the object to the pool for reuse
            pool.Return(obj);
        }
    }
```

In this example, an object pool is created using the DefaultObjectPool<T> class. The ReusableObjectPolicy defines how objects are created and reset when they are returned to the pool. This approach reduces the number of allocations, improving performance in scenarios where objects are frequently created and discarded.

2. Minimizing Large Object Heap (LOH) Allocations with Array Pooling

Large object heap (LOH) allocations can contribute to memory fragmentation and increased garbage collection pressure. By pooling large arrays, you can reduce the frequency of LOH allocations and improve memory efficiency.

Example: Using Array Pooling to Minimize LOH Allocations

```csharp
using System.Buffers;

public class ArrayPoolDemo
{
    public void DemonstrateArrayPooling()
    {
        // Rent a large array from the shared array pool
        var arrayPool = ArrayPool<byte>.Shared;
        byte[] buffer = arrayPool.Rent(100000); // Allocate a 100 KB buffer

        try
        {
            // Perform operations on the buffer
            for (int i = 0; i < buffer.Length; i++)
            {
```

```
            buffer[i] = (byte)(i % 256);
        }
    }
    finally
    {
        // Return the array to the pool to reduce LOH
        fragmentation
        arrayPool.Return(buffer);
    }
    }
}
```

In this example, the ArrayPool<byte>.Shared instance is used to rent a large array and return it to the pool after use. This approach minimizes LOH fragmentation by reusing large arrays instead of frequently allocating new ones.

3. Controlling Object Lifetimes with Weak References

Weak references allow developers to hold references to objects without preventing them from being collected by the garbage collector. This technique is useful for caching or scenarios where objects are not critical to the application's functionality.

Example: Using Weak References in a Cache

```csharp

using System;
using System.Collections.Generic;

public class WeakReferenceCache<T> where T : class
{
    private readonly Dictionary<int, WeakReference<T>> _cache = new();

    public void AddToCache(int key, T value)
    {
        _cache[key] = new WeakReference<T>(value);
```

```csharp
    }

    public bool TryGetFromCache(int key, out T value)
    {
        if (_cache.TryGetValue(key, out WeakReference<T>
        weakRef) && weakRef.TryGetTarget(out value))
        {
            return true;
        }

        value = null;
        return false;
    }
}

public class WeakReferenceDemo
{
    public void DemonstrateWeakReference()
    {
        var cache = new WeakReferenceCache<string>();

        // Add a value to the cache
        cache.AddToCache(1, "CachedValue");

        // Attempt to retrieve the cached value
        if (cache.TryGetFromCache(1, out var cachedValue))
        {
            Console.WriteLine($"Retrieved value: {cachedValue}");
        }
        else
        {
            Console.WriteLine("Value was collected by GC.");
        }
    }
}
```

In this example, a weak reference cache is implemented using the WeakReference<T> class. The cache allows objects to be collected by the garbage collector if they are no longer in use, preventing memory retention issues.

4. Efficient String Manipulation with Span<T>

Strings are immutable in .NET, which means that every modification creates a new string instance. This can lead to excessive memory allocations in scenarios involving frequent string manipulations. Span<char> provides an efficient way to work with slices of strings without creating new string instances.

Example: Parsing a Delimited String with Span<T>

```csharp
using System;

public class StringParser
{
    public void ParseDelimitedString(string input)
    {
        ReadOnlySpan<char> span = input.AsSpan();
        int index = span.IndexOf(',');

        if (index >= 0)
        {
            ReadOnlySpan<char> firstPart = span.Slice(0, index);
            ReadOnlySpan<char> secondPart = span.Slice(index + 1);

            Console.WriteLine($"First Part: {firstPart.ToString()}");
            Console.WriteLine($"Second Part: {secondPart.ToString()}");
        }
    }
}
```

In this example, ReadOnlySpan<char> is used to slice a delimited string without creating new string instances. This approach reduces memory allocations and improves performance in scenarios where large strings are frequently parsed or processed.

5. Ref Returns for Direct Access to Data

Ref returns allow methods to return a reference to a variable, enabling direct modifications without copying. This can significantly reduce memory allocations and improve performance when working with large data structures.

Example: Returning a Reference to an Array Element

```csharp
using System;

public class RefReturnDemo
{
    public ref int GetElementRef(int[] array, int index)
    {
        if (index < 0 || index >= array.Length)
        {
            throw new IndexOutOfRangeException();
        }

        return ref array[index]; // Return a reference to the array element
    }

    public void DemonstrateRefReturn()
    {
        int[] numbers = { 10, 20, 30 };
        ref int element = ref GetElementRef(numbers, 1);

        Console.WriteLine($"Original Value: {element}");
        element = 99; // Modify the element directly
        Console.WriteLine($"Modified Value: {numbers[1]}"); // Output: 99
    }
}
```

In this example, a method returns a reference to an array element, allowing the caller to modify the element directly. This avoids the overhead of copying large data structures and reduces memory allocations.

6. Efficient Data Access with Memory<T> and Asynchronous Methods

When working with asynchronous methods, using Memory<T> allows for efficient data access without creating unnecessary heap allocations. This is particularly useful in scenarios where large data buffers are being processed asynchronously.

Example: Using Memory<T> in an Asynchronous Method

```csharp
using System;
using System.Threading.Tasks;

public class MemoryAsyncDemo
{
    public async Task ProcessDataAsync(Memory<byte> buffer)
    {
        // Simulate asynchronous work
        await Task.Delay(1000);

        // Access the memory buffer using Span<T>
        Span<byte> span = buffer.Span;
        for (int i = 0; i < span.Length; i++)
        {
            span[i] = (byte)(span[i] + 1);
        }
    }

    public async Task DemonstrateMemoryAsync()
    {
        byte[] data = new byte[100];
        Memory<byte> buffer = data.AsMemory();

        // Process the buffer asynchronously
        await ProcessDataAsync(buffer);
        Console.WriteLine("Data processed asynchronously.");
    }
}
```

In this example, a method processes a memory buffer asynchronously using

Memory<byte>. This approach minimizes heap allocations and allows efficient access to the underlying buffer.

These practical examples demonstrate how advanced memory management techniques in .NET 6 can be applied to real-world scenarios. By using object pooling, array pooling, weak references, Span<T>, Memory<T>, and ref returns, developers can optimize memory usage, reduce allocations, and improve garbage collection efficiency.

Understanding and implementing these techniques allows developers to build high-performance applications that are both scalable and responsive. As you continue to refine your memory management strategies, keep these examples and best practices in mind to achieve optimal performance in your applications.

SIMD Programming and High-Performance Math Operations

Introduction to SIMD in .NET 6

Single Instruction, Multiple Data (SIMD) is a computing technique that allows a single instruction to process multiple data points simultaneously. In essence, SIMD enables parallel execution at the data level, taking advantage of specialized hardware instructions to perform operations on multiple data elements in one go. SIMD is particularly beneficial for improving performance in scenarios involving large datasets, repetitive calculations, or data-parallel tasks.

.NET 6 introduces enhanced support for SIMD programming through the System.Numerics and System.Runtime.Intrinsics namespaces, empowering developers to write high-performance code that leverages hardware acceleration.

1. What is SIMD?

SIMD (Single Instruction, Multiple Data) is a form of data-level parallelism where a single instruction operates on multiple data elements stored in vectors. Modern CPUs have dedicated vector units (such as SSE, AVX on Intel processors, or NEON on ARM processors) that support SIMD instructions. These instructions can execute arithmetic, logical, and bitwise operations across multiple data elements in a single instruction cycle.

Key Characteristics of SIMD:

- **Parallel Execution on Data Elements:** SIMD processes multiple elements in parallel, reducing the number of instructions and boosting throughput.
- **Vector-Based Operations:** SIMD uses vectors (contiguous data elements) to perform parallel operations, enhancing efficiency in scenarios like mathematical computations, image processing, and scientific simulations.
- **Hardware-Accelerated Performance:** SIMD leverages hardware vector units to achieve high-speed processing of large datasets.

2. **Why Use SIMD in .NET 6?**

.NET 6 provides built-in support for SIMD to allow developers to write high-performance applications that take advantage of hardware acceleration. SIMD can lead to substantial improvements in execution speed for tasks involving vector and matrix operations, numerical simulations, graphics, and cryptographic calculations.

Benefits of SIMD in .NET 6:

- **Improved Throughput:** SIMD enables concurrent execution of the same operation on multiple data points, reducing the time required to process large datasets.
- **Hardware-Level Optimizations:** SIMD leverages vector instructions supported by modern CPUs, including Intel's SSE (Streaming SIMD Extensions) and AVX (Advanced Vector Extensions), and ARM's NEON extensions.
- **Ideal for Data-Parallel Workloads:** SIMD is well-suited for scenarios like image processing, signal processing, matrix multiplications, and physics simulations.

3. **SIMD Support in .NET 6: System.Numerics.Vectors**

The System.Numerics.Vectors namespace in .NET 6 provides a high-level abstraction for SIMD operations through the Vector<T> class. This abstraction automatically adapts to the vector width supported by the underlying hardware, such as 128-bit or 256-bit vectors, making it easier to write portable SIMD code.

Key Classes in System.Numerics.Vectors:

- **Vector<T>:** A generic SIMD vector type that can store multiple elements of type T (e.g., int, float, double). Vector<T> automatically adapts to the maximum SIMD width supported by the hardware.
- **Vector2, Vector3, and Vector4:** Represent 2D, 3D, and 4D vectors, respectively. These classes are commonly used in graphics, physics, and geometric calculations.

Example: Basic SIMD Operations Using Vector<T>

```csharp
using System;
using System.Numerics;

public class SimdOperations
{
    public void PerformVectorAddition()
    {
        float[] array1 = { 1.0f, 2.0f, 3.0f, 4.0f };
        float[] array2 = { 5.0f, 6.0f, 7.0f, 8.0f };
        float[] result = new float[4];

        // Create Vector<T> instances from arrays
        Vector<float> vector1 = new Vector<float>(array1);
        Vector<float> vector2 = new Vector<float>(array2);

        // Perform SIMD addition
        Vector<float> vectorResult = vector1 + vector2;

        // Copy the result back to the array
        vectorResult.CopyTo(result);

        Console.WriteLine($"Result: {string.Join(", ",
```

```
        result)}"); // Output: Result: 6, 8, 10, 12
    }
}
```

In this example, the Vector<float> type is used to perform SIMD addition on two arrays. The addition is executed in parallel, leveraging the SIMD capabilities of the underlying CPU.

4. Low-Level SIMD Programming with System.Runtime.Intrinsics

For developers who need direct access to low-level SIMD instructions, .NET 6 provides the System.Runtime.Intrinsics namespace. This namespace exposes specific SIMD instructions supported by the underlying CPU, enabling developers to fine-tune performance-critical code.

Key Classes in System.Runtime.Intrinsics:

- **Vector128<T> and Vector256<T>:** Represent 128-bit and 256-bit SIMD vectors, respectively. These classes provide direct access to SIMD instructions based on the CPU's supported features.
- **Hardware Intrinsics (Sse, Sse2, Avx, Avx2, etc.):** Provide methods for specific SIMD instruction sets, such as SSE (Streaming SIMD Extensions), AVX (Advanced Vector Extensions), and NEON.

Example: Using SIMD Intrinsics with Vector128<T>

```csharp
using System;
using System.Runtime.Intrinsics;
using System.Runtime.Intrinsics.X86;

public class IntrinsicsOperations
{
    public void MultiplyVectors()
    {
        if (Sse.IsSupported)
```

```csharp
{
    // Define two 128-bit vectors with four
    // single-precision floating-point elements each
    Vector128<float> vector1 = Vector128.Create(1.0f,
    2.0f, 3.0f, 4.0f);
    Vector128<float> vector2 = Vector128.Create(5.0f,
    6.0f, 7.0f, 8.0f);

    // Multiply the vectors using SIMD
    Vector128<float> result = Sse.Multiply(vector1,
    vector2);

    // Extract and print the result
    for (int i = 0; i < 4; i++)
    {
        Console.WriteLine(result.GetElement(i)); //
        Output: 5, 12, 21, 32
    }
}
else
{
    Console.WriteLine("SSE not supported on this
    machine.");
}
}
}
```

In this example, the Sse.Multiply intrinsic is used to multiply two 128-bit vectors. This approach gives developers fine-grained control over SIMD instructions, enabling precise optimization for performance-critical code sections.

5. Best Practices for SIMD Programming in .NET 6

To leverage SIMD effectively in .NET 6, developers should follow best practices to ensure optimal performance and maintainable code:

- **Align Data to SIMD Width:** Align data structures and arrays to SIMD vector widths (e.g., 128-bit, 256-bit) to avoid inefficient memory access patterns.

- **Use Higher-Level Abstractions (Vector<T>):** Use the Vector<T> class to write portable SIMD code that adapts automatically to the hardware's supported SIMD width.
- **Avoid Complex Control Flow Inside SIMD Loops:** SIMD relies on executing the same operation on multiple elements concurrently, so avoid branching within SIMD loops to maintain parallelism.
- **Check for Hardware Support:** Use runtime checks like Sse.IsSupported or Avx.IsSupported to ensure that the target hardware supports the required SIMD instructions before executing them.

6. Common Use Cases for SIMD in .NET 6

SIMD can significantly enhance performance in a variety of applications. Here are some common use cases:

- **Numerical Computations and Matrix Operations:** SIMD is ideal for matrix multiplications, vector arithmetic, and other numerical computations that involve large datasets.
- **Image and Signal Processing:** SIMD can accelerate tasks like image transformations, filters, and convolution operations by processing multiple pixels or samples concurrently.
- **Physics Simulations and Game Development:** Game engines and physics simulations often involve complex vector and matrix math, making SIMD an excellent choice for real-time calculations.
- **Cryptography:** SIMD instructions can optimize cryptographic algorithms that perform repetitive arithmetic or logical operations on large blocks of data.

7. Performance Considerations for SIMD in .NET 6

While SIMD offers substantial performance benefits, developers should consider the following factors:

- **Hardware Support and Compatibility:** Not all SIMD instructions are supported on all CPUs. For example, AVX and AVX2 instructions are only

available on newer CPUs. Check for hardware support at runtime before using specific SIMD instructions.
- **Data Alignment and Access Patterns:** Unaligned memory access can lead to performance degradation. Ensure that data structures are aligned to the SIMD vector width, and use vector loads and stores appropriately.
- **Handling Remainder Elements:** SIMD operates on fixed-size vectors, so developers need to handle any remaining elements in datasets that don't fit perfectly into the vector size.

SIMD in .NET 6 provides developers with powerful tools to harness the parallel processing capabilities of modern CPUs. By leveraging System.Numerics.Vectors and System.Runtime.Intrinsics, developers can write high-performance code that takes full advantage of hardware acceleration.

Understanding the basics of SIMD, the available high-level and low-level abstractions, and best practices for SIMD programming is essential for building applications that can handle large datasets, perform complex calculations, and meet the demands of modern computing. Whether you're working on scientific simulations, graphics rendering, cryptography, or financial calculations, SIMD in .NET 6 offers the tools you need to achieve optimal performance.

Implementing SIMD-Based Algorithms

SIMD-based algorithms are designed to take advantage of Single Instruction, Multiple Data (SIMD) capabilities by processing multiple data points concurrently. This section delves into how to effectively implement SIMD-based algorithms in .NET 6 using both high-level and low-level approaches. We'll explore practical techniques and examples of implementing SIMD-based algorithms to optimize various types of computational tasks.

1. **High-Level SIMD with Vector<T>**

The easiest way to get started with SIMD programming in .NET 6 is to use the Vector<T> class provided in the System.Numerics.Vectors namespace. This class abstracts away the complexity of specific SIMD instruction sets and automatically adapts to the SIMD width of the hardware, making it a great starting point for general-purpose SIMD programming.

Example 1: Summing an Array Using Vector<T>

A common scenario where SIMD can help is in summing large arrays of numbers. Instead of using a simple loop, we can leverage SIMD to perform additions on multiple elements simultaneously.

```csharp
using System;
using System.Numerics;

public class SimdArraySum
{
    public float SumArray(float[] data)
    {
        // Define a Vector size based on the hardware's SIMD width
        int vectorSize = Vector<float>.Count;
        Vector<float> sumVector = Vector<float>.Zero;

        // Process the array in chunks of the vector size
        int i = 0;
        for (; i <= data.Length - vectorSize; i += vectorSize)
        {
            Vector<float> dataVector = new Vector<float>(data, i);
            sumVector += dataVector; // SIMD addition
        }

        // Sum up the elements of the sumVector
        float totalSum = 0;
        for (int j = 0; j < vectorSize; j++)
        {
            totalSum += sumVector[j];
```

```
        }

        // Handle remaining elements
        for (; i < data.Length; i++)
        {
            totalSum += data[i];
        }

        return totalSum;
    }
}
```

Explanation: In this example, we use Vector<T> to sum the elements of an array. The algorithm processes chunks of elements using SIMD and adds the results into a vector sum. After completing the SIMD additions, we handle any remaining elements separately.

2. Low-Level SIMD with System.Runtime.Intrinsics

For more control over specific SIMD instructions, you can use low-level intrinsics provided in the System.Runtime.Intrinsics namespace. This allows you to fine-tune the algorithm using explicit SIMD instructions tailored to the target CPU architecture.

Example 2: Multiplying Arrays Using SSE Intrinsics

Let's multiply two arrays element-wise using SIMD instructions through the System.Runtime.Intrinsics.X86 namespace.

```csharp
using System;
using System.Runtime.Intrinsics;
using System.Runtime.Intrinsics.X86;

public class SimdArrayMultiply
{
    public void MultiplyArrays(float[] array1, float[] array2, float[] result)
    {
```

```csharp
        if (array1.Length != array2.Length || array1.Length != result.Length)
        {
            throw new ArgumentException("Arrays must have the same length.");
        }

        int vectorSize = Vector128<float>.Count;
        int i = 0;

        if (Sse.IsSupported)
        {
            // Process arrays in chunks of the vector size
            for (; i <= array1.Length - vectorSize; i += vectorSize)
            {
                Vector128<float> vec1 = Vector128.Create(array1[i], array1[i + 1], array1[i + 2], array1[i + 3]);
                Vector128<float> vec2 = Vector128.Create(array2[i], array2[i + 1], array2[i + 2], array2[i + 3]);

                Vector128<float> vecResult = Sse.Multiply(vec1, vec2); // SIMD multiplication

                // Store the result back to the result array
                vecResult.CopyTo(result, i);
            }
        }

        // Handle remaining elements
        for (; i < array1.Length; i++)
        {
            result[i] = array1[i] * array2[i];
        }
    }
}
```

Explanation: This example demonstrates element-wise multiplication of two arrays using the SSE intrinsic Sse.Multiply. The method processes chunks of four elements at a time using 128-bit SIMD instructions and handles any remaining elements separately.

3. Real-World SIMD Algorithm: Vector Dot Product

The dot product of two vectors is a common mathematical operation in physics, graphics, and machine learning. SIMD can significantly accelerate this operation by processing multiple elements simultaneously.

Example 3: Calculating the Dot Product of Two Vectors

```csharp
using System;
using System.Numerics;

public class SimdDotProduct
{
    public float CalculateDotProduct(float[] vector1, float[] vector2)
    {
        if (vector1.Length != vector2.Length)
        {
            throw new ArgumentException("Vectors must have the same length.");
        }

        int vectorSize = Vector<float>.Count;
        Vector<float> dotProductVector = Vector<float>.Zero;
        int i = 0;

        // Process vectors in chunks of the vector size
        for (; i <= vector1.Length - vectorSize; i += vectorSize)
        {
            Vector<float> vec1 = new Vector<float>(vector1, i);
            Vector<float> vec2 = new Vector<float>(vector2, i);

            dotProductVector += vec1 * vec2; // SIMD multiplication and addition
        }
```

```csharp
            // Sum up the elements of the dotProductVector
            float dotProduct = 0;
            for (int j = 0; j < vectorSize; j++)
            {
                dotProduct += dotProductVector[j];
            }

            // Handle remaining elements
            for (; i < vector1.Length; i++)
            {
                dotProduct += vector1[i] * vector2[i];
            }

            return dotProduct;
    }
}
```

Explanation: In this example, we use SIMD to calculate the dot product of two vectors. The code multiplies corresponding elements of the vectors using Vector<float> and sums up the results.

4. Image Processing with SIMD: Grayscale Conversion

Image processing often involves applying the same operation to each pixel in an image. SIMD can help accelerate these operations by processing multiple pixels in parallel.

Example 4: Converting an RGB Image to Grayscale Using SIMD

```csharp
using System;
using System.Numerics;

public class SimdGrayscaleConversion
{
    public void ConvertToGrayscale(byte[] rgbImage, byte[] grayscaleImage)
    {
```

```csharp
if (rgbImage.Length / 3 != grayscaleImage.Length)
{
    throw new ArgumentException("Invalid image sizes.");
}

int vectorSize = Vector<byte>.Count;
int pixelCount = grayscaleImage.Length;

// Define SIMD constants for RGB weighting factors
Vector<float> redWeight = new Vector<float>(0.3f);
Vector<float> greenWeight = new Vector<float>(0.59f);
Vector<float> blueWeight = new Vector<float>(0.11f);

int i = 0;
for (; i <= pixelCount - vectorSize; i += vectorSize)
{
    // Load RGB channels as separate vectors
    var redChannel = new Vector<byte>(rgbImage, i * 3);
    var greenChannel = new Vector<byte>(rgbImage, i * 3
    + 1);
    var blueChannel = new Vector<byte>(rgbImage, i * 3 +
    2);

    // Convert to float vectors for weighted sum
    var red = Vector.ConvertToSingle(redChannel) *
    redWeight;
    var green = Vector.ConvertToSingle(greenChannel) *
    greenWeight;
    var blue = Vector.ConvertToSingle(blueChannel) *
    blueWeight;

    // Calculate grayscale value
    var grayscale = red + green + blue;

    // Convert back to byte and store in the result array
    var grayscaleBytes =
    Vector.ConvertToInt32(grayscale);
    grayscaleBytes.CopyTo(grayscaleImage, i);
}
```

```
    // Handle remaining pixels
    for (; i < pixelCount; i++)
    {
        int baseIndex = i * 3;
        grayscaleImage[i] = (byte)(0.3 * rgbImage[baseIndex]
        + 0.59 * rgbImage[baseIndex + 1] + 0.11 *
        rgbImage[baseIndex + 2]);
    }
  }
}
```

Explanation: This example converts an RGB image to grayscale using SIMD. It leverages SIMD instructions to apply the same weighting factors to each pixel in parallel, thereby improving performance over a scalar implementation.

5. Best Practices for Implementing SIMD Algorithms

When implementing SIMD-based algorithms in .NET 6, it's essential to follow best practices to ensure code maintainability, portability, and performance:

- **Align Data to Vector Size:** Ensure that your data arrays are aligned to the SIMD vector size (e.g., 16 bytes for 128-bit SIMD). This reduces the overhead of unaligned memory access.
- **Handle Remainder Elements Separately:** Since SIMD processes fixed-size chunks, handle any leftover elements separately to avoid out-of-bounds errors.
- **Use Higher-Level Abstractions (Vector<T>) When Possible:** For general-purpose SIMD optimizations, use Vector<T>. It abstracts away the complexities of specific SIMD instruction sets and adapts to the hardware's capabilities.
- **Verify Hardware Support:** Use runtime checks to ensure that the target hardware supports the required SIMD instructions. This prevents runtime errors and ensures portability across different CPU architectures.

Implementing SIMD-based algorithms in .NET 6 can significantly improve the performance of data-parallel tasks. By leveraging high-level abstractions like Vector<T> or low-level intrinsics from the System.Runtime.Intrinsics namespace, developers can achieve substantial speed-ups for computationally intensive operations.

Understanding how to effectively apply SIMD and following best practices ensures that your applications are optimized for both performance and maintainability. Whether you're working on scientific computing, image processing, financial analysis, or game development, SIMD-based algorithms in .NET 6 provide the tools needed to build high-performance solutions.

Performance Benefits of SIMD Operations

The performance benefits of SIMD (Single Instruction, Multiple Data) operations stem from their ability to execute a single instruction on multiple data points simultaneously. SIMD leverages the parallel processing capabilities of modern CPUs, enabling developers to achieve significant speed-ups in data-parallel computations. In .NET 6, the System.Numerics and System.Runtime.Intrinsics namespaces allow developers to take full advantage of SIMD for high-performance applications.

This section explores the key performance benefits of SIMD, demonstrating how it optimizes execution speed, reduces resource usage, and improves efficiency in various types of applications.

1. Parallelism at the Data Level

The core idea behind SIMD is to perform the same operation on multiple pieces of data in parallel. This type of parallelism is especially powerful for workloads that involve repetitive calculations on large datasets, such as vector and matrix operations, image processing, and physics simulations. By processing multiple elements in a single instruction, SIMD drastically

SIMD PROGRAMMING AND HIGH-PERFORMANCE MATH OPERATIONS

reduces the number of iterations required, leading to faster execution times.

Example: Array Addition with and Without SIMD

Let's compare the execution of a basic array addition using traditional scalar code versus SIMD code.

Scalar Code Example:

```csharp
public float[] AddArraysScalar(float[] array1, float[] array2)
{
    int length = array1.Length;
    float[] result = new float[length];

    for (int i = 0; i < length; i++)
    {
        result[i] = array1[i] + array2[i];
    }

    return result;
}
```

SIMD Code Example:

```csharp
using System.Numerics;

public float[] AddArraysSimd(float[] array1, float[] array2)
{
    int length = array1.Length;
    float[] result = new float[length];

    int vectorSize = Vector<float>.Count;
    int i = 0;

    // Perform addition using SIMD for chunks of vector size
    for (; i <= length - vectorSize; i += vectorSize)
    {
```

```csharp
        Vector<float> vec1 = new Vector<float>(array1, i);
        Vector<float> vec2 = new Vector<float>(array2, i);

        Vector<float> sum = vec1 + vec2;
        sum.CopyTo(result, i);
    }

    // Handle remaining elements
    for (; i < length; i++)
    {
        result[i] = array1[i] + array2[i];
    }

    return result;
}
```

Performance Benefit: The SIMD code processes multiple elements per loop iteration, reducing the total number of iterations and increasing throughput. Depending on the hardware and vector width, SIMD can lead to 4x, 8x, or higher speed-ups compared to scalar code.

2. Reduction in Instruction Count

One of the key benefits of SIMD is that it reduces the number of instructions executed by processing multiple data points in a single operation. For instance, if a CPU supports 256-bit SIMD instructions, each instruction can operate on eight 32-bit floating-point values at once. This results in a significant reduction in the overall number of instructions executed, improving both speed and efficiency.

Real-World Example: Dot Product Calculation

Calculating the dot product of two vectors involves multiplying corresponding elements and summing them up. SIMD reduces the instruction count by performing multiple multiplications and additions concurrently.

Scalar Approach:

```csharp
```

SIMD PROGRAMMING AND HIGH-PERFORMANCE MATH OPERATIONS

```csharp
public float DotProductScalar(float[] vector1, float[] vector2)
{
    float result = 0;
    for (int i = 0; i < vector1.Length; i++)
    {
        result += vector1[i] * vector2[i];
    }
    return result;
}
```

SIMD Approach:

csharp

```csharp
using System.Numerics;

public float DotProductSimd(float[] vector1, float[] vector2)
{
    int vectorSize = Vector<float>.Count;
    Vector<float> sum = Vector<float>.Zero;

    int i = 0;
    for (; i <= vector1.Length - vectorSize; i += vectorSize)
    {
        Vector<float> vec1 = new Vector<float>(vector1, i);
        Vector<float> vec2 = new Vector<float>(vector2, i);
        sum += vec1 * vec2;
    }

    float result = 0;
    for (int j = 0; j < vectorSize; j++)
    {
        result += sum[j];
    }

    for (; i < vector1.Length; i++)
    {
        result += vector1[i] * vector2[i];
```

```
        }

        return result;
}
```

Performance Benefit: The SIMD-based dot product performs multiple multiplications and additions in a single operation, reducing the instruction count and improving performance.

3. Optimized Memory Access and Cache Utilization

SIMD optimizes memory access by processing data in contiguous blocks, improving cache locality and reducing the number of memory accesses. This is particularly beneficial in data-parallel tasks where memory bandwidth is often a limiting factor. By fetching and processing larger chunks of data at once, SIMD reduces cache misses and improves overall memory access efficiency.

Example: Processing Image Data with SIMD

In image processing, each pixel can be represented as a set of RGB values. SIMD allows processing multiple pixels simultaneously, reducing memory access overhead and improving cache utilization.

SIMD Grayscale Conversion Example:

```csharp
using System;
using System.Numerics;

public class SimdGrayscaleConverter
{
    public void ConvertToGrayscale(byte[] rgbImage, byte[] grayscaleImage)
    {
        int pixelCount = grayscaleImage.Length;
        int vectorSize = Vector<byte>.Count;

        Vector<float> redWeight = new Vector<float>(0.3f);
```

```
        Vector<float> greenWeight = new Vector<float>(0.59f);
        Vector<float> blueWeight = new Vector<float>(0.11f);

        int i = 0;
        for (; i <= pixelCount - vectorSize; i += vectorSize)
        {
            var redChannel = new Vector<byte>(rgbImage, i * 3);
            var greenChannel = new Vector<byte>(rgbImage, i * 3
            + 1);
            var blueChannel = new Vector<byte>(rgbImage, i * 3 +
            2);

            var red = Vector.ConvertToSingle(redChannel) *
            redWeight;
            var green = Vector.ConvertToSingle(greenChannel) *
            greenWeight;
            var blue = Vector.ConvertToSingle(blueChannel) *
            blueWeight;

            var grayscale = red + green + blue;
            var grayscaleBytes =
            Vector.ConvertToInt32(grayscale);
            grayscaleBytes.CopyTo(grayscaleImage, i);
        }

        // Handle remaining pixels
        for (; i < pixelCount; i++)
        {
            int baseIndex = i * 3;
            grayscaleImage[i] = (byte)(0.3 * rgbImage[baseIndex]
            + 0.59 * rgbImage[baseIndex + 1] + 0.11 *
            rgbImage[baseIndex + 2]);
        }
    }
}
```

Performance Benefit: SIMD improves memory access patterns and cache utilization by fetching and processing multiple pixels in contiguous memory blocks.

4. Lower Power Consumption

By reducing the number of instructions and improving memory access patterns, SIMD can also lower the CPU's power consumption. When fewer instructions are executed, and data is processed more efficiently, the CPU spends less time in active states, resulting in lower energy usage. This is crucial in applications that require high efficiency, such as mobile devices and battery-powered embedded systems.

5. Reduced Execution Time and Improved Throughput

The most obvious and significant benefit of SIMD is the reduction in execution time. By processing multiple data points in parallel, SIMD dramatically increases throughput, enabling applications to handle more data in less time. This can lead to significant performance improvements in areas such as:

- **Scientific Simulations:** Faster computation of large-scale mathematical models, fluid dynamics, or weather simulations.
- **Financial Calculations:** High-speed analysis of large datasets for real-time market analysis and financial predictions.
- **Graphics and Game Development:** Real-time physics calculations, vector math, and image transformations for smoother gameplay and visual effects.

6. Performance Considerations

While SIMD offers numerous benefits, it's essential to keep the following considerations in mind:

- **Alignment of Data:** For optimal performance, data should be aligned with the vector size supported by the hardware (e.g., 16-byte alignment for 128-bit vectors).
- **Hardware-Specific Instructions:** The availability of SIMD instructions depends on the target CPU architecture. Use runtime checks (Sse.IsSupported, Avx.IsSupported) to verify that the target hardware supports the required SIMD instructions.

- **Handling Remaining Elements:** SIMD typically processes data in fixed-size chunks. Any remaining elements that do not fit within a SIMD vector must be handled separately.
- **Optimizing for Different Vector Widths:** Modern CPUs support different vector widths, such as 128-bit, 256-bit, and 512-bit vectors. Consider the target hardware and optimize SIMD implementations accordingly.

SIMD operations in .NET 6 provide significant performance benefits by exploiting data-level parallelism. By reducing the instruction count, optimizing memory access, and leveraging hardware vector instructions, SIMD improves execution speed and throughput for a wide range of applications. The performance gains are most evident in scenarios involving large datasets, repetitive computations, and tasks requiring high-speed data processing.

Through careful implementation and attention to best practices, developers can harness the full potential of SIMD in .NET 6 to build high-performance applications that are both efficient and scalable. Whether you are developing scientific simulations, financial analysis tools, graphics applications, or real-time systems, SIMD offers the capabilities to achieve substantial improvements in speed and efficiency.

Real-World Use Cases and Code Examples

SIMD (Single Instruction, Multiple Data) is widely used in various industries to improve the performance of computationally intensive applications. In this section, we explore real-world use cases where SIMD operations provide significant performance benefits. We will also provide practical code examples that demonstrate how to apply SIMD techniques in .NET 6 to optimize real-world scenarios.

1. Financial Services: Real-Time Data Analysis

Financial services rely heavily on fast computations for tasks such as market analysis, risk assessment, and financial modeling. Many of these tasks involve operations on large datasets, making them ideal candidates for SIMD optimizations.

Use Case: Calculating Exponential Moving Average (EMA)

The Exponential Moving Average (EMA) is a popular technical indicator used in financial analysis. It gives more weight to recent prices, making it more responsive to new information.

SIMD Optimized Code for EMA Calculation:

```csharp
using System;
using System.Numerics;

public class SimdFinancialAnalysis
{
    public void CalculateEma(float[] prices, float smoothingFactor, float[] emaResult)
    {
        if (prices.Length != emaResult.Length)
            throw new ArgumentException("Input arrays must have the same length.");

        int vectorSize = Vector<float>.Count;
        Vector<float> weight = new Vector<float>(smoothingFactor);
        int length = prices.Length;

        // Initialize EMA with the first price
        emaResult[0] = prices[0];
        Vector<float> emaVector = new Vector<float>(emaResult[0]);

        for (int i = 1; i <= length - vectorSize; i += vectorSize)
```

```
    {
        Vector<float> priceVector = new
        Vector<float>(prices, i);
        emaVector = weight * priceVector +
        (Vector<float>.One - weight) * emaVector;

        // Store result
        emaVector.CopyTo(emaResult, i);
    }

    // Handle remaining elements
    for (int i = length - vectorSize; i < length; i++)
    {
        emaResult[i] = smoothingFactor * prices[i] + (1 -
        smoothingFactor) * emaResult[i - 1];
    }
  }
}
```

Explanation: This code uses SIMD to perform the EMA calculation on large price datasets. The algorithm processes elements in chunks using vector operations, reducing the number of iterations and improving computation speed.

2. Image Processing: Convolution Filters

Convolution filters are fundamental operations in image processing used to apply effects like blurring, edge detection, and sharpening. These operations involve a kernel that is applied to every pixel and its surrounding neighbors. SIMD is highly effective in accelerating these tasks by processing multiple pixels concurrently.

Use Case: Applying a Gaussian Blur Filter

Gaussian blur is a widely used effect that smooths images by averaging pixel values with their neighbors using a Gaussian weight distribution.

SIMD Optimized Code for Gaussian Blur:

```csharp
using System;
using System.Numerics;

public class SimdImageProcessing
{
    private readonly float[] _gaussianKernel = new float[] {
    0.06136f, 0.24477f, 0.38774f, 0.24477f, 0.06136f };

    public void ApplyGaussianBlur(float[] image, float[]
    blurredImage, int width, int height)
    {
        int vectorSize = Vector<float>.Count;
        int kernelRadius = _gaussianKernel.Length / 2;

        for (int y = 0; y < height; y++)
        {
            for (int x = 0; x <= width - vectorSize; x +=
            vectorSize)
            {
                Vector<float> sumVector = Vector<float>.Zero;

                for (int k = -kernelRadius; k <= kernelRadius;
                k++)
                {
                    int offsetX = x + k;
                    if (offsetX >= 0 && offsetX < width)
                    {
                        Vector<float> pixelVector = new
                        Vector<float>(image, y * width +
                        offsetX);
                        Vector<float> weight = new
                        Vector<float>(_gaussianKernel[k +
                        kernelRadius]);
                        sumVector += weight * pixelVector;
                    }
                }

                // Store the blurred result
```

SIMD PROGRAMMING AND HIGH-PERFORMANCE MATH OPERATIONS

```
                sumVector.CopyTo(blurredImage, y * width + x);
            }

            // Handle remaining pixels outside of SIMD range
            for (int x = width - vectorSize; x < width; x++)
            {
                float sum = 0f;
                for (int k = -kernelRadius; k <= kernelRadius; k++)
                {
                    int offsetX = x + k;
                    if (offsetX >= 0 && offsetX < width)
                    {
                        sum += _gaussianKernel[k + kernelRadius]
                            * image[y * width + offsetX];
                    }
                }
                blurredImage[y * width + x] = sum;
            }
        }
    }
}
```

Explanation: In this example, SIMD is used to perform a Gaussian blur by applying a convolution kernel to the image. The code processes pixels in vector-sized chunks, reducing the number of iterations required and improving cache utilization.

3. Physics Simulations: Particle Systems

Physics simulations often involve large-scale computations, such as calculating the interactions between particles in a particle system. These simulations typically involve vector math, making them an ideal candidate for SIMD optimizations.

Use Case: Updating Particle Velocities in a Particle System

In particle systems, each particle has a position, velocity, and acceleration. Updating the velocity of each particle based on its acceleration is a common operation.

SIMD Optimized Code for Particle Velocity Update:

csharp

```
using System;
using System.Numerics;

public class SimdPhysicsSimulation
{
    public void UpdateParticleVelocities(Vector3[] velocities,
    Vector3[] accelerations, float deltaTime)
    {
        int vectorSize = Vector<float>.Count;
        Vector<float> deltaTimeVector = new
        Vector<float>(deltaTime);

        for (int i = 0; i <= velocities.Length - vectorSize; i
        += vectorSize)
        {
            Vector<float> velX = new
            Vector<float>(ExtractComponent(velocities, i, 0));
            Vector<float> velY = new
            Vector<float>(ExtractComponent(velocities, i, 1));
            Vector<float> velZ = new
            Vector<float>(ExtractComponent(velocities, i, 2));

            Vector<float> accX = new
            Vector<float>(ExtractComponent(accelerations, i, 0));
            Vector<float> accY = new
            Vector<float>(ExtractComponent(accelerations, i, 1));
            Vector<float> accZ = new
            Vector<float>(ExtractComponent(accelerations, i, 2));

            velX += accX * deltaTimeVector;
            velY += accY * deltaTimeVector;
            velZ += accZ * deltaTimeVector;

            StoreComponent(velocities, i, velX, 0);
            StoreComponent(velocities, i, velY, 1);
            StoreComponent(velocities, i, velZ, 2);
```

SIMD PROGRAMMING AND HIGH-PERFORMANCE MATH OPERATIONS

```
    }

    // Handle remaining particles
    for (int i = velocities.Length - vectorSize; i <
    velocities.Length; i++)
    {
        velocities[i] += accelerations[i] * deltaTime;
    }
}

private float[] ExtractComponent(Vector3[] vectors, int
index, int component)
{
    float[] componentValues = new float[Vector<float>.Count];
    for (int i = 0; i < Vector<float>.Count; i++)
    {
        componentValues[i] = component switch
        {
            0 => vectors[index + i].X,
            1 => vectors[index + i].Y,
            _ => vectors[index + i].Z,
        };
    }
    return componentValues;
}

private void StoreComponent(Vector3[] vectors, int index,
Vector<float> componentVector, int component)
{
    for (int i = 0; i < Vector<float>.Count; i++)
    {
        if (component == 0) vectors[index + i].X =
        componentVector[i];
        else if (component == 1) vectors[index + i].Y =
        componentVector[i];
        else vectors[index + i].Z = componentVector[i];
    }
}
}
```

Explanation: This code demonstrates how to use SIMD to update the velocities of particles in a particle system based on their accelerations. The algorithm processes the X, Y, and Z components of multiple particles simultaneously, improving performance for large-scale simulations.

4. Cryptography: Hash Computation

Cryptographic algorithms often involve repetitive arithmetic and bitwise operations on large data blocks, making them ideal for SIMD optimization. Hash functions, for example, are used extensively in data integrity checks, digital signatures, and authentication protocols.

Use Case: Optimizing a Simple Hash Function with SIMD

SIMD Optimized Code for Hash Computation:

```csharp

using System;
using System.Numerics;

public class SimdHashComputation
{
    public int ComputeHash(byte[] data)
    {
        int hash = 0;
        int vectorSize = Vector<int>.Count;
        int i = 0;

        Vector<int> primeVector = new Vector<int>(31);

        for (; i <= data.Length - vectorSize; i += vectorSize)
        {
            Vector<int> byteVector = new Vector<int>(new int[vectorSize]);
            for (int j = 0; j < vectorSize; j++)
            {
                byteVector[j] = data[i + j];
            }

            Vector<int> productVector = byteVector * primeVector;
            hash += Vector.Dot(productVector, Vector<int>.One);
```

```
        }

        // Handle remaining bytes
        for (; i < data.Length; i++)
        {
            hash += data[i] * 31;
        }

        return hash;
    }
}
```

Explanation: This code computes a simple hash function using SIMD. It multiplies blocks of bytes by a prime number and accumulates the results in parallel, improving throughput for large data inputs.

These real-world use cases and examples demonstrate how SIMD can be effectively applied in various domains such as financial services, image processing, physics simulations, and cryptography. By leveraging SIMD capabilities in .NET 6, developers can achieve significant performance improvements in applications that involve large datasets, repetitive calculations, or data-parallel tasks.

Understanding these use cases and implementing SIMD-based algorithms can help developers build high-performance applications that meet the demands of today's data-intensive workloads. Through careful design and optimization, SIMD enables developers to unlock the full potential of modern hardware and achieve substantial gains in speed and efficiency.

P/Invoke and Native Interoperability for Performance Gains

When to Use P/Invoke in .NET 6 Applications

P/Invoke (Platform Invocation Services) is a powerful feature in .NET that allows managed code to call native functions implemented in external dynamic link libraries (DLLs). It enables .NET applications to interact directly with the underlying operating system or with native libraries written in C, C++, or other unmanaged languages. While .NET provides a robust runtime and a wide range of high-performance libraries, there are scenarios where P/Invoke becomes necessary to achieve specific performance gains or access low-level system functionality.

In this section, we'll explore when and why you should consider using P/Invoke in .NET 6 applications, along with the potential benefits and challenges.

1. Why Use P/Invoke?

P/Invoke is primarily used to extend the capabilities of .NET applications by allowing direct calls to native libraries and operating system functions. While managed code offers significant benefits such as memory safety, garbage collection, and cross-platform compatibility, there are situations where accessing unmanaged code via P/Invoke is advantageous.

Reasons to Use P/Invoke:

- **Access to System-Level Functions:** P/Invoke provides access to low-level operating system APIs and system calls that are not directly exposed by the .NET runtime or its managed libraries.
- **Utilizing Existing Native Libraries:** Many high-performance libraries and APIs are written in unmanaged languages like C or C++. P/Invoke allows you to reuse these libraries without rewriting them in managed code.
- **Performance Gains for Low-Level Operations:** In scenarios where fine-grained control over memory, hardware, or system resources is required, P/Invoke enables you to write efficient low-level code that can improve performance.
- **Cross-Platform Compatibility:** With .NET 6's cross-platform capabilities, P/Invoke allows you to write platform-specific code that leverages native libraries for optimal performance on different operating systems.

2. Key Scenarios for Using P/Invoke in .NET 6

Below are common scenarios where using P/Invoke in .NET 6 applications is highly beneficial:

1. Interfacing with Native APIs

When developing applications that require interaction with the underlying operating system, P/Invoke allows you to call native system APIs directly. This is useful for tasks like interacting with hardware, accessing file systems, or invoking native Windows, macOS, or Linux functions.

Example: Calling Windows API Functions Using P/Invoke

```csharp
using System;
using System.Runtime.InteropServices;

public class NativeMethods
{
    // Import the Beep function from kernel32.dll (Windows API)
    [DllImport("kernel32.dll", SetLastError = true)]
```

```csharp
    public static extern bool Beep(uint dwFreq, uint dwDuration);

    // Import the MessageBox function from user32.dll (Windows
    API)
    [DllImport("user32.dll", CharSet = CharSet.Unicode)]
    public static extern int MessageBox(IntPtr hWnd, string
    text, string caption, uint type);
}

public class PInvokeDemo
{
    public void CallNativeFunctions()
    {
        // Call Beep function to produce a beep sound
        NativeMethods.Beep(750, 300);

        // Call MessageBox function to display a message box
        NativeMethods.MessageBox(IntPtr.Zero, "Hello from
        P/Invoke!", "P/Invoke Demo", 0);
    }
}
```

Explanation: In this example, P/Invoke is used to call two Windows API functions: Beep and MessageBox. This provides direct access to system-level functionality not available in managed .NET libraries.

2. Leveraging High-Performance Native Libraries

If you are working with computationally intensive tasks, such as numerical analysis, image processing, or cryptography, and there are well-optimized native libraries available, P/Invoke can be used to call these libraries directly. This allows you to take advantage of their performance optimizations without having to rewrite the algorithms in managed code.

Example: Using a C Math Library for High-Performance Calculations

```csharp
csharp

using System;
using System.Runtime.InteropServices;
```

```csharp
public class NativeMathLibrary
{
    // Import a native C function for calculating the square root
    [DllImport("libmath.so", EntryPoint = "sqrt",
    CallingConvention = CallingConvention.Cdecl)]
    public static extern double Sqrt(double value);
}

public class PInvokeMathDemo
{
    public void CalculateSquareRoot()
    {
        double value = 16.0;
        double result = NativeMathLibrary.Sqrt(value);
        Console.WriteLine($"Square root of {value} is {result}");
    }
}
```

Explanation: In this example, P/Invoke is used to call the native sqrt function from a C library (libmath.so), which provides a high-performance implementation of the square root calculation. This can be especially useful when working with existing native libraries that are optimized for specific hardware or platforms.

3. Accessing Hardware and Device Drivers

When building applications that need to interface with hardware devices, such as sensors, network cards, or USB devices, P/Invoke allows you to call native device drivers or APIs directly. This is essential for applications that require precise control over hardware interactions.

Example: Accessing System Information via Native Functions

```csharp
using System;
using System.Runtime.InteropServices;
```

```csharp
public class SystemInfo
{
    [StructLayout(LayoutKind.Sequential)]
    public struct SYSTEM_INFO
    {
        public ushort processorArchitecture;
        public ushort reserved;
        public uint pageSize;
        public IntPtr minimumApplicationAddress;
        public IntPtr maximumApplicationAddress;
        public IntPtr activeProcessorMask;
        public uint numberOfProcessors;
        public uint processorType;
        public uint allocationGranularity;
        public ushort processorLevel;
        public ushort processorRevision;
    }

    [DllImport("kernel32.dll", SetLastError = true)]
    public static extern void GetSystemInfo(out SYSTEM_INFO lpSystemInfo);
}

public class HardwareInfoDemo
{
    public void DisplaySystemInfo()
    {
        SystemInfo.SYSTEM_INFO sysInfo;
        SystemInfo.GetSystemInfo(out sysInfo);
        Console.WriteLine($"Number of Processors: {sysInfo.numberOfProcessors}");
        Console.WriteLine($"Page Size: {sysInfo.pageSize} bytes");
    }
}
```

Explanation: This example demonstrates how to use P/Invoke to call the GetSystemInfo function from the Windows API to retrieve system information. This kind of access is essential for applications that need detailed hardware or system-level data.

4. Handling Low-Latency or Real-Time Requirements

In scenarios that require low-latency or real-time operations, such as multimedia processing, gaming, or network packet handling, native code often provides more predictable performance and lower overhead. P/Invoke allows you to write or reuse native code to achieve the necessary performance.

5. Interacting with Legacy Systems

Many organizations have legacy systems or components written in unmanaged languages. P/Invoke enables you to integrate these legacy components with modern .NET 6 applications, avoiding the cost and complexity of rewriting them in managed code.

3. Advantages of Using P/Invoke

Using P/Invoke in .NET 6 can offer several benefits:

- **Direct Access to Native Code:** P/Invoke allows you to call native functions directly, making it possible to leverage the full power of the underlying operating system and hardware.
- **Performance Optimization:** P/Invoke enables access to highly optimized native libraries, which can provide significant performance improvements for computationally intensive tasks.
- **Interoperability:** P/Invoke supports seamless interaction between managed .NET code and unmanaged code, facilitating integration with existing native libraries, system APIs, and legacy systems.
- **Expanded Functionality:** Through P/Invoke, developers can extend the capabilities of .NET applications beyond the scope of the .NET runtime and managed libraries.

4. Challenges and Considerations

While P/Invoke provides powerful capabilities, there are some challenges and considerations to be aware of:

- **Complexity and Maintenance:** P/Invoke involves working with unmanaged code, which can introduce complexity in terms of marshaling

data, error handling, and managing memory. Maintaining P/Invoke declarations and ensuring compatibility across platforms requires careful attention.
- **Platform-Specific Code:** P/Invoke is often used to call platform-specific APIs (e.g., Windows-only functions). This can lead to code that is not portable across different operating systems. In cross-platform applications, it's essential to conditionally include P/Invoke code based on the target platform.
- **Marshaling Overhead:** When using P/Invoke, data must be marshaled between managed and unmanaged memory. This marshaling process can introduce overhead, especially when working with complex data structures or large datasets.
- **Security Considerations:** Calling unmanaged code through P/Invoke requires proper security measures to prevent vulnerabilities such as buffer overflows, injection attacks, or unauthorized access to system resources.

5. Best Practices for Using P/Invoke in .NET 6

To effectively use P/Invoke in .NET 6 applications, consider the following best practices:

- **Minimize P/Invoke Calls:** Use P/Invoke only when necessary and avoid frequent calls to unmanaged code, as each call incurs marshaling overhead.
- **Optimize Data Marshaling:** When passing data between managed and unmanaged code, choose the most efficient marshaling techniques. For example, use simple data types or IntPtr when possible, and avoid unnecessary conversions or copying of large data structures.
- **Handle Errors and Exceptions:** Native functions can return error codes or raise exceptions that need to be handled in managed code. Use the SetLastError attribute to capture error codes, and wrap P/Invoke calls in try-catch blocks to handle exceptions gracefully.
- **Maintain Platform Portability:** If your application targets multiple plat-

forms, use conditional compilation (#if directives) or runtime checks (RuntimeInformation.IsOSPlatform) to include platform-specific P/Invoke code as needed.
- **Document P/Invoke Declarations:** Clearly document each P/Invoke declaration, including the expected input and output parameters, data types, and calling conventions, to improve code readability and maintainability.

P/Invoke is a valuable feature in .NET 6 that enables direct access to native functions, APIs, and libraries, expanding the capabilities of managed applications. It is particularly beneficial in scenarios that require system-level access, integration with existing native libraries, or performance optimizations through low-level code.

By understanding when to use P/Invoke and following best practices, developers can create high-performance applications that leverage the full power of native code while maintaining the safety and convenience of the .NET runtime. Whether you are working on hardware interfacing, financial calculations, multimedia processing, or cross-platform development, P/Invoke in .NET 6 provides the flexibility and efficiency needed to achieve your goals.

Best Practices for Calling Native Code Efficiently

Using P/Invoke in .NET 6 to call native code is a powerful capability, but to achieve efficient and stable applications, it's crucial to follow certain best practices. These practices help to minimize performance overhead, ensure stability, and maintain cross-platform compatibility.

Here's a comprehensive look at the best practices for calling native code efficiently in .NET 6.

1. Minimize the Frequency of P/Invoke Calls

Each P/Invoke call incurs a certain amount of overhead due to the transition between managed and unmanaged code. This transition involves marshaling data, adjusting the call stack, and handling calling conventions, which can introduce performance bottlenecks if not managed carefully.

Best Practice:

- **Batch Operations:** When possible, group operations into a single P/Invoke call rather than making multiple small calls. For instance, if you need to process multiple items, consider passing an array or buffer to a single native function that performs all necessary operations in one call.

Example: Efficient vs. Inefficient P/Invoke Calls

```csharp
// Inefficient: Multiple P/Invoke calls
for (int i = 0; i < data.Length; i++)
{
    NativeMethods.ProcessItem(data[i]);
}

// Efficient: Single P/Invoke call with an array
NativeMethods.ProcessAllItems(data, data.Length);
```

2. Optimize Data Marshaling

Marshaling is the process of converting data between managed and unmanaged memory. Improper marshaling can lead to significant performance penalties, especially when dealing with large or complex data structures.

Best Practices for Marshaling:

- **Use Simple Data Types:** For parameters and return values, prefer using primitive data types (e.g., int, float, double) that do not require complex

marshaling.
- **Pass Pointers or Handles:** When dealing with large amounts of data, pass pointers (such as IntPtr) or handles instead of copying data structures back and forth between managed and unmanaged memory.
- **Use Structs Wisely:** When passing complex structures, define them using [StructLayout(LayoutKind.Sequential)] to ensure that the managed and unmanaged memory layouts match.
- **Avoid Frequent String Marshaling:** Marshaling strings incurs extra overhead due to encoding conversions. Pass strings as IntPtr or use a fixed-size character buffer when possible.

Example: Optimized Struct Marshaling

```csharp

[StructLayout(LayoutKind.Sequential)]
public struct NativeStruct
{
    public int Field1;
    public float Field2;
}

[DllImport("native.dll")]
public static extern void ProcessNativeStruct(ref NativeStruct nativeStruct);

public void CallNativeCode()
{
    NativeStruct myStruct = new NativeStruct { Field1 = 42, Field2 = 3.14f };
    ProcessNativeStruct(ref myStruct);
}
```

3. Handle Memory Management Carefully

When using P/Invoke, memory management becomes a critical responsibility. Incorrect handling of unmanaged resources can lead to memory leaks, corruption, and security vulnerabilities. In .NET, you need to be aware of who owns the memory and when it should be released.

Best Practices for Memory Management:

- **Use SafeHandle for Resource Management:** Instead of using raw IntPtr, use SafeHandle subclasses to manage native resources like file handles, database connections, or unmanaged memory. This ensures that resources are properly released even in case of exceptions.
- **Free Allocated Memory:** If you allocate unmanaged memory using functions like Marshal.AllocHGlobal, ensure that it is freed using Marshal.FreeHGlobal or equivalent functions.
- **Be Careful with Pointers:** When using pointers in native code, be sure that the memory referenced by those pointers is still valid during the entire duration of the native call.

Example: Using SafeHandle for File Management

```csharp
csharp

public class NativeMethods
{
    [DllImport("kernel32.dll", SetLastError = true, CharSet = CharSet.Auto)]
    public static extern SafeFileHandle CreateFile(
        string lpFileName,
        uint dwDesiredAccess,
        uint dwShareMode,
        IntPtr lpSecurityAttributes,
        uint dwCreationDisposition,
        uint dwFlagsAndAttributes,
        IntPtr hTemplateFile);
}

public void CallNativeFileApi()
{
    using (var fileHandle = NativeMethods.CreateFile(
        "example.txt",
```

```
        0x80000000,  // GENERIC_READ
        0,           // No sharing
        IntPtr.Zero,
        3,           // OPEN_EXISTING
        0x80,        // FILE_ATTRIBUTE_NORMAL
        IntPtr.Zero))
    {
        if (fileHandle.IsInvalid)
        {
            // Handle error
        }

        // Use fileHandle...
    }
}
```

4. Match Calling Conventions Correctly

The calling convention determines how parameters are passed between managed and unmanaged code. Mismatched calling conventions can lead to stack corruption, memory leaks, or crashes. The default calling convention in .NET for P/Invoke is StdCall, but native functions may use other conventions like Cdecl.

Best Practices:

- **Specify Calling Convention:** Always explicitly specify the calling convention in your DllImport attribute to avoid ambiguity.
- **Verify Calling Convention of the Native Library:** Ensure that the calling convention used in the native library matches the one specified in your managed code.

Example: Specifying Calling Convention

csharp

```
[DllImport("native.dll", CallingConvention = CallingConvention.Cdecl)]
```

```
public static extern int AddNumbers(int a, int b);
```

5. Check for Platform Compatibility

When using P/Invoke in cross-platform applications, remember that certain native functions and libraries may only be available on specific operating systems. For example, Windows API functions are not available on Linux or macOS. Use conditional compilation or runtime checks to maintain compatibility.

Best Practices:

- **Use Conditional Compilation (#if Directives):** Wrap platform-specific code with #if directives to include or exclude code based on the target platform.
- **Use RuntimeInformation for Runtime Checks:** Determine the current platform at runtime using the RuntimeInformation class and execute platform-specific logic as needed.

Example: Cross-Platform P/Invoke with Conditional Compilation

```csharp
public class CrossPlatformNativeMethods
{
    #if WINDOWS
    [DllImport("user32.dll", CharSet = CharSet.Unicode)]
    public static extern int MessageBox(IntPtr hWnd, string text, string caption, uint type);
    #elif LINUX
    [DllImport("libX11.so.6")]
    public static extern IntPtr XOpenDisplay(IntPtr displayName);
    #endif
}

public void CallPlatformSpecificFunction()
{
```

```
    if (RuntimeInformation.IsOSPlatform(OSPlatform.Windows))
    {
        CrossPlatformNativeMethods.MessageBox(IntPtr.Zero,
        "Hello, Windows!", "P/Invoke Demo", 0);
    }
    else if (RuntimeInformation.IsOSPlatform(OSPlatform.Linux))
    {
        IntPtr display =
        CrossPlatformNativeMethods.XOpenDisplay(IntPtr.Zero);
        // Handle display...
    }
}
```

6. Handle Errors and Return Values Appropriately

Native functions often use error codes or specific return values to indicate success or failure. When calling native functions through P/Invoke, it is essential to properly check and handle these return values to prevent undefined behavior or crashes.

Best Practices for Error Handling:

- **Check Error Codes:** For functions that return error codes, use the SetLastError attribute and call Marshal.GetLastWin32Error to retrieve the error code in managed code.
- **Validate Pointer Return Values:** For functions that return pointers, validate that the returned pointer is not null or invalid before using it in managed code.

Example: Handling Errors with P/Invoke

```csharp

[DllImport("kernel32.dll", SetLastError = true)]
public static extern bool CloseHandle(IntPtr hObject);

public void CloseNativeHandle(IntPtr handle)
```

```
{
    if (!CloseHandle(handle))
    {
        int errorCode = Marshal.GetLastWin32Error();
        Console.WriteLine($"Failed to close handle. Error code:
        {errorCode}");
    }
}
```

Calling native code through P/Invoke in .NET 6 can provide significant performance benefits and expand the capabilities of managed applications. However, to achieve these benefits without introducing complexity or instability, it is crucial to follow these best practices. Efficient use of P/Invoke involves optimizing marshaling, managing memory carefully, handling errors appropriately, and maintaining cross-platform compatibility.

By adhering to these best practices, developers can harness the full potential of native code while minimizing the risks and challenges associated with unmanaged code. This allows .NET applications to interact seamlessly with system-level APIs, hardware devices, and high-performance native libraries, resulting in more powerful and efficient software solutions.

Integrating C++ and C# for High-Performance Computing

Integrating C++ and C# can lead to substantial performance improvements by leveraging the low-level control and high efficiency of C++ alongside the flexibility and productivity of C#. This approach is commonly used in high-performance computing scenarios, where computationally intensive tasks benefit from the speed and fine-grained optimizations possible with C++.

.NET 6 offers multiple ways to integrate C++ and C# to achieve high-performance computing, including Platform Invocation (P/Invoke),

C++/CLI (Common Language Infrastructure), and .NET's own interop capabilities. This section will focus on understanding these integration methods, their use cases, and best practices to maximize performance gains.

1. Why Integrate C++ with C#?

C++ is a low-level, unmanaged language that provides fine-grained control over memory and hardware. By integrating C++ with C#, developers can:

- **Leverage C++ for Performance-Critical Code:** C++ provides superior performance for tasks like mathematical computations, image processing, real-time physics simulations, and low-latency applications.
- **Access Legacy C++ Libraries:** Many well-optimized libraries, such as those for numerical analysis, image processing, or cryptography, are written in C++. Reusing these libraries allows for faster development and higher efficiency.
- **Utilize Low-Level System and Hardware APIs:** C++ provides direct access to system-level APIs and hardware-specific features that may not be exposed in managed code.

2. Integration Techniques for High-Performance Computing

There are three primary techniques to integrate C++ and C# in .NET 6:

- **Using P/Invoke to Call C++ Functions**
- **Using C++/CLI for Mixed-Mode Interoperability**
- **Using COM Interop for Component-Based Integration**

Using P/Invoke to Call C++ Functions

P/Invoke (Platform Invocation) allows C# code to call functions in unmanaged DLLs. It is an ideal solution when you need to access C++ functions from a native DLL directly.

Best Use Case: When you have a native C++ library compiled into a DLL, and you want to call its functions from C#.

Example: Calling a Simple C++ Function from C#

Suppose you have the following C++ code compiled into a DLL named MathLibrary.dll:

```cpp
Copy code
// MathLibrary.cpp - C++ Code
extern "C" __declspec(dllexport) int Add(int a, int b)
{
    return a + b;
}
```

To call this C++ function from C#, you can use P/Invoke as follows:

```csharp
Copy code
using System;
using System.Runtime.InteropServices;

public class MathLibrary
{
    [DllImport("MathLibrary.dll", CallingConvention = CallingConvention.Cdecl)]
    public static extern int Add(int a, int b);
}

public class PInvokeDemo
{
    public void PerformAddition()
    {
        int result = MathLibrary.Add(10, 20);
        Console.WriteLine($"Result of addition: {result}");
    }
}
```

Explanation: This example uses P/Invoke to call the Add function in the MathLibrary.dll C++ DLL. The CallingConvention.Cdecl attribute specifies the calling convention used by the C++ function.

Using C++/CLI for Mixed-Mode Interoperability

C++/CLI is an extension of C++ that allows the creation of mixed-mode assemblies containing both managed and unmanaged code. It is particularly useful when you need seamless interaction between C++ and C# code.

Best Use Case: When you need tight integration between C++ and C#, and direct access to C++ objects and classes.

Example: Wrapping C++ Code in C++/CLI

Suppose you have a native C++ class in MathLibrary:

cpp

```cpp
// MathLibrary.h - C++ Code
class MathOperations
{
public:
    int Multiply(int a, int b)
    {
        return a * b;
    }
};
```

Now, wrap this class in a C++/CLI wrapper:

cpp

```cpp
// MathWrapper.cpp - C++/CLI Code
#include "MathLibrary.h"

public ref class MathWrapper
{
private:
    MathOperations* _mathOps;

public:
```

```
    MathWrapper()
    {
        _mathOps = new MathOperations();
    }

    ~MathWrapper()
    {
        delete _mathOps;
    }

    int Multiply(int a, int b)
    {
        return _mathOps->Multiply(a, b);
    }
};
```

You can then call this C++/CLI wrapper class from C#:

```csharp
Copy code
public class CppCliDemo
{
    public void PerformMultiplication()
    {
        var mathWrapper = new MathWrapper();
        int result = mathWrapper.Multiply(5, 6);
        Console.WriteLine($"Result of multiplication: {result}");
    }
}
```

Explanation: This example uses C++/CLI to wrap a native C++ class and expose it to C#. C++/CLI enables seamless integration with C++ classes, allowing C# to call C++ code as if it were managed.

Using COM Interop for Component-Based Integration

COM (Component Object Model) is another way to integrate C++ and C# code. By creating a COM-visible C++ library, you can call C++ code from C# using COM Interop.

Best Use Case: When you need to expose reusable C++ components to C# or other languages that support COM.

Example: Exposing a C++ Class as a COM Object

Suppose you have a C++ class that you want to expose as a COM object:

```cpp
// MathCom.cpp - C++ COM Code
class __declspec(uuid("...")) MathCom : public IUnknown
{
public:
    int Divide(int a, int b)
    {
        return a / b;
    }
};
```

You can then register this COM object and call it from C# using Interop:

```csharp
using System.Runtime.InteropServices;

[ComImport]
[Guid("...")]
[InterfaceType(ComInterfaceType.InterfaceIsIUnknown)]
public interface IMathCom
{
    int Divide(int a, int b);
}

public class ComInteropDemo
{
    public void PerformDivision()
    {
        var mathCom = (IMathCom)new MathCom();
        int result = mathCom.Divide(10, 2);
        Console.WriteLine($"Result of division: {result}");
```

```
    }
}
```

Explanation: This example uses COM Interop to call a C++ COM object from C#. The ComImport and Guid attributes are used to define the COM interface in C#.

3. Best Practices for C++ and C# Integration

To maximize the performance and reliability of your C++ and C# integration, consider these best practices:

1. **Optimize Data Passing Between C++ and C#:** Avoid passing large data structures back and forth between managed and unmanaged code. Instead, use pointers or buffers to minimize memory copying.
2. **Use SafeHandle for Resource Management:** When working with native resources in C++, use SafeHandle to ensure proper cleanup of unmanaged resources in C#.
3. **Be Mindful of Memory Leaks:** When using P/Invoke or C++/CLI, it's essential to free any allocated unmanaged memory to prevent memory leaks. Consider using RAII (Resource Acquisition Is Initialization) in C++ and finalizers or IDisposable in C#.
4. **Ensure Thread Safety:** When interacting with C++ code that involves threading or shared data, ensure proper synchronization to avoid race conditions or deadlocks.
5. **Leverage C++ for Performance-Critical Operations:** Identify performance-critical sections of code that would benefit from low-level optimizations in C++, and keep the rest of the code in C# for productivity and maintainability.
6. **Use Platform-Specific Optimizations:** Take advantage of platform-specific optimizations in C++ (like SSE/AVX instructions) for CPU-intensive tasks, and expose these optimizations to C# through P/Invoke or C++/CLI.

4. Performance Considerations for C++ and C# Integration

When integrating C++ and C# for high-performance computing, consider the following performance factors:

- **Overhead of P/Invoke and COM Calls:** While P/Invoke and COM provide convenient integration, each call incurs marshaling overhead. To mitigate this, minimize the frequency of cross-boundary calls and pass pointers or handles for large datasets.
- **Data Alignment and Memory Layouts:** Ensure that data structures are aligned correctly between C++ and C# to avoid marshaling overhead and potential data corruption.
- **Direct Memory Access via Unsafe Code:** In certain high-performance scenarios, using unsafe code in C# to directly manipulate memory via pointers can reduce the cost of marshaling.

Integrating C++ and C# in .NET 6 allows developers to harness the full power of C++ for performance-critical tasks while leveraging C# for productivity and rapid development. Techniques such as P/Invoke, C++/CLI, and COM Interop enable seamless communication between managed and unmanaged code, opening up new possibilities for high-performance applications.

By understanding the various integration techniques and following best practices, developers can create powerful, efficient applications that take advantage of both the low-level control of C++ and the managed capabilities of .NET. Whether you're building scientific simulations, financial analysis tools, or real-time gaming engines, the integration of C++ and C# offers a flexible and effective solution for achieving high performance.

Real-World Examples of Interoperability

Integrating C++ with C# using P/Invoke, C++/CLI, and COM Interop opens up numerous possibilities for enhancing application performance and capabilities. In this section, we will explore several real-world examples that illustrate how interoperability can be effectively utilized in various domains, including scientific computing, graphics processing, and legacy system integration.

1. Scientific Computing: Using Optimized C++ Libraries

Scientific computing often requires complex mathematical operations and high-performance calculations. Many well-established libraries, such as the GNU Scientific Library (GSL) or Intel Math Kernel Library (MKL), are written in C++. By leveraging these libraries through P/Invoke, developers can significantly boost performance in .NET applications.

Example: Integrating GSL for Numerical Methods

Suppose you want to use GSL for solving linear systems or performing numerical integrations. First, ensure you have GSL installed and accessible from your application.

C++ Function (GSL) Example:

```cpp
extern "C" {
    #include <gsl/gsl_matrix.h>
    #include <gsl/gsl_linalg.h>

    __declspec(dllexport) void SolveLinearSystem(double* A, double* b, double* x, int n) {
        gsl_matrix_view m = gsl_matrix_view_array(A, n, n);
        gsl_vector_view v = gsl_vector_view_array(b, n);
        gsl_vector_view x_view = gsl_vector_view_array(x, n);
        gsl_permutation* p = gsl_permutation_alloc(n);
        int signum;
```

```
        // Decompose matrix
        gsl_linalg_LU_decomp(&m.matrix, p, &signum);
        // Solve the system
        gsl_linalg_LU_solve(&m.matrix, p, &v.vector,
        &x_view.vector);

        gsl_permutation_free(p);
    }
}
```

C# P/Invoke Code Example:

```csharp
using System;
using System.Runtime.InteropServices;

public class GslInterop
{
    [DllImport("gsl_wrapper.dll", CallingConvention =
    CallingConvention.Cdecl)]
    public static extern void SolveLinearSystem(double[] A,
    double[] b, double[] x, int n);
}

public class ScientificDemo
{
    public void SolveSystem()
    {
        int n = 3;
        double[] A = { 3, 2, -1, 2, 3, 1, -1, 1, 4 };
        double[] b = { 1, 2, 3 };
        double[] x = new double[n];

        GslInterop.SolveLinearSystem(A, b, x, n);

        Console.WriteLine("Solution: " + string.Join(", ", x));
    }
```

}

Explanation: This example demonstrates how to call a C++ function from the GNU Scientific Library to solve a linear system. The C++ function SolveLinearSystem uses GSL to perform matrix decomposition and solve the system of equations. The C# code uses P/Invoke to call this function, passing arrays for the matrix and vectors.

2. Graphics Processing: Using OpenCV for Image Manipulation

OpenCV is a powerful library for computer vision tasks, and it is often used in image processing applications. By integrating OpenCV with C# through P/Invoke, developers can leverage its extensive capabilities for image analysis and manipulation.

Example: Applying Image Filters Using OpenCV

Assuming OpenCV is set up on your system, you can create a simple C++ function to apply a Gaussian blur filter.

C++ Function (OpenCV) Example:

```cpp
#include <opencv2/opencv.hpp>

extern "C" {
    __declspec(dllexport) void ApplyGaussianBlur(unsigned char*
    inputImage, unsigned char* outputImage, int width, int
    height) {
        cv::Mat inputMat(height, width, CV_8UC3, inputImage);
        cv::Mat outputMat;

        cv::GaussianBlur(inputMat, outputMat, cv::Size(5, 5), 0);
        std::memcpy(outputImage, outputMat.data, width * height
        * 3);
    }
}
```

C# P/Invoke Code Example:

```csharp
using System;
using System.Runtime.InteropServices;

public class OpenCvInterop
{
    [DllImport("opencv_wrapper.dll", CallingConvention =
    CallingConvention.Cdecl)]
    public static extern void ApplyGaussianBlur(byte[]
    inputImage, byte[] outputImage, int width, int height);
}

public class ImageProcessingDemo
{
    public void ProcessImage(byte[] inputImage, int width, int
    height)
    {
        byte[] outputImage = new byte[width * height * 3]; //
        Assuming 3 channels (RGB)

        OpenCvInterop.ApplyGaussianBlur(inputImage, outputImage,
        width, height);

        // Use the outputImage for further processing or display
    }
}
```

Explanation: This example shows how to apply a Gaussian blur filter to an image using OpenCV in C++. The ApplyGaussianBlur function receives raw image data and processes it using OpenCV functions. The C# code calls this function to perform the image processing efficiently.

3. Legacy System Integration: Accessing Existing C++ Code

In many organizations, legacy systems are still in use, often built using C++. Integrating these legacy components with modern .NET applications allows for reusing existing code and minimizing the need for a complete rewrite.

Example: Accessing a Legacy C++ Logging System

Assume you have a legacy C++ logging library that you want to use in a new C# application.

C++ Logging Function Example:

```cpp
extern "C" {
    __declspec(dllexport) void LogMessage(const char* message) {
        std::cout << message << std::endl;
    }
}
```

C# P/Invoke Code Example:

```csharp
using System;
using System.Runtime.InteropServices;

public class LegacyLogger
{
    [DllImport("legacy_logging.dll", CallingConvention = CallingConvention.Cdecl)]
    public static extern void LogMessage(string message);
}

public class LoggerDemo
{
    public void Log()
    {
        LegacyLogger.LogMessage("This is a message from the C# application.");
    }
}
```

Explanation: This example illustrates how to call a simple C++ logging function from a legacy DLL. The LogMessage function writes messages to the console, and the C# code uses P/Invoke to log messages through the legacy system.

4. High-Performance Computing: Using C++ for Numerical Computation

In high-performance computing scenarios, complex numerical calculations often require the efficiency of C++. By using P/Invoke, developers can write performance-critical code in C++ and call it from C# applications.

Example: Using a C++ Library for Matrix Multiplication

Suppose you have a C++ function for matrix multiplication that needs to be accessed from C#.

C++ Matrix Multiplication Example:

```cpp
extern "C" {
    __declspec(dllexport) void MultiplyMatrices(double* A,
    double* B, double* C, int n) {
        for (int i = 0; i < n; i++) {
            for (int j = 0; j < n; j++) {
                C[i * n + j] = 0;
                for (int k = 0; k < n; k++) {
                    C[i * n + j] += A[i * n + k] * B[k * n + j];
                }
            }
        }
    }
}
```

C# P/Invoke Code Example:

```csharp
using System;
using System.Runtime.InteropServices;

public class MatrixInterop
```

```csharp
{
    [DllImport("matrix_operations.dll", CallingConvention = 
    CallingConvention.Cdecl)]
    public static extern void MultiplyMatrices(double[] A, 
    double[] B, double[] C, int n);
}

public class MatrixMultiplicationDemo
{
    public void Multiply()
    {
        int n = 3;
        double[] A = { 1, 2, 3, 4, 5, 6, 7, 8, 9 };
        double[] B = { 9, 8, 7, 6, 5, 4, 3, 2, 1 };
        double[] C = new double[n * n];

        MatrixInterop.MultiplyMatrices(A, B, C, n);

        Console.WriteLine("Matrix C:");
        for (int i = 0; i < n; i++)
        {
            for (int j = 0; j < n; j++)
            {
                Console.Write(C[i * n + j] + " ");
            }
            Console.WriteLine();
        }
    }
}
```

Explanation: This example demonstrates how to perform matrix multiplication using a C++ function. The matrices are passed as arrays from C# to the native function, enabling high-performance calculations while leveraging existing C++ code.

Real-world examples of interoperability between C++ and C# illustrate the versatility and performance benefits of integrating native code with managed applications. By leveraging techniques like P/Invoke, C++/CLI, and COM Interop, developers can enhance their applications in various domains, from scientific computing to image processing and legacy system integration.

These integration strategies not only allow the reuse of existing code but also enable the performance optimizations that are critical in high-demand environments. By following best practices and understanding the nuances of native code integration, developers can create efficient, high-performance applications that capitalize on the strengths of both C++ and C#.

Low-Level Programming with Unsafe Code

Introduction to Unsafe Code and Pointers in C#

In the world of .NET, C# is predominantly a safe, managed language that provides developers with built-in safeguards against memory corruption and other common programming errors. However, there are scenarios where developers need to interact directly with memory, manipulate data at a low level, or optimize performance-critical sections of code. This is where unsafe code and pointers come into play.

Unsafe code in C# allows developers to bypass certain safety checks imposed by the Common Language Runtime (CLR) and work with memory directly using pointers, similar to what is possible in languages like C and C++. This capability can lead to performance improvements and enable functionality that would otherwise be difficult or impossible to achieve in managed code.

1. What is Unsafe Code?

Unsafe code is a feature in C# that allows for direct memory manipulation. When using unsafe code, the CLR does not enforce the same level of memory access protection as it does with safe code, enabling operations such as pointer arithmetic, direct memory access, and the use of unmanaged types. This flexibility can result in enhanced performance, particularly in scenarios that require fine-tuned control over memory and processing.

Key Characteristics of Unsafe Code:

- **Bypasses Memory Safety Checks:** Unsafe code allows developers to circumvent the automatic memory management and safety checks provided by the CLR, which can lead to faster execution in certain contexts.
- **Direct Memory Manipulation:** Using pointers, developers can access and manipulate memory locations directly, which can be useful for interfacing with native code or performing operations on large data structures.
- **Requires Special Compiler Settings:** Unsafe code must be explicitly marked with the unsafe keyword, and the project must be compiled with the /unsafe option enabled.

2. Understanding Pointers in C#

Pointers are variables that store the memory address of another variable. In C#, pointers can only be used in unsafe contexts. Pointers are similar to references but provide more control and flexibility, enabling operations such as pointer arithmetic and direct memory access.

Key Types of Pointers:

- **Pointer Types:** C# supports pointer types that correspond to the built-in data types. For example, int* is a pointer to an integer, and char* is a pointer to a character.
- **Void Pointers:** The void* type is a special pointer that can point to any data type, but it cannot be dereferenced directly without casting.
- **Function Pointers:** C# also supports function pointers, which allow you to point to methods. This feature is particularly useful for callbacks and interop scenarios.

3. Declaring and Using Pointers

To use pointers in C#, you must declare a variable as a pointer type. This declaration requires the unsafe keyword, both at the method and project levels.

Example: Declaring Pointers

```csharp
unsafe
{
    int value = 42;
    int* pointer = &value; // Getting the address of value
    Console.WriteLine($"Value: {value}, Pointer: {pointer}, Dereferenced Value: {*pointer}");
}
```

Explanation: In this example, we declare an integer variable value, obtain its memory address using the & operator, and assign it to an integer pointer pointer. The * operator is then used to dereference the pointer and retrieve the value it points to.

4. Pointer Arithmetic

Pointer arithmetic allows you to perform calculations on pointers to navigate through memory. This capability is particularly useful for iterating through arrays or buffers in an efficient manner.

Example: Pointer Arithmetic with Arrays

```csharp
unsafe
{
    int[] numbers = { 1, 2, 3, 4, 5 };
    fixed (int* ptr = numbers) // Pin the array in memory
    {
        for (int i = 0; i < 5; i++)
        {
            Console.WriteLine($"Value at index {i}: {*(ptr + i)}"); // Accessing array elements via pointer
        }
    }
}
```

Explanation: In this example, we use the fixed statement to pin the numbers array in memory, preventing the garbage collector from moving it. We then use pointer arithmetic to access each element of the array through its pointer.

5. Using Unsafe Code for Performance

Unsafe code can be beneficial for performance optimization, especially in scenarios involving large data processing, memory-intensive operations, or when interfacing with native APIs.

Example: Fast Memory Copy with Unsafe Code

```csharp
unsafe
{
    byte[] source = new byte[1024];
    byte[] destination = new byte[1024];

    fixed (byte* srcPtr = source)
    fixed (byte* destPtr = destination)
    {
        // Perform a fast memory copy
        Buffer.MemoryCopy(srcPtr, destPtr, destination.Length,
        source.Length);
    }
}
```

Explanation: This example demonstrates a fast memory copy operation using pointers. The Buffer.MemoryCopy method is called to copy bytes from the source to the destination using pointers. This approach can outperform managed copy operations, particularly for large buffers.

6. Safety and Best Practices

While unsafe code provides powerful capabilities, it also introduces risks related to memory corruption, access violations, and security vulnerabilities. To mitigate these risks, consider the following best practices:

- **Limit the Scope of Unsafe Code:** Use unsafe code sparingly and limit its scope to performance-critical sections of your application. This approach minimizes the risk of introducing instability into your codebase.
- **Use fixed Statements Wisely:** When working with arrays or strings, use the fixed statement to pin data in memory while accessing it through pointers. This prevents the garbage collector from relocating the memory during the operation.
- **Validate Pointer Usage:** Always check pointers for null or invalid values before dereferencing them to avoid runtime exceptions or crashes.
- **Encapsulate Unsafe Code:** Consider encapsulating unsafe code within classes or methods to provide a controlled interface for accessing unsafe operations, enhancing code maintainability and readability.
- **Profile Performance Improvements:** When using unsafe code for performance optimizations, use profiling tools to measure the impact on performance and ensure that the benefits outweigh the risks and complexity introduced.

Unsafe code and pointers in C# offer developers a powerful toolset for low-level programming and performance optimization. By allowing direct memory manipulation and bypassing the safety checks of the CLR, unsafe code can significantly improve execution speed in scenarios where high performance is essential.

Understanding how to safely and effectively use unsafe code, along with pointers, is crucial for harnessing its benefits while minimizing risks. As you explore low-level programming in C#, you can unlock new levels of performance and functionality in your applications, making them well-suited for high-performance computing tasks and scenarios. Whether you're working with numerical computations, graphics processing, or any performance-sensitive domain, leveraging unsafe code effectively can lead to substantial improvements.

LOW-LEVEL PROGRAMMING WITH UNSAFE CODE

Advanced Techniques for Low-Level Memory Access in C#

Low-level memory access in C# through unsafe code and pointers opens up powerful capabilities for performance optimization and system-level programming. While we have already covered the basics of unsafe code, pointers, and their applications, this section delves deeper into advanced techniques for efficient memory management and manipulation. These techniques are crucial for high-performance computing, game development, graphics processing, and scenarios where performance is paramount.

1. Using Memory Mapped Files for Interprocess Communication

Memory-mapped files allow multiple processes to share data by mapping a file or a portion of a file to the memory space of a process. This technique is especially useful for interprocess communication (IPC) and can be combined with unsafe code for low-level memory manipulation.

Creating and Using Memory-Mapped Files:

Example: Writing and Reading with Memory-Mapped Files

```csharp
using System;
using System.IO.MemoryMappedFiles;
using System.Runtime.InteropServices;

public class MemoryMappedFileExample
{
    const int MapSize = 1024; // Size of the memory-mapped file

    public void WriteToMemoryMappedFile()
    {
        using (var mmf =
        MemoryMappedFile.CreateNew("MyMappedFile", MapSize))
        {
            using (var accessor = mmf.CreateViewAccessor())
            {
                unsafe
```

```csharp
        {
            // Pin the buffer in memory
            byte[] buffer = new byte[MapSize];
            fixed (byte* pBuffer = buffer)
            {
                // Write data directly to the
                memory-mapped file
                for (int i = 0; i < MapSize; i++)
                {
                    pBuffer[i] = (byte)(i % 256); //
                    Example data
                }
                accessor.Write(0, pBuffer, 0, MapSize);
                // Write to the memory-mapped file
            }
        }
      }
    }
}

public void ReadFromMemoryMappedFile()
{
    using (var mmf =
    MemoryMappedFile.OpenExisting("MyMappedFile"))
    {
        using (var accessor = mmf.CreateViewAccessor())
        {
            unsafe
            {
                byte[] buffer = new byte[MapSize];
                fixed (byte* pBuffer = buffer)
                {
                    accessor.Read(0, pBuffer, 0, MapSize);
                    // Read from the memory-mapped file
                    for (int i = 0; i < MapSize; i++)
                    {
                        Console.WriteLine($"Value at index
                        {i}: {pBuffer[i]}");
                    }
                }
```

```
                }
            }
        }
    }
}
```

Explanation: In this example, we create a memory-mapped file named "MyMappedFile" and write data to it using unsafe code. The fixed statement is used to pin the buffer in memory, allowing direct access to its address. We then read the data back from the memory-mapped file and print the values. This technique allows for efficient data sharing between processes without the need for complex serialization or IPC mechanisms.

2. Working with Unmanaged Memory

The Marshal class provides methods to allocate and free unmanaged memory. This allows for fine-grained control over memory usage, which can be crucial in performance-sensitive applications.

Example: Allocating and Freeing Unmanaged Memory

```csharp
using System;
using System.Runtime.InteropServices;

public class UnmanagedMemoryExample
{
    public void AllocateAndUseUnmanagedMemory()
    {
        // Allocate unmanaged memory for an array of integers
        int size = 10;
        IntPtr unmanagedPointer = Marshal.AllocHGlobal(size * sizeof(int));

        try
        {
```

```csharp
            // Initialize unmanaged memory
            for (int i = 0; i < size; i++)
            {
                Marshal.WriteInt32(unmanagedPointer, i *
                sizeof(int), i);
            }

            // Read and display unmanaged memory values
            for (int i = 0; i < size; i++)
            {
                int value = Marshal.ReadInt32(unmanagedPointer,
                i * sizeof(int));
                Console.WriteLine($"Value at index {i}:
                {value}");
            }
        }
        finally
        {
            // Free unmanaged memory
            Marshal.FreeHGlobal(unmanagedPointer);
        }
    }
}
```

Explanation: This example demonstrates how to allocate unmanaged memory using Marshal.AllocHGlobal, initialize it with values, and read those values back. It's crucial to ensure that unmanaged memory is freed using Marshal.FreeHGlobal to avoid memory leaks. This technique is particularly useful when interfacing with native APIs that require raw memory buffers.

3. Using Span<T> and Memory<T> for Slicing Data

With the introduction of Span<T> and Memory<T> in C#, developers can work with slices of memory in a safe manner while still achieving high performance. Span<T> allows for memory access without the need for unsafe code, making it easier to manage slices of arrays, strings, and other data structures.

Example: Using Span<T> for Efficient Data Manipulation

LOW-LEVEL PROGRAMMING WITH UNSAFE CODE

```csharp
using System;

public class SpanExample
{
    public void ProcessData()
    {
        int[] data = { 1, 2, 3, 4, 5 };
        Span<int> dataSpan = new Span<int>(data);

        // Perform operations on the span
        for (int i = 0; i < dataSpan.Length; i++)
        {
            dataSpan[i] *= 2; // Example operation: doubling
            each value
        }

        // Display updated data
        Console.WriteLine("Processed Data: " + string.Join(", ",
        dataSpan.ToArray()));
    }
}
```

Explanation: This example illustrates how to use Span<T> to manipulate a slice of an array efficiently. Span<T> provides a safe way to access and modify memory, allowing for efficient data manipulation without the need for unsafe code.

4. Memory Optimization Techniques

When working with low-level memory access, performance optimizations are essential. Here are some advanced techniques to consider:

- **Memory Alignment:** Ensure that your data structures are aligned properly to reduce cache misses and improve access speeds. Aligning data structures can also reduce the likelihood of access violations.

- **Pooling Memory:** Implement memory pooling to reuse allocated memory instead of allocating and freeing it repeatedly. This can significantly reduce the overhead of memory management, especially in performance-sensitive applications.
- **Batch Processing:** When performing operations on large datasets, consider processing them in batches. This reduces the overhead of function calls and allows better cache utilization.
- **Use Unsafe Contexts Wisely:** While unsafe code provides flexibility, use it judiciously. Reserve unsafe operations for critical performance sections of your application, and encapsulate them to minimize risk.
- **Profile and Optimize:** Use profiling tools to analyze memory usage and identify bottlenecks in your application. Focus on optimizing sections that have the most significant impact on performance.

Low-level memory access in C# through unsafe code and pointers offers powerful capabilities for performance optimization, especially in high-performance computing scenarios. By utilizing advanced techniques such as memory-mapped files, unmanaged memory management, and Span<T>, developers can efficiently manipulate data while maintaining control over memory usage.

Understanding how to effectively leverage these techniques enables the development of high-performance applications that meet the demands of computationally intensive tasks. By combining the safety of managed code with the power of low-level programming, C# developers can create applications that are both efficient and robust. Whether working in scientific computing, graphics processing, or systems programming, mastering low-level memory access is essential for achieving optimal performance in .NET applications.

When to Use Unsafe Code for Performance

Unsafe code in C# offers developers the ability to interact directly with memory and perform operations that bypass the safety mechanisms of the Common Language Runtime (CLR). While this feature provides powerful capabilities, it should be used judiciously and only in scenarios where the performance benefits outweigh the potential risks and complexities associated with unsafe operations.

This section outlines the situations in which using unsafe code is advantageous, detailing the performance gains that can be achieved and the considerations that should guide its use.

1. Performance-Critical Sections

Unsafe code is particularly useful in performance-critical sections of an application where every millisecond counts. These sections often involve intensive computations, real-time processing, or scenarios where large amounts of data are manipulated.

Examples of Performance-Critical Scenarios:

- **Numerical Computation:** Operations such as matrix multiplications, FFT (Fast Fourier Transform), or complex numerical algorithms can benefit from direct memory access and manipulation through unsafe code.
- **Graphics Processing:** Real-time graphics rendering, image manipulation, and pixel processing often require low-level access to memory for optimal performance.
- **Game Development:** In games, performance is crucial for rendering, physics calculations, and managing large datasets. Unsafe code can reduce overhead when working with game objects or raw data buffers.

Example: High-Performance Matrix Multiplication Using Unsafe Code

```csharp
unsafe public class MatrixMultiplication
{
    public void MultiplyMatrices(int* A, int* B, int* C, int rowsA, int colsA, int colsB)
    {
        for (int i = 0; i < rowsA; i++)
        {
            for (int j = 0; j < colsB; j++)
            {
                C[i * colsB + j] = 0;
                for (int k = 0; k < colsA; k++)
                {
                    C[i * colsB + j] += A[i * colsA + k] * B[k * colsB + j];
                }
            }
        }
    }
}
```

In this example, unsafe pointers are used for direct memory access, enhancing the performance of matrix multiplication compared to managed arrays.

2. Direct Memory Manipulation

When you need precise control over memory layout and access patterns, unsafe code provides the flexibility to manipulate memory directly. This capability can be critical in scenarios where performance is impacted by memory allocation overhead or garbage collection.

Situations for Direct Memory Manipulation:

- **Interfacing with Unmanaged Code:** When working with native libraries that require specific memory layouts or pointers, unsafe code enables you to pass memory addresses directly.
- **Optimizing Buffer Operations:** For applications that require frequent

LOW-LEVEL PROGRAMMING WITH UNSAFE CODE

reading and writing to memory buffers (e.g., in network programming or file I/O), unsafe code can streamline these operations, reducing the overhead of managed memory management.

Example: Efficient Buffer Handling Using Unsafe Code

```csharp
unsafe public class BufferHandler
{
    public void FillBuffer(byte* buffer, int length)
    {
        for (int i = 0; i < length; i++)
        {
            *(buffer + i) = (byte)(i % 256); // Fill buffer with
            pattern
        }
    }
}
```

In this example, a byte buffer is filled directly through a pointer, minimizing the overhead associated with bounds checking and managed array operations.

3. Working with Large Data Structures

When handling large data structures, the overhead of bounds checking and garbage collection can impact performance. Unsafe code allows you to bypass these checks, making it easier to work with large arrays, structures, or other data types.

Examples of Large Data Structures:

- **Image Data Processing:** Manipulating large images or video frames may require access to raw pixel data without the overhead of managed collections.
- **Scientific Simulations:** In simulations that require large matrices or datasets, unsafe code can optimize memory access patterns and improve

computational speed.

Example: Manipulating Image Data Using Unsafe Code

```csharp

unsafe public class ImageProcessor
{
    public void ConvertToGrayscale(byte* pixelData, int width, int height)
    {
        for (int y = 0; y < height; y++)
        {
            for (int x = 0; x < width; x++)
            {
                int index = (y * width + x) * 3; // Assuming RGB format
                byte r = *(pixelData + index);
                byte g = *(pixelData + index + 1);
                byte b = *(pixelData + index + 2);
                byte gray = (byte)((r * 0.3) + (g * 0.59) + (b * 0.11));
                *(pixelData + index) = gray;     // Update red channel
                *(pixelData + index + 1) = gray; // Update green channel
                *(pixelData + index + 2) = gray; // Update blue channel
            }
        }
    }
}
```

This example shows how to directly manipulate pixel data for image processing, providing high performance by avoiding managed array overhead.

4. Interfacing with Hardware and Native APIs

In scenarios where your application needs to interact closely with hardware, drivers, or native APIs, unsafe code is often necessary. This is

LOW-LEVEL PROGRAMMING WITH UNSAFE CODE

especially true for applications requiring low-level access to devices or performance-critical components.

Examples of Hardware Interfacing:

- **Device Drivers:** Accessing hardware components such as sensors, network interfaces, or custom hardware interfaces may require pointers and direct memory manipulation.
- **Real-time Systems:** Applications with real-time processing requirements, such as audio or video processing, may need to interact directly with hardware for efficient performance.

Example: Accessing Hardware Resources

```csharp
unsafe public class HardwareAccess
{
    public void ReadFromDevice(int* deviceAddress, int* buffer,
    int length)
    {
        for (int i = 0; i < length; i++)
        {
            *(buffer + i) = *(deviceAddress + i); // Read from
            hardware device
        }
    }
}
```

In this example, unsafe pointers are used to read data directly from a device memory address, optimizing the data retrieval process.

5. Profiling and Benchmarking

When considering the use of unsafe code for performance enhancements, profiling and benchmarking are essential. Always profile your application to identify bottlenecks and determine if the added complexity of unsafe code results in significant performance gains.

Best Practices for Profiling:

- **Use Profiling Tools:** Employ tools like Visual Studio Profiler, JetBrains dotTrace, or PerfView to analyze your application's performance and identify hot paths that may benefit from unsafe code.
- **Benchmark Before and After:** Measure performance before introducing unsafe code and after implementation to quantify the improvements and ensure that they justify the complexity and risks involved.

Unsafe code in C# provides powerful capabilities for low-level memory manipulation, performance optimization, and direct interaction with native APIs. Understanding when and how to use unsafe code is critical for achieving performance gains in high-performance computing scenarios, scientific simulations, graphics processing, and hardware interfacing.

By recognizing the situations where unsafe code is beneficial—such as in performance-critical sections, direct memory manipulation, and working with large data structures—developers can leverage the full potential of C# while ensuring that performance and safety are balanced effectively. Proper profiling and benchmarking practices further enhance the decision-making process, enabling developers to create robust and efficient applications in the .NET ecosystem.

Code Snippets and Best Practices for Unsafe Code in C#

When working with unsafe code in C#, having practical code snippets and understanding best practices is essential for efficient and safe memory manipulation. Below are various examples demonstrating how to use unsafe code effectively, along with best practices to ensure reliability and performance.

LOW-LEVEL PROGRAMMING WITH UNSAFE CODE

1. Basic Unsafe Code Example

Unsafe code allows you to use pointers, enabling direct memory access and manipulation. Here's a simple example that demonstrates the basic usage of unsafe code.

Code Snippet: Basic Pointer Manipulation

```csharp
unsafe
{
    int number = 10;
    int* pointer = &number; // Get the address of number
    Console.WriteLine($"Value: {number}, Pointer: {pointer}, 
    Dereferenced Value: {*pointer}");
}
```

Best Practice: Always ensure that pointers are not dereferenced if they can potentially be null. Use checks wherever possible to avoid runtime exceptions.

2. Working with Fixed Buffers

The fixed statement is essential for pinning memory locations so that the garbage collector does not relocate them during operations. This is especially useful when working with arrays or strings.

Code Snippet: Using Fixed with Arrays

```csharp
unsafe
{
    int[] array = { 1, 2, 3, 4, 5 };
    fixed (int* pArray = array) // Pin the array in memory
    {
        for (int i = 0; i < 5; i++)
        {
            Console.WriteLine($"Value at index {i}: {*(pArray +
```

```
            i)}");
        }
    }
}
```

Best Practice: Use fixed to pin memory when you need to pass arrays to unmanaged code, ensuring that the garbage collector does not move the data during the operation.

3. Allocating and Freeing Unmanaged Memory

When working with unmanaged memory, always ensure that you allocate and free memory appropriately to avoid memory leaks.

Code Snippet: Allocating Unmanaged Memory

```csharp
using System;
using System.Runtime.InteropServices;

public class UnmanagedMemoryDemo
{
    unsafe public void AllocateAndUseMemory()
    {
        int size = 5;
        IntPtr unmanagedMemory = Marshal.AllocHGlobal(size * sizeof(int));
        try
        {
            int* pArray = (int*)unmanagedMemory.ToPointer();
            for (int i = 0; i < size; i++)
            {
                pArray[i] = i * 10; // Initialize values
            }

            for (int i = 0; i < size; i++)
            {
                Console.WriteLine($"Value at index {i}:
```

```
                {pArray[i]}");
            }
        }
        finally
        {
            Marshal.FreeHGlobal(unmanagedMemory); // Free
            unmanaged memory
        }
    }
}
```

Best Practice: Always wrap unmanaged memory allocation and access in a try-finally block to ensure that memory is freed, even if an exception occurs.

4. Using Span<T> for Safe Memory Manipulation

With the introduction of Span<T> in .NET, developers can manipulate memory safely while avoiding the overhead of unsafe code. However, when necessary, Span<T> can be combined with unsafe code for performance-critical operations.

Code Snippet: Using Span<T>

```csharp
public void ProcessDataSpan(int[] data)
{
    Span<int> span = data; // Implicit conversion to Span<int>
    for (int i = 0; i < span.Length; i++)
    {
        span[i] *= 2; // Modify data in-place
    }
}
```

Best Practice: Prefer using Span<T> when possible, as it provides a safe way to work with slices of memory without the need for unsafe code, making your code more maintainable.

5. Buffer Manipulation Using Unsafe Code

In high-performance applications, manipulating byte buffers directly can yield significant performance benefits. Here's how to use unsafe code for efficient buffer handling.

Code Snippet: Direct Buffer Manipulation

```csharp
unsafe public class BufferManipulator
{
    public void FillBuffer(byte[] buffer)
    {
        fixed (byte* pBuffer = buffer) // Pin the buffer
        {
            for (int i = 0; i < buffer.Length; i++)
            {
                pBuffer[i] = (byte)(i % 256); // Fill buffer
                with pattern
            }
        }
    }
}
```

Best Practice: Use the fixed statement to pin buffers before performing direct memory manipulation, ensuring that the garbage collector does not relocate the memory during the operation.

6. Error Handling in Unsafe Code

When using unsafe code, error handling becomes crucial to prevent crashes and ensure stability. Always validate pointers and consider using try-catch blocks for exception handling.

Code Snippet: Error Handling in Unsafe Code

```csharp
```

LOW-LEVEL PROGRAMMING WITH UNSAFE CODE

```csharp
unsafe public void SafePointerAccess(int* pValue)
{
    if (pValue == null)
    {
        Console.WriteLine("Pointer is null.");
        return;
    }

    try
    {
        Console.WriteLine($"Pointer Value: {*pValue}");
    }
    catch (Exception ex)
    {
        Console.WriteLine($"Error accessing pointer: 
        {ex.Message}");
    }
}
```

Best Practice: Always check pointers for null or invalid values before dereferencing them. Implement error handling strategies to manage exceptions that may arise during pointer operations.

7. Leveraging Inline Assembly for Performance Optimization

While C# does not natively support inline assembly, unsafe code combined with P/Invoke can enable the use of assembly routines for performance-critical operations.

Code Snippet: Calling an Assembly Routine via P/Invoke

```
csharp

[DllImport("MyAssembly.dll", CallingConvention = 
CallingConvention.Cdecl)]
public static extern void FastMultiply(int* a, int* b, int* 
result);
```

```
unsafe public void UseFastMultiply(int[] arrayA, int[] arrayB,
int[] resultArray)
{
    fixed (int* pA = arrayA, pB = arrayB, pResult = resultArray)
    {
        FastMultiply(pA, pB, pResult);
    }
}
```

Best Practice: If you are utilizing assembly routines for performance, document the interface and ensure that the assembly code is well-tested to avoid introducing errors into your application.

Unsafe code in C# provides the capability to perform low-level memory operations and optimizations that can greatly enhance application performance. By using pointers, fixed buffers, unmanaged memory, and techniques such as direct buffer manipulation, developers can create highly efficient applications suited for high-performance computing tasks.

However, with great power comes great responsibility. It is crucial to follow best practices such as proper error handling, memory management, and validating pointers to ensure stability and reliability in your applications. By carefully leveraging unsafe code, you can achieve substantial performance gains while maintaining the integrity and safety of your software.

Data Structures and Algorithms for High Performance

Choosing the Right Data Structures in .NET 6

In software development, selecting the appropriate data structure is a critical decision that can significantly impact the performance, maintainability, and scalability of an application. Data structures provide a means to organize, manage, and store data efficiently, and their choice can determine how effectively algorithms run in terms of time and space complexity. This chapter will explore how to choose the right data structures in .NET 6, considering performance implications and common use cases.

1. Understanding the Basics of Data Structures

Data structures can be broadly classified into two categories: **primitive** and **composite**.

- **Primitive Data Structures**: These are the basic types provided by .NET, such as integers, floats, characters, and booleans. They serve as the building blocks for more complex data structures.
- **Composite Data Structures**: These are built using primitive data structures and can be more complex, such as arrays, lists, dictionaries, trees, and graphs. Composite data structures can store multiple values and provide various methods for accessing and manipulating that data.

2. Common Data Structures in .NET 6

Here are some commonly used data structures in .NET 6, along with their characteristics and appropriate use cases:

2.1. Arrays

- **Characteristics**: Arrays are fixed-size collections of elements of the same type. They provide fast access (O(1) time complexity) to elements by index but have a fixed size once created.
- **Use Cases**: Use arrays when the size of the collection is known ahead of time and remains constant. They are ideal for storing data that needs quick indexed access, such as in mathematical computations or image processing.

2.2. Lists

- **Characteristics**: The List<T> class in .NET is a dynamic array that can grow or shrink in size. Lists allow for easy addition and removal of elements, with average access time being O(1) and insertion or deletion being O(n) in the worst case.
- **Use Cases**: Use lists when you need a resizable collection where the size can change dynamically, such as in scenarios where data is frequently added or removed.

2.3. Dictionaries

- **Characteristics**: The Dictionary<TKey, TValue> class provides a collection of key-value pairs. It uses a hash table for storage, offering average O(1) time complexity for lookups, insertions, and deletions.
- **Use Cases**: Use dictionaries when you need to quickly retrieve values based on a unique key, such as when implementing caching, indexing, or frequency counting.

2.4. Sets

- **Characteristics**: The HashSet<T> class represents a collection of unique elements, offering O(1) time complexity for add, remove, and contains operations.
- **Use Cases**: Use sets when you need to maintain a collection of distinct elements, such as in situations where you want to eliminate duplicates from a dataset.

2.5. Queues and Stacks

- **Characteristics**: The Queue<T> class represents a first-in, first-out (FIFO) collection, while the Stack<T> class represents a last-in, first-out (LIFO) collection. Both data structures provide O(1) time complexity for adding and removing elements.
- **Use Cases**: Use queues for scenarios requiring order preservation, such as task scheduling or handling asynchronous events. Use stacks for situations involving backtracking, such as undo mechanisms or expression evaluation.

2.6. Trees

- **Characteristics**: Trees, such as binary trees and binary search trees (BSTs), are hierarchical structures with nodes connected by edges. They provide O(log n) time complexity for insertion, deletion, and search operations (in balanced trees).
- **Use Cases**: Use trees when you need to store hierarchical data or implement algorithms that require quick searching, such as in databases, file systems, or UI components.

2.7. Graphs

- **Characteristics**: Graphs consist of nodes (vertices) and edges connecting them. They can be directed or undirected, weighted or unweighted. Graph operations can be more complex, often requiring O(V + E) time

for traversal algorithms like Depth-First Search (DFS) or Breadth-First Search (BFS).
- **Use Cases**: Use graphs to model relationships between entities, such as social networks, transportation systems, or web page linking structures.

3. Performance Considerations When Choosing Data Structures

When selecting a data structure, consider the following performance factors:

- **Time Complexity**: Analyze the expected time complexity of operations like insertion, deletion, and lookup. Choose a structure that provides optimal performance for the most frequently executed operations in your application.
- **Space Complexity**: Consider the memory overhead of each data structure, especially in applications dealing with large datasets. Structures like List<T> and Dictionary<TKey, TValue> may consume more memory than simple arrays.
- **Access Patterns**: Understand how data will be accessed and manipulated. For example, if you need frequent indexed access, arrays or lists are more appropriate. If you need to frequently search for items, dictionaries or sets are better choices.
- **Concurrency**: Consider whether your application will be multi-threaded. If so, you may need to choose thread-safe data structures like ConcurrentDictionary<TKey, TValue> to avoid race conditions.

4. Use Cases and Examples

To illustrate the application of these principles, let's explore some specific use cases:

4.1. Real-Time Data Processing

In applications like stock trading systems, where real-time performance is crucial, using a SortedDictionary<TKey, TValue> can provide quick lookups and maintain order based on stock prices.

Example: Storing and Accessing Stock Prices

```csharp
var stockPrices = new SortedDictionary<string, double>();
stockPrices["AAPL"] = 150.25;
stockPrices["GOOGL"] = 2800.50;
Console.WriteLine($"AAPL Price: {stockPrices["AAPL"]}");
```

4.2. Caching Results

In scenarios where data is frequently queried, a Dictionary<TKey, TValue> can serve as an efficient cache to store previously computed results for quick access.

Example: Caching Computed Results

```csharp
var cache = new Dictionary<int, double>();
if (!cache.TryGetValue(input, out double result))
{
    result = PerformComplexCalculation(input);
    cache[input] = result; // Store result in cache
}
```

4.3. Managing User Sessions

For web applications, managing user sessions can be efficiently handled using a ConcurrentDictionary<string, Session> to store session data in a thread-safe manner.

Example: Thread-Safe Session Management

```csharp
var userSessions = new ConcurrentDictionary<string, Session>();
userSessions["session1"] = new Session { UserId = 1, Expiration = DateTime.Now.AddMinutes(30) };
```

4.4. Implementing Undo Functionality

In applications like text editors, a Stack<string> can be used to manage undo actions, allowing users to revert to previous states.

Example: Managing Undo Operations

```csharp
var undoStack = new Stack<string>();
undoStack.Push("Initial State");
undoStack.Push("State After Edit");
// Undo the last action
string lastState = undoStack.Pop();
```

5. Choosing the Right Data Structure: A Summary

When choosing the right data structure in .NET 6, consider:

- The specific operations required (insertion, deletion, access, etc.).
- The expected size and variability of the dataset.
- The performance characteristics of each data structure in terms of time and space complexity.
- The concurrency requirements of your application.

Selecting the appropriate data structure is fundamental to building efficient, scalable applications in .NET 6. By understanding the characteristics and use cases of various data structures, developers can make informed decisions that lead to better performance and maintainability.

This chapter has provided a comprehensive overview of common data structures in .NET 6, their performance considerations, and practical examples of how to use them effectively. As you design and implement your applications, always align your choice of data structures with the specific needs and constraints of your project to maximize efficiency and achieve optimal performance.

Optimizing Algorithms for Scalability

Scalability is a crucial aspect of modern software development, particularly for applications that need to handle increasing amounts of data or user requests. As systems grow in size and complexity, the algorithms used must efficiently manage resources and respond quickly to changing demands. In this chapter, we will explore strategies for optimizing algorithms in .NET 6 to ensure scalability, including analyzing time and space complexity, utilizing efficient data structures, and implementing best practices for algorithm design.

1. Understanding Algorithm Complexity

Before diving into optimization techniques, it's important to understand the concepts of time and space complexity, which serve as the foundation for evaluating algorithm efficiency.

- **Time Complexity**: This measures how the runtime of an algorithm increases with the size of the input data. It is expressed using Big O notation (e.g., $O(1)$, $O(n)$, $O(\log n)$, $O(n^2)$), which provides an upper bound on the growth rate of an algorithm's execution time.
- **Space Complexity**: This measures how the memory consumption of an algorithm increases with the size of the input data. Like time complexity, it is also expressed using Big O notation.

By analyzing the time and space complexity of algorithms, developers can identify potential bottlenecks and areas for improvement.

2. Choosing the Right Algorithm

Selecting the appropriate algorithm for a given task is vital for optimizing performance and scalability. Different algorithms can yield vastly different performance characteristics depending on the input size and distribution.

Example: Searching Algorithms

- **Linear Search (O(n))**: This algorithm checks each element in a list one by one, making it inefficient for large datasets.
- **Binary Search (O(log n))**: This algorithm quickly narrows down the search space by repeatedly dividing the dataset in half, but it requires that the dataset be sorted.

Example Code: Binary Search in C#

```csharp
public int BinarySearch(int[] sortedArray, int target)
{
    int left = 0;
    int right = sortedArray.Length - 1;

    while (left <= right)
    {
        int mid = left + (right - left) / 2;

        if (sortedArray[mid] == target)
        {
            return mid; // Target found
        }
        else if (sortedArray[mid] < target)
        {
            left = mid + 1; // Search in the right half
        }
        else
        {
            right = mid - 1; // Search in the left half
        }
    }

    return -1; // Target not found
}
```

3. Optimizing Algorithm Efficiency

Once you have selected an algorithm, you can apply various optimization techniques to enhance its efficiency. Here are several strategies for optimizing algorithms for scalability:

3.1. Avoiding Redundant Computations

Recalculating values that have already been computed can lead to inefficiencies. Use caching or memoization to store results of expensive function calls.

Example: Fibonacci Calculation with Memoization

```csharp
public class Fibonacci
{
    private Dictionary<int, long> _memo = new Dictionary<int, long>();

    public long ComputeFibonacci(int n)
    {
        if (n <= 1) return n;
        if (_memo.ContainsKey(n)) return _memo[n];

        long result = ComputeFibonacci(n - 1) + ComputeFibonacci(n - 2);
        _memo[n] = result; // Cache the result
        return result;
    }
}
```

3.2. Reducing Time Complexity

Sometimes, the time complexity of an algorithm can be improved by altering its approach. Techniques such as divide-and-conquer or dynamic programming can often reduce time complexity significantly.

Example: Merge Sort (O(n log n))

```csharp
public void MergeSort(int[] array, int left, int right)
{
```

```csharp
    if (left < right)
    {
        int mid = left + (right - left) / 2;
        MergeSort(array, left, mid);
        MergeSort(array, mid + 1, right);
        Merge(array, left, mid, right);
    }
}

private void Merge(int[] array, int left, int mid, int right)
{
    // Implementation of the merge operation...
}
```

3.3. Leveraging Parallelism and Concurrency

For computationally intensive algorithms, leveraging parallel processing can lead to significant performance improvements. The Task Parallel Library (TPL) in .NET allows for easy parallelization of tasks.

Example: Parallel Processing with TPL

csharp

```
public void ProcessDataInParallel(int[] data)
{
    Parallel.For(0, data.Length, i =>
    {
        // Process each element concurrently
        data[i] = PerformComplexOperation(data[i]);
    });
}
```

4. Using Efficient Data Structures

The choice of data structures directly impacts the performance of algorithms. Select data structures that complement your algorithm's access patterns.

Example: HashSet for Fast Lookups If you frequently need to check for the existence of elements, using a HashSet<T> instead of a list can drastically reduce the time complexity from O(n) to O(1).

Example Code: Using HashSet for Membership Testing

```csharp
public void CheckMembership(int[] numbers, int target)
{
    var numberSet = new HashSet<int>(numbers);
    bool exists = numberSet.Contains(target);
    Console.WriteLine($"Number {target} exists: {exists}");
}
```

5. Profiling and Benchmarking

To ensure that your optimizations are effective, it's crucial to profile and benchmark your algorithms. Use profiling tools to analyze execution time, memory usage, and identify hotspots.

Best Practices for Profiling:

- **Use Profiling Tools:** Leverage tools like Visual Studio Profiler or JetBrains dotTrace to measure the performance of your algorithms.
- **Write Benchmarks:** Implement benchmarking tests using libraries like BenchmarkDotNet to compare the performance of different algorithms and data structures.
- **Focus on Hot Paths:** Identify the most frequently executed sections of code (hot paths) and optimize those first for maximum impact on overall performance.

6. Real-World Examples of Algorithm Optimization

Example 1: Database Query Optimization In a web application, optimizing database queries can significantly improve performance. Instead of performing multiple round-trips to the database, consider batching queries or using stored procedures. Indexing the database columns used in queries can also reduce lookup times.

Example 2: Image Processing Pipeline In an image processing application, using parallel processing to apply filters to different regions of an image can enhance performance. Instead of processing the image sequentially, divide it into sections and process each section in parallel.

Optimizing algorithms for scalability is essential in today's data-driven applications. By understanding algorithm complexity, selecting the right algorithms and data structures, and applying optimization techniques, developers can build applications that efficiently handle increasing loads and larger datasets.

Profiling and benchmarking are key components of the optimization process, ensuring that the improvements made lead to tangible performance gains. As you develop applications in .NET 6, keep scalability in mind and implement best practices that allow your algorithms to adapt to growing demands effectively. By mastering these concepts, you will be well-equipped to create robust, high-performance applications that stand the test of time.

Case Studies in Algorithm Optimization

Optimizing algorithms for performance and scalability is crucial in various industries and applications. This section explores real-world case studies where algorithm optimization has been implemented successfully, detailing the challenges faced, the strategies employed, and the results achieved. These examples will highlight the importance of algorithm selection, data structures, and optimization techniques in practical scenarios.

1. E-Commerce: Optimizing Search Functionality

Challenge: In an e-commerce platform, the search functionality was slow and unable to handle a high volume of queries during peak traffic times.

Customers experienced delays in finding products, leading to frustration and potentially lost sales.

Optimization Strategy: To address this issue, the team decided to optimize the search algorithm and data structure. They replaced a linear search algorithm with a more efficient inverted index approach, combined with a trie structure for handling autocomplete suggestions.

- **Inverted Index:** An inverted index is a data structure that maps words or terms to their locations in the dataset (e.g., product names and descriptions). This structure allows for fast lookups by eliminating the need to scan through every product.
- **Trie for Autocomplete:** A trie is a tree-like structure used to store a dynamic set of strings. By implementing a trie, the team could efficiently retrieve product suggestions based on user input.

Results:

- **Performance Improvement:** Search queries that previously took several seconds were reduced to milliseconds.
- **Enhanced User Experience:** The platform experienced increased user satisfaction, leading to a higher conversion rate during peak shopping times.

2. Financial Services: Real-Time Risk Assessment

Challenge: A financial services firm needed to calculate real-time risk metrics for its trading operations. The existing algorithm was too slow to process large volumes of transaction data, resulting in delayed insights that could lead to financial losses.

Optimization Strategy: The team analyzed the existing algorithm and identified several bottlenecks:

- They switched from a naïve implementation to a more efficient data structure (e.g., a balanced binary search tree) to store transaction

records, allowing for faster insertion and querying of data.
- They implemented parallel processing using the Task Parallel Library (TPL) to perform calculations across multiple CPU cores, leveraging the power of multicore processors.

Results:

- **Time Complexity Reduction:** The time complexity for risk calculations improved from $O(n^2)$ to $O(n \log n)$ due to the use of a balanced binary search tree.
- **Real-Time Insights:** The firm could now perform risk assessments in real time, enabling quicker decision-making and a reduction in financial exposure.

3. Healthcare: Optimizing Patient Data Retrieval

Challenge: In a healthcare application, retrieving patient data from a large database was slow, leading to delays in critical care situations. The application struggled to manage large datasets effectively.

Optimization Strategy: The development team implemented several optimizations:

- They created an index on frequently queried fields (e.g., patient ID, last name) to speed up searches.
- They used caching to store recently accessed patient records in memory, reducing database load and improving retrieval times.

Results:

- **Query Performance Improvement:** Database queries that took several seconds were reduced to milliseconds.
- **Improved Patient Care:** Medical staff could access patient data faster, which was critical for timely interventions and improved patient outcomes.

4. Telecommunications: Optimizing Network Traffic Analysis

Challenge: A telecommunications company needed to analyze network traffic data in real time to detect anomalies and optimize performance. The existing algorithm was too slow to keep up with the volume of data generated by thousands of users.

Optimization Strategy: To improve performance, the team implemented the following strategies:

- They transitioned from a basic linear scan of network packets to a more sophisticated algorithm utilizing a hash table for quick lookups and frequency counting of packet types.
- They used multi-threading to distribute the analysis workload across multiple cores, allowing for concurrent processing of traffic data.

Results:

- **Increased Throughput:** The system was able to analyze and respond to network traffic in real time, significantly increasing throughput.
- **Reduced Latency:** Anomaly detection time was reduced from minutes to seconds, enabling proactive measures to maintain service quality.

5. Gaming: Optimizing Pathfinding Algorithms

Challenge: In a game development project, the pathfinding algorithm for non-player characters (NPCs) was consuming too much CPU time, especially in complex environments with many obstacles. This caused noticeable lag and degraded the overall gaming experience.

Optimization Strategy: The development team focused on optimizing the A* pathfinding algorithm:

- They improved the heuristic used in the A* algorithm to better guide the search towards the target, reducing the number of nodes processed.
- They implemented a hierarchical pathfinding system where the game world was divided into regions, allowing for quicker high-level decisions

about path direction before drilling down into local details.

Results:

- **Performance Gains:** CPU usage for pathfinding was reduced by up to 50%, significantly lowering lag during gameplay.
- **Enhanced Experience:** Players enjoyed a smoother experience with more responsive NPC behavior, leading to higher engagement and positive feedback.

These case studies demonstrate the importance of algorithm optimization across various domains, including e-commerce, finance, healthcare, telecommunications, and gaming. By choosing the right algorithms and data structures, applying performance optimization techniques, and leveraging technologies like parallel processing, organizations can achieve significant performance improvements.

Optimizing algorithms not only enhances efficiency and scalability but also improves user experience and operational effectiveness. As you implement optimizations in your own applications, consider these strategies and learn from these real-world examples to drive performance and scalability in your projects. By continuously evaluating and refining your algorithms, you can ensure that your applications remain responsive and capable of handling growing data and user demands.

Comparing Time Complexity and Memory Usage

When developing algorithms, it is essential to evaluate both time complexity and memory usage, as these factors significantly influence performance and scalability. Time complexity measures the amount of computational time an algorithm takes to complete as a function of the size of its input, while memory usage assesses the amount of memory consumed during the algorithm's execution. Understanding the trade-offs between these two metrics is crucial for optimizing algorithms in real-world applications.

1. Understanding Time Complexity

Time complexity provides a theoretical estimate of how the execution time of an algorithm increases with the size of the input. It is typically expressed using Big O notation, which describes the upper bound of the runtime growth rate. The most common time complexities include:

- **O(1) - Constant Time:** The execution time remains the same regardless of the input size.
- **O(log n) - Logarithmic Time:** The execution time grows logarithmically as the input size increases. Common in algorithms that reduce the problem size by half with each step, such as binary search.
- **O(n) - Linear Time:** The execution time increases linearly with the input size.
- **O(n log n) - Linearithmic Time:** Common in efficient sorting algorithms like mergesort and heapsort.
- **O(n^2) - Quadratic Time:** The execution time grows proportionally to the square of the input size. Common in algorithms with nested loops, such as bubble sort.
- **O(2^n) - Exponential Time:** The execution time doubles with each addition to the input size. Common in recursive algorithms that solve problems by solving multiple subproblems, such as the naïve solution to the Fibonacci sequence.

2. Understanding Memory Usage

Memory usage refers to the amount of memory an algorithm requires during its execution. Similar to time complexity, memory usage can also be analyzed using Big O notation. Key categories of memory complexity include:

- **O(1) - Constant Space:** The algorithm requires a fixed amount of memory, regardless of the input size.
- **O(n) - Linear Space:** The memory requirement grows linearly with the input size.
- **O(n^2) - Quadratic Space:** The memory requirement grows proportionally to the square of the input size, often seen in algorithms that create a 2D data structure (e.g., adjacency matrix for graphs).

3. Trade-offs Between Time and Space Complexity

When designing algorithms, there is often a trade-off between time complexity and space complexity. Some common scenarios include:

- **Optimizing for Speed vs. Memory:** Algorithms that use more memory (like caching or precomputing results) can significantly reduce runtime, as they avoid recalculating values.
- **Iterative vs. Recursive Solutions:** Recursive algorithms may be more straightforward to implement but can lead to higher memory usage due to the call stack. Iterative solutions may consume less memory at the cost of increased complexity.
- **Data Structure Selection:** The choice of data structures can impact both time and space complexity. For example, using a hash table allows for O(1) average-time complexity for lookups, but it consumes more memory than a simple array.

Example: Consider a function to compute Fibonacci numbers.

- **Naïve Recursive Solution:** This approach has exponential time complexity O(2^n) and uses O(n) space due to recursive call stacks.
- **Iterative Solution:** This approach has linear time complexity O(n) and uses constant space O(1) since it only requires a few variables.

4. Practical Comparison of Time and Space Complexity

When optimizing algorithms, it's important to evaluate both time and

space complexity side by side. Let's explore some common algorithms and their complexities to illustrate this comparison:
Example 1: Linear Search vs. Binary Search

- **Linear Search:**
- Time Complexity: O(n)
- Space Complexity: O(1)
- **Binary Search:**
- Time Complexity: O(log n)
- Space Complexity: O(1) (iterative) or O(log n) (recursive due to call stack)

Conclusion: Binary search is more efficient than linear search in terms of time complexity, especially for large datasets, but both have similar space complexity in their iterative forms.
Example 2: Mergesort vs. Quicksort

- **Mergesort:**
- Time Complexity: O(n log n)
- Space Complexity: O(n) (due to temporary arrays used during merging)
- **Quicksort:**
- Time Complexity: O(n log n) on average but O(n^2) in the worst case.
- Space Complexity: O(log n) for the recursive call stack.

While both algorithms have similar time complexities, mergesort requires more space due to its temporary arrays, while quicksort can be more memory-efficient with its in-place sorting.
5. Evaluating Algorithm Performance
When choosing algorithms for a specific task, consider the following:

- **Nature of the Input:** Understand the size and characteristics of the input data. Algorithms that perform well on average might not do so in the worst-case scenario.

- **Resource Constraints:** Evaluate the available memory and processing power. If memory is limited, prefer algorithms with lower space complexity.
- **Use Cases:** Determine the specific requirements of your application. For example, if you require fast lookups, consider using hash tables, even if they consume more memory.

6. Tools for Measuring Performance

To effectively compare time and space complexity in real-world applications, utilize profiling tools and benchmarks:

- **Profiling Tools:** Use tools like Visual Studio Profiler, JetBrains dotTrace, or PerfView to analyze your application's performance, identify bottlenecks, and understand memory usage patterns.
- **Benchmark Libraries:** Implement benchmark tests using libraries like BenchmarkDotNet to measure and compare the execution time of different algorithms.

Choosing the right algorithm requires a thorough understanding of both time complexity and memory usage. By comparing these factors and considering trade-offs, developers can select algorithms that optimize performance while meeting the resource constraints of their applications.

Evaluating algorithms in the context of their specific use cases, input characteristics, and resource availability ensures that your applications can scale effectively and efficiently. With the right tools and strategies, you can develop high-performance applications in .NET 6 that respond quickly to user demands and handle large datasets seamlessly.

High-Performance Networking in .NET 6

Leveraging Kestrel for High-Performance HTTP Servers in .NET 6

Kestrel is the cross-platform web server included with ASP.NET Core, designed specifically for high-performance scenarios. It is built on the foundation of the libuv library and optimized for handling asynchronous I/O operations, making it an ideal choice for applications that require low latency and high throughput. In this chapter, we will explore how to leverage Kestrel for building high-performance HTTP servers in .NET 6, covering its architecture, configuration, performance optimization techniques, and best practices.

1. Understanding Kestrel's Architecture

Kestrel's architecture is designed for speed and efficiency, making it suitable for modern web applications and APIs. The key components of Kestrel's architecture include:

- **Asynchronous I/O:** Kestrel uses asynchronous I/O operations, allowing it to handle multiple connections simultaneously without blocking threads. This design minimizes thread contention and improves resource utilization.
- **Connection Handling:** Kestrel supports multiple concurrent connections using a single-threaded model that efficiently handles requests and responses. It uses a connection pool to manage resources and reduce

the overhead of creating new threads for each request.
- **HTTP/2 and WebSockets Support:** Kestrel natively supports HTTP/2 and WebSockets, enabling faster communication and real-time interactions in web applications. HTTP/2 multiplexing allows multiple requests to be sent over a single connection, reducing latency and improving throughput.
- **Middleware Pipeline:** Kestrel operates within the ASP.NET Core middleware pipeline, allowing developers to customize request handling by adding middleware components. This flexibility enables the implementation of cross-cutting concerns such as authentication, logging, and error handling.

2. Setting Up Kestrel in .NET 6

To get started with Kestrel, you need to create an ASP.NET Core application. The following steps outline how to set up Kestrel in a new .NET 6 project:

1. **Create a New ASP.NET Core Project:** Use the .NET CLI or Visual Studio to create a new ASP.NET Core Web API project.

```bash
dotnet new webapi -n MyKestrelApp
```

1. **Configure Kestrel in Program.cs:** The Program.cs file is where you can configure Kestrel settings.

```csharp
using Microsoft.AspNetCore.Builder;
using Microsoft.Extensions.DependencyInjection;
```

```
var builder = WebApplication.CreateBuilder(args);

// Add services to the container
builder.Services.AddControllers();

var app = builder.Build();

// Configure the HTTP request pipeline
app.UseHttpsRedirection();
app.UseAuthorization();
app.MapControllers();

app.Run();
```

1. **Run the Application:** You can run the application using the .NET CLI:

bash

dotnet run

1. **Access the Kestrel Server:** By default, Kestrel will listen on http://localhost:5000 and https://localhost:5001. You can access your API endpoints through these URLs.

3. Configuring Kestrel for Performance

Kestrel offers several configuration options that allow you to optimize performance for your specific use case. Some of the important settings include:

- **Listening Ports:** You can configure Kestrel to listen on multiple ports or specify the protocols (HTTP/1.1, HTTP/2).

- **Limits and Timeouts:** Configure limits for the maximum request body size, connection timeouts, and keep-alive settings to control resource usage and improve responsiveness.

Example: Configuring Kestrel Settings in appsettings.json:

```json
{
  "Kestrel": {
    "EndPoints": {
      "Http": {
        "Url": "http://localhost:5000"
      },
      "Https": {
        "Url": "https://localhost:5001"
      }
    },
    "Limits": {
      "MaxRequestBodySize": 10485760, // 10 MB
      "RequestHeadersTimeout": "00:00:30" // 30 seconds
    }
  }
}
```

Example: Accessing Configuration in Program.cs:

```csharp
var builder = WebApplication.CreateBuilder(args);

// Configure Kestrel using appsettings.json
builder.WebHost.UseKestrel(options =>
{
    options.Limits.MaxRequestBodySize = 10485760; // 10 MB
    options.Limits.RequestHeadersTimeout =
    TimeSpan.FromSeconds(30);
});
```

4. Performance Optimization Techniques

To achieve maximum performance with Kestrel, consider the following optimization techniques:

4.1. Use Asynchronous Programming

Utilizing asynchronous programming patterns allows Kestrel to handle more requests concurrently, improving overall throughput. Use async and await keywords in your controller actions and middleware.

Example: Asynchronous Controller Action

```csharp
[HttpGet]
public async Task<IActionResult> GetDataAsync()
{
    var data = await FetchDataFromDatabaseAsync();
    return Ok(data);
}
```

4.2. Enable HTTP/2 Support

HTTP/2 offers improved performance over HTTP/1.1 by enabling multiplexing and reducing latency. Ensure that your Kestrel server is configured to support HTTP/2.

Example: Enabling HTTP/2

```csharp
builder.WebHost.UseKestrel(options =>
{
    options.ConfigureEndpointDefaults(lo =>
    {
        lo.Protocols = HttpProtocols.Http2; // Enable HTTP/2
    });
});
```

4.3. Optimize Middleware Usage

Minimize the number of middleware components and avoid unnecessary processing in the request pipeline. Only include middleware that is essential for your application.

Example: Simplifying Middleware Pipeline

```csharp
app.UseHttpsRedirection(); // Essential for security
app.UseAuthorization(); // Required for secure routes
```

4.4. Leverage Connection Pooling

Kestrel automatically uses connection pooling to manage client connections efficiently. However, configuring your application to maintain a healthy pool of connections can further enhance performance.

5. Monitoring and Troubleshooting Kestrel Performance

Monitoring the performance of your Kestrel server is vital to identify bottlenecks and optimize resource usage. Use tools and techniques like:

- **Logging:** Implement logging to capture request and response times, error messages, and other relevant metrics.
- **Application Insights:** Integrate Application Insights for detailed telemetry, monitoring, and performance analysis of your application.
- **Performance Profiling:** Use profiling tools to analyze CPU and memory usage, helping you identify and optimize inefficient code paths.

6. Real-World Example: Building a High-Performance API

Consider a scenario where you need to build a high-performance API for a real-time data analytics platform. This platform must handle thousands of concurrent users, process large datasets, and provide rapid response times.

Solution Overview:

- **Use Kestrel as the Web Server:** Kestrel's asynchronous capabilities and support for HTTP/2 make it ideal for high-traffic scenarios.
- **Optimize Data Access:** Implement caching strategies to reduce database load and speed up data retrieval.

- **Leverage Asynchronous Programming:** Ensure all API endpoints use asynchronous methods to improve throughput and resource utilization.
- **Monitoring:** Implement logging and monitoring to continuously assess performance and identify potential issues.

Example: High-Performance Data Retrieval API

```csharp
[ApiController]
[Route("api/[controller]")]
public class DataController : ControllerBase
{
    private readonly IDataService _dataService;

    public DataController(IDataService dataService)
    {
        _dataService = dataService;
    }

    [HttpGet("{id}")]
    public async Task<IActionResult> GetDataAsync(int id)
    {
        var data = await _dataService.GetDataAsync(id);
        if (data == null) return NotFound();
        return Ok(data);
    }
}
```

Kestrel is a powerful web server that enables developers to build high-performance HTTP servers in .NET 6. By understanding its architecture, configuration options, and optimization techniques, you can harness its full potential to create responsive, scalable applications.

Utilizing Kestrel effectively requires an understanding of how to optimize algorithms and use asynchronous programming, while also considering memory usage and resource management. By leveraging these strategies, you can build robust applications that handle significant traffic while maintaining excellent performance.

As you develop applications with Kestrel, continuously monitor performance, adapt to changing requirements, and refine your strategies to ensure optimal operation in real-world environments.

Building Asynchronous and Scalable Sockets in .NET 6

Asynchronous programming is a core aspect of developing high-performance applications, especially when it comes to network communication. Sockets are the foundation of network communication in .NET, and using them asynchronously allows for non-blocking operations that can handle many connections simultaneously. In this section, we will explore how to build asynchronous and scalable socket applications in .NET 6, discussing the relevant concepts, implementation techniques, and best practices.

1. Understanding Sockets in .NET

Sockets provide a way to communicate over a network using the TCP/IP protocol. They allow for both client-server and peer-to-peer communication. The System.Net.Sockets namespace in .NET provides classes for both TCP and UDP socket programming.

- **TCP Sockets:** These sockets establish a reliable, connection-oriented communication channel. They guarantee that data packets are delivered in the correct order and without duplication.
- **UDP Sockets:** These sockets are connectionless and do not guarantee reliable delivery, making them suitable for applications where speed is crucial, such as video streaming or online gaming.

2. Setting Up Asynchronous Sockets

In .NET 6, you can create asynchronous sockets using the SocketAsyncEventArgs class or by leveraging higher-level abstractions like the TcpClient and TcpListener classes. Here, we will focus on using TcpListener for server-side socket programming.

Example: Creating an Asynchronous TCP Server

```csharp
using System;
using System.Net;
using System.Net.Sockets;
using System.Text;
using System.Threading.Tasks;

public class AsyncTcpServer
{
    private readonly TcpListener _listener;

    public AsyncTcpServer(IPAddress ipAddress, int port)
    {
        _listener = new TcpListener(ipAddress, port);
    }

    public async Task StartAsync()
    {
        _listener.Start();
        Console.WriteLine("Server started. Waiting for connections...");

        while (true)
        {
            var client = await _listener.AcceptTcpClientAsync();
            _ = HandleClientAsync(client); // Handle client connection asynchronously
        }
    }

    private async Task HandleClientAsync(TcpClient client)
```

```csharp
{
    Console.WriteLine("Client connected.");
    using (var stream = client.GetStream())
    {
        var buffer = new byte[1024];
        int bytesRead;

        while ((bytesRead = await stream.ReadAsync(buffer,
        0, buffer.Length)) != 0)
        {
            string message = Encoding.UTF8.GetString(buffer,
            0, bytesRead);
            Console.WriteLine($"Received: {message}");

            // Echo the message back to the client
            await stream.WriteAsync(buffer, 0, bytesRead);
        }
    }

    Console.WriteLine("Client disconnected.");
    client.Close();
}
```

Explanation:

- The AsyncTcpServer class sets up a TCP listener on a specified IP address and port.
- The StartAsync method listens for incoming connections and handles each client connection asynchronously using the HandleClientAsync method.
- Data is read from the client stream and echoed back, demonstrating basic communication.

3. Implementing Asynchronous Client Sockets

On the client side, you can use TcpClient to connect to the server asynchronously. This allows for non-blocking operations, enabling the client application to perform other tasks while waiting for responses.

Example: Creating an Asynchronous TCP Client

```csharp
using System;
using System.Net.Sockets;
using System.Text;
using System.Threading.Tasks;

public class AsyncTcpClient
{
    private readonly TcpClient _client;

    public AsyncTcpClient(string serverIp, int port)
    {
        _client = new TcpClient(serverIp, port);
    }

    public async Task SendMessageAsync(string message)
    {
        byte[] data = Encoding.UTF8.GetBytes(message);
        var stream = _client.GetStream();

        await stream.WriteAsync(data, 0, data.Length);
        Console.WriteLine($"Sent: {message}");

        // Read response
        var buffer = new byte[1024];
        int bytesRead = await stream.ReadAsync(buffer, 0, buffer.Length);
        string response = Encoding.UTF8.GetString(buffer, 0, bytesRead);
        Console.WriteLine($"Received: {response}");
    }

    public void Close()
    {
        _client.Close();
    }
```

}

Explanation:

- The AsyncTcpClient class connects to the server and sends messages asynchronously.
- The SendMessageAsync method writes data to the server and reads the response, demonstrating a complete request-response cycle.

4. Scaling with Asynchronous Sockets

To build scalable applications using asynchronous sockets, consider the following strategies:

4.1. Connection Pooling

Implement a connection pool for managing multiple connections efficiently. This allows your application to reuse existing connections, reducing the overhead of creating new ones.

4.2. Task-Based Asynchronous Pattern (TAP)

Leverage the Task-based Asynchronous Pattern in your socket programming. Using async and await makes it easier to write non-blocking code while keeping it readable.

4.3. Load Balancing

For high-traffic applications, consider implementing a load balancer that distributes incoming connections across multiple server instances. This can improve overall throughput and responsiveness.

4.4. Thread Safety

Ensure that your socket operations are thread-safe. Use appropriate locking mechanisms when accessing shared resources to avoid race conditions and ensure data integrity.

5. Handling Errors and Exceptions

As with any network programming, error handling is crucial. Handle potential exceptions during socket operations to ensure that your application remains robust and user-friendly.

Example: Error Handling in Socket Communication

csharp

```
try
{
    var server = new AsyncTcpServer(IPAddress.Any, 8080);
    await server.StartAsync();
}
catch (SocketException ex)
{
    Console.WriteLine($"SocketException: {ex.Message}");
}
catch (Exception ex)
{
    Console.WriteLine($"Unexpected exception: {ex.Message}");
}
```

Best Practices for Error Handling:

- Log exceptions to help diagnose issues during development and production.
- Implement retry logic for transient errors, especially in network communications.
- Gracefully handle disconnections and provide feedback to users where applicable.

6. Performance Considerations

When building high-performance socket applications, consider the following performance metrics:

- **Latency:** Measure the time taken for a message to travel from client to server and back. Aim for low latency to enhance user experience.
- **Throughput:** Assess how many requests can be processed per second. Optimize algorithms and minimize bottlenecks to maximize throughput.

- **Resource Utilization:** Monitor CPU and memory usage to identify inefficiencies in your socket implementations.

Building asynchronous and scalable sockets in .NET 6 is essential for creating high-performance networked applications. By leveraging the capabilities of the System.Net.Sockets namespace, developers can create robust client-server architectures that efficiently handle multiple connections and provide responsive interactions.

Through effective configuration, error handling, and performance optimization techniques, you can build socket applications that not only meet current demands but also scale effectively as user traffic increases. As you implement these strategies, you will be well-equipped to develop high-performance networking solutions that enhance the capabilities of your .NET applications.

Performance Enhancements in .NET 6 Networking APIs

.NET 6 introduces several performance enhancements to its networking APIs, making it easier for developers to build high-performance applications. These enhancements include optimizations in existing classes, improvements to asynchronous programming patterns, and new features that facilitate efficient network communication. In this section, we will explore key performance improvements in the .NET 6 networking APIs, how they can be leveraged in your applications, and best practices for achieving optimal performance.

1. Enhanced Socket APIs

The System.Net.Sockets namespace has been optimized to improve the performance of socket programming. Key enhancements include:

- **SocketAsyncEventArgs Improvements:** The SocketAsyncEventArgs class has been optimized for better performance when handling asynchronous socket operations. The enhancements allow for reduced memory allocations and improved handling of multiple concurrent connections.
- **Improved Connection Handling:** Kestrel and the underlying socket implementations in .NET 6 are designed to handle more connections with lower latency. This is particularly beneficial for applications that require high concurrency, such as web servers and real-time data applications.

Example: Using SocketAsyncEventArgs for Improved Performance

```csharp
public async Task HandleConnectionAsync(Socket socket)
{
    var args = new SocketAsyncEventArgs();
    args.SetBuffer(new byte[1024], 0, 1024);
    args.Completed += (sender, e) => ProcessReceive(e);

    if (!socket.ReceiveAsync(args))
    {
        ProcessReceive(args); // Process immediately if
        completed synchronously
    }
}

private void ProcessReceive(SocketAsyncEventArgs e)
{
    if (e.SocketError == SocketError.Success)
    {
        // Process the received data
        // Start another async receive operation if necessary
        HandleConnectionAsync(e.ConnectSocket);
    }
}
```

2. HTTP/2 Support and Performance

.NET 6 enhances support for HTTP/2 in Kestrel, providing several performance benefits over HTTP/1.1:

- **Multiplexing:** HTTP/2 allows multiple streams to be sent over a single TCP connection, reducing latency by enabling concurrent requests and responses. This capability can significantly improve performance for applications with multiple simultaneous requests.
- **Header Compression:** HTTP/2 compresses headers, reducing the amount of data sent over the network and improving response times, especially for high-latency connections.

Example: Enabling HTTP/2 in Kestrel

```csharp
builder.WebHost.UseKestrel(options =>
{
    options.ConfigureEndpointDefaults(lo =>
    {
        lo.Protocols = HttpProtocols.Http2; // Enable HTTP/2
    });
});
```

3. Improved DNS Resolution

.NET 6 introduces enhancements to DNS resolution that can lead to faster and more reliable hostname lookups:

- **Synchronous and Asynchronous Methods:** The Dns class now provides both synchronous and asynchronous methods for resolving hostnames. Using asynchronous methods can help avoid blocking the calling thread and improve responsiveness in applications.
- **Caching Mechanism:** A built-in caching mechanism for DNS lookups reduces the overhead of repeated lookups for the same hostname, enhancing performance in applications that make frequent network

requests.

Example: Using Asynchronous DNS Resolution

csharp

```
public async Task<string> ResolveHostAsync(string hostName)
{
    var addresses = await Dns.GetHostAddressesAsync(hostName);
    return addresses.FirstOrDefault()?.ToString();
}
```

4. Connection Resiliency

.NET 6 provides enhancements to ensure that applications can recover gracefully from transient network failures:

- **Improved Handling of Connection Failures:** The networking APIs now include built-in support for automatic retries in certain scenarios, such as failed HTTP requests, which can significantly improve reliability without requiring additional code.
- **Cancellation Support:** The introduction of CancellationToken support across various networking APIs allows developers to cancel ongoing network operations, enhancing responsiveness and user experience.

Example: Using CancellationToken with HTTP Client

csharp

```
public async Task<string> FetchDataAsync(string url, CancellationToken cancellationToken)
{
    using var httpClient = new HttpClient();
    var response = await httpClient.GetAsync(url, cancellationToken);
    response.EnsureSuccessStatusCode();
```

```
        return await response.Content.ReadAsStringAsync();
}
```

5. Enhanced TLS Performance

.NET 6 introduces improvements to TLS (Transport Layer Security), which enhance the security and performance of network communications:

- **Reduced Handshake Times:** TLS handshakes have been optimized, resulting in faster connection setups, especially for secure HTTP connections.
- **Support for Modern Cryptography:** .NET 6 updates its cryptographic libraries to support the latest standards, ensuring that applications can take advantage of improved security protocols and algorithms without sacrificing performance.

Example: Configuring HTTPS with Kestrel

```csharp
builder.WebHost.UseKestrel(options =>
{
    options.Listen(IPAddress.Any, 5001, listenOptions =>
    {
        listenOptions.UseHttps("cert.pfx", "password");
    });
});
```

6. Best Practices for Leveraging Performance Enhancements

To maximize the performance benefits offered by the networking APIs in .NET 6, consider the following best practices:

- **Use Asynchronous Programming:** Take advantage of asynchronous methods throughout your application to prevent blocking operations and improve responsiveness.
- **Optimize Connection Usage:** Reuse existing connections where possi-

ble, and leverage connection pooling to reduce the overhead associated with establishing new connections.
- **Leverage HTTP/2 Features:** Enable HTTP/2 in your applications to take advantage of multiplexing, header compression, and other performance optimizations.
- **Implement Error Handling:** Ensure robust error handling and implement retry logic for transient network errors to improve application reliability.
- **Monitor Performance:** Use performance monitoring tools to gather metrics on network latency, throughput, and resource utilization, enabling you to identify bottlenecks and optimize performance accordingly.

The enhancements to networking APIs in .NET 6 provide developers with powerful tools for building high-performance applications. By leveraging the features of Kestrel, utilizing asynchronous programming patterns, and optimizing DNS resolution, TLS performance, and connection resiliency, you can create responsive and scalable networked applications.

Understanding and implementing these performance enhancements will enable you to build robust applications that can handle the demands of modern networking, ensuring that they remain efficient, reliable, and user-friendly. As you design and implement your networking solutions, keep these strategies in mind to achieve optimal performance and scalability in your .NET 6 applications.

Real-World Examples: High-Performance Network Applications

In today's digital landscape, high-performance network applications are critical for delivering seamless user experiences, handling large volumes of data, and supporting real-time interactions. This section presents several real-world examples of high-performance network applications built using .NET 6, showcasing how the framework's features and enhancements facilitate the development of scalable, efficient solutions.

1. Real-Time Chat Application

Use Case: A real-time chat application enables users to communicate instantly, share files, and send notifications. The application must handle multiple concurrent connections efficiently and provide low-latency messaging.

Implementation:

- **WebSockets:** The application uses WebSockets for bi-directional communication, allowing the server to push updates to clients without requiring them to constantly poll the server.
- **Kestrel Server:** Built on Kestrel, the server efficiently manages thousands of concurrent connections and uses asynchronous programming to handle incoming messages.

Example Code: WebSocket Server

```csharp
csharp

public class ChatHub : Hub
{
    public async Task SendMessage(string user, string message)
    {
        await Clients.All.SendAsync("ReceiveMessage", user, message);
    }
}

// In Startup.cs or Program.cs
app.UseEndpoints(endpoints =>
{
    endpoints.MapHub<ChatHub>("/chatHub");
```

});

Performance Highlights:

- **Low Latency:** WebSockets reduce latency compared to traditional HTTP requests, providing a more responsive user experience.
- **Scalability:** The application can handle a significant number of users, thanks to the asynchronous nature of Kestrel and WebSocket connections.

2. Streaming Video Platform

Use Case: A streaming video platform requires high-performance delivery of video content to users, with features like adaptive streaming based on network conditions.

Implementation:

- **HTTP/2 Support:** The application leverages HTTP/2 to serve video segments, allowing multiple streams to be sent over a single connection.
- **Adaptive Bitrate Streaming:** The server monitors user bandwidth and adjusts the quality of the video stream dynamically, enhancing user experience.

Example Code: Serving Video Segments

```csharp
app.MapGet("/video/{id}", async (HttpContext context, string id) =>
{
    var filePath = GetVideoFilePath(id); // Logic to retrieve video file path
    context.Response.ContentType = "video/mp4";
    await context.Response.SendFileAsync(filePath);
});
```

Performance Highlights:

- **Improved Throughput:** HTTP/2's multiplexing capabilities reduce latency and improve the speed at which video segments are delivered.
- **User Experience:** Adaptive streaming ensures smooth playback across varying network conditions, reducing buffering times.

3. Online Gaming Server

Use Case: An online multiplayer game requires a server capable of handling real-time communication between players, maintaining game state, and processing player actions.

Implementation:

- **UDP Sockets:** The game server uses UDP for quick communication of player actions and game events, prioritizing speed over reliability.
- **Asynchronous Processing:** The server processes player inputs asynchronously, ensuring that game state updates and event handling do not block communication.

Example Code: UDP Server

```csharp
public class GameServer
{
    private readonly UdpClient _udpClient;

    public GameServer(int port)
    {
        _udpClient = new UdpClient(port);
    }

    public async Task StartAsync()
    {
        while (true)
```

```csharp
        {
            var result = await _udpClient.ReceiveAsync();
            ProcessGameEvent(result.Buffer);
        }
    }

    private void ProcessGameEvent(byte[] data)
    {
        // Logic to update game state based on received data
    }
}
```

Performance Highlights:

- **Low Latency:** Using UDP allows for rapid communication, which is essential in fast-paced gaming environments.
- **High Concurrency:** The server can handle multiple players and events concurrently, maintaining a smooth gaming experience.

4. Financial Trading Application

Use Case: A financial trading application requires real-time updates on market data, quick execution of trades, and efficient handling of user transactions.

Implementation:

- **SignalR for Real-Time Updates:** The application uses SignalR to provide real-time updates to clients about stock prices, trade executions, and alerts.
- **High-Performance APIs:** Kestrel serves as the web server, handling numerous concurrent requests efficiently.

Example Code: Real-Time Stock Updates with SignalR

```csharp
public class StockHub : Hub
{
    public async Task SendStockUpdate(string stockSymbol,
    decimal price)
    {
        await Clients.All.SendAsync("ReceiveStockUpdate",
        stockSymbol, price);
    }
}

// In Startup.cs or Program.cs
app.UseEndpoints(endpoints =>
{
    endpoints.MapHub<StockHub>("/stockHub");
});
```

Performance Highlights:

- **Real-Time Data Delivery:** SignalR provides immediate updates to users, essential for timely trading decisions.
- **Scalability:** Kestrel's asynchronous handling of requests enables the application to scale effectively under heavy load.

5. IoT Data Collection Platform

Use Case: An IoT data collection platform gathers data from numerous sensors deployed in various locations. The system requires efficient data ingestion and real-time processing.

Implementation:

- **HTTP and MQTT Protocols:** The platform supports both HTTP and MQTT for data transmission, allowing devices to send data efficiently, either as bulk uploads or in small messages.
- **Asynchronous Data Processing:** Incoming data is processed asynchronously to ensure quick response times and to avoid bottlenecks.

Example Code: HTTP Endpoint for Data Collection

```csharp
app.MapPost("/api/sensor/data", async (SensorData data) =>
{
    // Logic to process and store incoming sensor data
});
```

Performance Highlights:

- **Efficient Data Ingestion:** Supporting multiple protocols allows devices to send data using the most suitable method.
- **Real-Time Processing:** Asynchronous processing of incoming data ensures that the system can handle spikes in data transmission without lag.

These real-world examples illustrate how .NET 6 can be leveraged to build high-performance network applications across various domains, including real-time communication, streaming, gaming, finance, and IoT. By utilizing the features and enhancements provided by the .NET framework, such as Kestrel's efficient handling of connections, support for asynchronous programming, and optimized networking APIs, developers can create robust and scalable applications.

As you develop high-performance network applications, consider the specific requirements of your use case, leverage the capabilities of .NET 6, and implement best practices to ensure optimal performance and user experience. By doing so, you will be well-equipped to build applications that meet the demands of modern users and businesses alike.

Efficient File and I/O Handling

Optimizing File Operations and Asynchronous I/O in .NET 6

Efficient file handling and I/O operations are critical for application performance, especially in data-intensive applications such as web services, data processing systems, and desktop applications. .NET 6 provides robust features and enhancements for optimizing file operations and managing asynchronous I/O, enabling developers to create applications that efficiently read, write, and manage file data. This chapter will explore strategies for optimizing file operations, leveraging asynchronous I/O, and employing best practices for effective file management.

1. **Understanding File I/O in .NET**

File I/O (Input/Output) operations refer to the methods and techniques used to read from and write to files stored on a disk. In .NET, the System.IO namespace provides classes for working with files and directories, including:

- **FileStream:** Provides a stream for reading from and writing to files, allowing for both synchronous and asynchronous operations.
- **StreamReader and StreamWriter:** Simplified classes for reading and writing text files.
- **File and Directory classes:** Provide static methods for file and directory manipulation, such as creating, copying, and deleting files.

2. Synchronous vs. Asynchronous File Operations

- **Synchronous Operations:** Traditional file I/O operations are blocking, meaning that the executing thread waits until the operation completes. While straightforward to implement, synchronous file operations can lead to performance bottlenecks, especially in applications requiring high responsiveness.
- **Asynchronous Operations:** Asynchronous file I/O operations allow the executing thread to continue executing while the file operation completes in the background. This approach improves application responsiveness and resource utilization, particularly in UI applications or server-side applications handling multiple requests.

3. Optimizing File Operations

To ensure efficient file operations in .NET applications, consider the following strategies:

3.1. Buffered I/O

Buffered I/O improves performance by reading or writing data in larger chunks rather than byte by byte. By using BufferedStream, you can wrap a file stream to buffer data, minimizing the number of I/O operations.

Example: Using BufferedStream for Efficient File Writing

```csharp
using (var fileStream = new FileStream("example.txt", FileMode.Create, FileAccess.Write))
using (var bufferedStream = new BufferedStream(fileStream))
using (var writer = new StreamWriter(bufferedStream))
{
    for (int i = 0; i < 10000; i++)
    {
        writer.WriteLine($"Line {i}");
    }
}
```

3.2. File System Access Patterns

Understanding file access patterns is essential for optimizing file operations. Sequential access is typically more efficient than random access. Structure your file operations to minimize seek time and leverage sequential reads and writes where possible.

3.3. Use Memory-Mapped Files

Memory-mapped files provide an efficient way to handle large files by mapping a portion of the file directly into memory. This allows for fast random access without the overhead of traditional file I/O operations.

Example: Using Memory-Mapped Files

```csharp
using (var mmf = MemoryMappedFile.CreateNew("MyMap", 10000))
{
    using (var accessor = mmf.CreateViewAccessor())
    {
        accessor.Write(0, 12345); // Write data to the
        memory-mapped file
        int value = accessor.ReadInt32(0); // Read data from the
        memory-mapped file
    }
}
```

4. Leveraging Asynchronous I/O

.NET 6 provides a rich set of asynchronous file I/O operations, enabling developers to perform file operations without blocking the main execution thread.

4.1. Asynchronous File Reading and Writing

Utilize the asynchronous methods provided by the FileStream, StreamReader, and StreamWriter classes to perform file operations asynchronously.

Example: Asynchronous File Reading

EFFICIENT FILE AND I/O HANDLING

```csharp
public async Task<string> ReadFileAsync(string path)
{
    using (var stream = new FileStream(path, FileMode.Open,
    FileAccess.Read, FileShare.Read, bufferSize: 4096, useAsync:
    true))
    using (var reader = new StreamReader(stream))
    {
        return await reader.ReadToEndAsync();
    }
}
```

Example: Asynchronous File Writing

```csharp
public async Task WriteFileAsync(string path, string content)
{
    using (var stream = new FileStream(path, FileMode.Create,
    FileAccess.Write, FileShare.None, bufferSize: 4096,
    useAsync: true))
    using (var writer = new StreamWriter(stream))
    {
        await writer.WriteAsync(content);
    }
}
```

4.2. Async File APIs in .NET 6

The introduction of async file APIs in .NET 6 provides additional enhancements for reading and writing files asynchronously, enabling better performance and responsiveness.

- **File.ReadAllTextAsync:** Reads all text from a file asynchronously.
- **File.WriteAllTextAsync:** Writes text to a file asynchronously.

Example: Using Async File APIs

```csharp
public async Task<string> ReadAllTextAsync(string path)
{
    return await File.ReadAllTextAsync(path);
}

public async Task WriteAllTextAsync(string path, string content)
{
    await File.WriteAllTextAsync(path, content);
}
```

5. Best Practices for File I/O Optimization

To ensure optimal file I/O performance, follow these best practices:

- **Use Asynchronous Methods:** Always prefer asynchronous file I/O methods to prevent blocking and enhance application responsiveness, especially in UI applications or web servers.
- **Batch File Operations:** When processing multiple files, batch operations together to reduce the overhead of individual I/O calls.
- **Consider File Size and Structure:** For large files, consider breaking them into smaller chunks for processing, as this can help manage memory usage and improve performance.
- **Implement Caching:** For frequently accessed files, implement caching strategies to reduce the need for repeated disk access, enhancing performance.
- **Monitor and Measure Performance:** Use profiling tools to monitor file I/O performance and identify bottlenecks. Optimize based on measured results rather than assumptions.

6. Real-World Example: File Processing Application

Consider a scenario where you need to build a file processing application that reads large datasets from CSV files, processes the data, and writes results back to disk. Optimizing file operations and using asynchronous I/O

EFFICIENT FILE AND I/O HANDLING

can significantly enhance performance in such applications.

Implementation:

- **Asynchronous File Reading:** Use asynchronous file reading methods to load data into memory without blocking the main thread.
- **Buffered Processing:** Implement buffered processing to handle large datasets efficiently.
- **Asynchronous Writing:** Write processed results back to disk asynchronously to prevent blocking.

Example Code: Asynchronous CSV File Processing

```csharp
public async Task ProcessCsvFileAsync(string inputPath, string outputPath)
{
    var data = new List<string>();

    // Asynchronously read the input file
    using (var stream = new FileStream(inputPath, FileMode.Open, FileAccess.Read, FileShare.Read, bufferSize: 4096, useAsync: true))
    using (var reader = new StreamReader(stream))
    {
        while (!reader.EndOfStream)
        {
            var line = await reader.ReadLineAsync();
            // Process the line (e.g., parse CSV)
            data.Add(line); // Simple example; replace with
            actual processing logic
        }
    }

    // Asynchronously write to the output file
    using (var stream = new FileStream(outputPath, FileMode.Create, FileAccess.Write, FileShare.None,
```

```
    bufferSize: 4096, useAsync: true))
using (var writer = new StreamWriter(stream))
{
    foreach (var line in data)
    {
        await writer.WriteLineAsync(line); // Write
        processed data back
    }
}
}
```

Optimizing file operations and leveraging asynchronous I/O in .NET 6 is crucial for building high-performance applications that efficiently manage file data. By understanding the capabilities of the System.IO namespace and applying best practices, developers can significantly enhance the performance and responsiveness of their applications.

Implementing asynchronous file operations, utilizing buffering techniques, and employing efficient file access patterns will lead to better resource utilization and improved user experience. As you develop your applications, consider these strategies to ensure that file handling remains a strong aspect of your overall performance optimization efforts.

Managing High-Volume Data Processing Efficiently in .NET 6

In an era where data is generated at an unprecedented rate, managing high-volume data processing efficiently is critical for applications across various domains, including finance, healthcare, e-commerce, and IoT. .NET 6 provides robust tools and frameworks to handle large datasets effectively, ensuring that applications can scale and perform well under

EFFICIENT FILE AND I/O HANDLING

heavy loads. This section will explore strategies for managing high-volume data processing, including techniques for efficient data handling, optimizing performance, and utilizing asynchronous processing.

1. Understanding High-Volume Data Processing

High-volume data processing refers to the techniques and practices employed to handle, analyze, and transform large amounts of data efficiently. The key challenges in high-volume data processing include:

- **Data Ingestion:** Rapidly capturing data from various sources, such as sensors, APIs, or user interactions.
- **Data Storage:** Efficiently storing large datasets in a manner that allows for quick access and retrieval.
- **Data Processing:** Applying transformations, calculations, or analytics on large datasets in a timely manner.
- **Data Output:** Storing processed data or sending it to downstream systems or users effectively.

2. Efficient Data Ingestion Techniques

When dealing with high-volume data, the ingestion process must be optimized to handle large streams of incoming data. Consider the following strategies:

2.1. Use of Streaming APIs

.NET 6 provides the System.IO.Pipelines namespace, which allows for efficient handling of streaming data. This API is designed for high-performance scenarios where data is processed in streams, minimizing memory allocations and enhancing throughput.

Example: Using Pipelines for Data Ingestion

```csharp
using System.IO.Pipelines;
```

```csharp
public async Task ProcessStreamAsync(Stream inputStream)
{
    var pipe = new Pipe();
    var writer = pipe.Writer;
    var reader = pipe.Reader;

    // Writing data to the pipe
    _ = Task.Run(async () =>
    {
        try
        {
            while (true)
            {
                var buffer = new byte[4096];
                int bytesRead = await
                inputStream.ReadAsync(buffer, 0, buffer.Length);
                if (bytesRead == 0) break;

                await writer.WriteAsync(buffer.AsMemory(0,
                    bytesRead));
            }
        }
        finally
        {
            writer.Complete();
        }
    });

    // Reading data from the pipe
    while (true)
    {
        var result = await reader.ReadAsync();
        var buffer = result.Buffer;

        // Process the data
        foreach (var segment in buffer)
        {
            // Process each segment of data
        }
```

```
        reader.AdvanceTo(buffer.End);
        if (result.IsCompleted) break;
    }

    reader.Complete();
}
```

2.2. Batch Processing

Batch processing involves grouping multiple data records into a single batch for processing, which can significantly improve performance by reducing the overhead of individual processing requests.

Example: Batch Processing in Data Ingestion

csharp

```
public async Task ProcessBatchesAsync(IEnumerable<DataRecord> records)
{
    var batchSize = 1000;
    var batch = new List<DataRecord>(batchSize);

    foreach (var record in records)
    {
        batch.Add(record);
        if (batch.Count >= batchSize)
        {
            await ProcessBatchAsync(batch);
            batch.Clear();
        }
    }

    // Process any remaining records
    if (batch.Count > 0)
    {
        await ProcessBatchAsync(batch);
    }
}
```

```csharp
private Task ProcessBatchAsync(List<DataRecord> batch)
{
    // Perform processing logic for the batch
    return Task.CompletedTask;
}
```

3. Data Storage Strategies

Choosing the right storage strategy is critical for efficiently managing high-volume data:

3.1. NoSQL Databases

Consider using NoSQL databases like MongoDB or Cassandra for storing unstructured or semi-structured data. These databases are designed to handle large volumes of data with high write and read throughput.

Example: Using MongoDB with .NET

```csharp
public async Task InsertRecordsAsync(IMongoCollection<DataRecord> collection, IEnumerable<DataRecord> records)
{
    await collection.InsertManyAsync(records);
}
```

3.2. Data Warehousing Solutions

For analytical processing, utilize data warehousing solutions such as Azure Synapse Analytics or Amazon Redshift. These platforms are optimized for querying large datasets and support parallel processing.

4. Optimizing Data Processing

To ensure efficient processing of large datasets, apply the following optimization techniques:

4.1. Parallel Processing

Leverage parallel processing capabilities in .NET to split data processing

EFFICIENT FILE AND I/O HANDLING

tasks across multiple threads or tasks. The Task Parallel Library (TPL) can help distribute workloads effectively.

Example: Using Parallel.ForEach for Data Processing

```csharp
public void ProcessData(IEnumerable<DataRecord> records)
{
    Parallel.ForEach(records, record =>
    {
        // Process each record concurrently
    });
}
```

4.2. Asynchronous Data Processing

Asynchronous methods can enhance responsiveness and resource utilization by allowing other operations to proceed while waiting for I/O-bound tasks to complete.

Example: Asynchronous Processing of Large Datasets

```csharp
public async Task
ProcessLargeDatasetAsync(IEnumerable<DataRecord> records)
{
    var tasks = records.Select(record =>
    ProcessRecordAsync(record));
    await Task.WhenAll(tasks);
}

private async Task ProcessRecordAsync(DataRecord record)
{
    // Asynchronous processing logic
}
```

4.3. Efficient Querying

When querying large datasets, optimize your queries by:

- Using indexes to speed up lookups.
- Retrieving only necessary columns to reduce data transfer.
- Implementing pagination to handle large result sets efficiently.

5. Data Output and Integration

After processing high-volume data, consider how to efficiently output the results:

5.1. Writing to Databases

Utilize bulk insert operations for writing large datasets to databases. This approach minimizes the number of round trips and improves performance.

Example: Bulk Insertion with Entity Framework

```csharp
using (var context = new MyDbContext())
{
    await context.BulkInsertAsync(records); // Use a library
    like Entity Framework Extensions for bulk operations
}
```

5.2. File Outputs

For applications that require exporting data to files (e.g., CSV, JSON), ensure that file writes are performed asynchronously to avoid blocking.

Example: Asynchronous File Output

```csharp
public async Task WriteDataToFileAsync(string path,
IEnumerable<DataRecord> records)
{
    using (var writer = new StreamWriter(path))
    {
        foreach (var record in records)
        {
            await writer.WriteLineAsync(record.ToString());
```

```
        }
     }
}
```

6. Real-World Example: Data Ingestion and Processing Pipeline

Consider a data ingestion and processing pipeline for a social media analytics application that collects user interactions, analyzes trends, and generates reports.

Implementation Overview:

1. **Data Ingestion:** Collect data from various sources (APIs, user interactions) using asynchronous methods and pipelines.
2. **Data Processing:** Process incoming data in batches using parallel processing techniques to analyze trends.
3. **Storage:** Store processed data in a NoSQL database for quick retrieval and further analysis.
4. **Reporting:** Generate reports by querying the database and exporting results to CSV files asynchronously.

Managing high-volume data processing efficiently in .NET 6 involves understanding the nuances of data ingestion, storage, processing, and output. By leveraging asynchronous I/O, optimizing file operations, and employing best practices such as batching and parallel processing, developers can build robust applications capable of handling large datasets effectively.

As data continues to grow, adopting these strategies will ensure that your applications remain responsive, scalable, and efficient, enabling them to meet the demands of modern data processing requirements. With the powerful features provided by .NET 6, you are well-equipped to handle high-volume data scenarios and deliver exceptional performance in your applications.

Practical Examples: Batch Processing and Stream Optimization in .NET 6

Batch processing and stream optimization are essential techniques for managing high-volume data efficiently in .NET 6 applications. By processing data in batches and optimizing data streams, developers can significantly improve application performance, resource utilization, and responsiveness. This section provides practical examples that illustrate these concepts in action.

1. Batch Processing Examples

Batch processing involves grouping multiple records together for processing, which can reduce overhead and improve efficiency. This approach is particularly useful in scenarios where individual processing of records would incur significant performance penalties.

1.1. Batch Insertion into a Database

When inserting a large number of records into a database, using batch operations can greatly enhance performance by minimizing round trips to the database server. Here's how to implement batch insertion using Entity Framework Core.

Example: Batch Insertion with Entity Framework

```csharp
public async Task BatchInsertRecordsAsync(List<DataRecord> records)
{
    using (var context = new MyDbContext())
    {
        // Split records into batches of 1000
```

EFFICIENT FILE AND I/O HANDLING

```csharp
        const int batchSize = 1000;
        for (int i = 0; i < records.Count; i += batchSize)
        {
            var batch = records.Skip(i).Take(batchSize).ToList();
            await context.AddRangeAsync(batch);
            await context.SaveChangesAsync();
        }
    }
}
```

Explanation:

- This method processes records in batches of 1000, reducing the number of calls to SaveChangesAsync(), which improves performance for large datasets.
- Using AddRangeAsync allows for adding multiple entities in a single operation, optimizing database interaction.

1.2. Batch Processing for File Operations

When dealing with large files, reading and processing data in batches can minimize memory usage and improve processing time.

Example: Batch Processing of Lines in a Text File

```csharp
public async Task ProcessFileInBatchesAsync(string filePath)
{
    const int batchSize = 1000;
    var lines = new List<string>(batchSize);

    using (var reader = new StreamReader(filePath))
    {
        while (!reader.EndOfStream)
        {
            for (int i = 0; i < batchSize &&
            !reader.EndOfStream; i++)
```

```csharp
        {
            lines.Add(await reader.ReadLineAsync());
        }

        // Process the batch of lines
        await ProcessBatchAsync(lines);
        lines.Clear();
    }
  }
}

private Task ProcessBatchAsync(List<string> lines)
{
    // Implement processing logic for the batch of lines
    return Task.CompletedTask;
}
```

Explanation:

- This method reads lines from a text file in batches, processing each batch before moving on to the next. This approach conserves memory and enhances performance, especially for large files.

2. Stream Optimization Examples

Stream optimization focuses on improving the performance of data transmission by utilizing efficient buffering and asynchronous operations. In .NET 6, streams can be optimized using various techniques.

Optimizing Stream Writes with Buffered Streams

Using a BufferedStream to write data to a file can reduce the number of I/O operations and improve performance by buffering output data.

Example: Using BufferedStream for File Writing

```csharp
csharp
Copy code
public async Task WriteDataWithBufferingAsync(string filePath,
IEnumerable<string> data)
```

```csharp
{
    using (var fileStream = new FileStream(filePath,
    FileMode.Create, FileAccess.Write, FileShare.None))
    using (var bufferedStream = new BufferedStream(fileStream))
    using (var writer = new StreamWriter(bufferedStream))
    {
        foreach (var line in data)
        {
            await writer.WriteLineAsync(line);
        }
    }
}
```

Explanation:

- By wrapping the FileStream in a BufferedStream, the application can reduce the frequency of disk writes, improving performance when writing large volumes of data.

Streamlining Data Processing with Pipelines

The System.IO.Pipelines namespace enables efficient and low-latency handling of data streams. This API is particularly useful for high-performance scenarios involving I/O-bound operations.

Example: Using Pipelines for Data Processing

csharp

```
public async Task ProcessDataWithPipelinesAsync(Stream inputStream)
{
    var pipe = new Pipe();

    // Writing to the pipe
    _ = Task.Run(async () =>
    {
        var writer = pipe.Writer;
```

```csharp
            try
            {
                while (true)
                {
                    var buffer = new byte[4096];
                    int bytesRead = await
                    inputStream.ReadAsync(buffer, 0, buffer.Length);
                    if (bytesRead == 0) break;

                    await writer.WriteAsync(buffer.AsMemory(0,
                    bytesRead));
                }
            }
            finally
            {
                writer.Complete();
            }
        });

        // Reading from the pipe
        var reader = pipe.Reader;
        while (true)
        {
            var result = await reader.ReadAsync();
            var buffer = result.Buffer;

            // Process data in the buffer
            foreach (var segment in buffer)
            {
                // Implement data processing logic here
            }

            reader.AdvanceTo(buffer.End);
            if (result.IsCompleted) break;
        }

        reader.Complete();
    }
```

Explanation:

EFFICIENT FILE AND I/O HANDLING

- This example demonstrates how to read from an input stream and write to a pipe asynchronously, allowing for efficient and high-throughput data processing without blocking the main thread.

3. Combining Batch Processing and Stream Optimization

In many real-world scenarios, combining batch processing with stream optimization yields the best performance results. For instance, when processing large files from a source like an API or a database, you can read data in batches, process them, and write the results back efficiently.

Example: Batch Processing with Stream Optimization

```csharp
public async Task ProcessLargeFileWithOptimizationsAsync(string inputPath, string outputPath)
{
    const int batchSize = 1000;
    var dataBatch = new List<string>(batchSize);

    using (var reader = new StreamReader(inputPath))
    using (var writer = new StreamWriter(outputPath))
    {
        while (!reader.EndOfStream)
        {
            for (int i = 0; i < batchSize &&
            !reader.EndOfStream; i++)
            {
                var line = await reader.ReadLineAsync();
                if (line != null) dataBatch.Add(line);
            }

            // Process the batch and write to output
            foreach (var processedData in
            dataBatch.Select(ProcessLine))
            {
                await writer.WriteLineAsync(processedData);
            }
```

```
            dataBatch.Clear();
        }
    }
}

private string ProcessLine(string line)
{
    // Implement your processing logic here
    return line.ToUpper(); // Example transformation
}
```

Explanation:

- This method reads lines from a large input file in batches, processes each line, and writes the results to an output file using asynchronous I/O. This combination minimizes memory usage while maximizing throughput.

Batch processing and stream optimization are vital strategies for managing high-volume data processing efficiently in .NET 6. By leveraging techniques such as buffered I/O, asynchronous methods, and the System.IO.Pipelines API, developers can significantly enhance the performance of their applications.

Practical implementations of these strategies enable effective data handling, ensuring that applications can scale and respond to user demands without sacrificing performance. As you design your data processing solutions, consider these techniques to build robust applications that can handle the challenges of modern data management. By adopting these practices, you will be well-equipped to create high-performance applications that efficiently process large volumes of data in .NET 6.

Real-World Case Studies and Challenges

Case Studies from Financial Modeling and Game Development

In this chapter, we will explore real-world case studies in two distinct domains: financial modeling and game development. Each case study will illustrate how developers utilize .NET 6 features, address challenges, and implement high-performance solutions tailored to the specific needs of each domain. By examining these examples, we will gain insights into best practices, strategies for overcoming obstacles, and the importance of efficient design in high-stakes environments.

1. Case Study: Financial Modeling Application

Overview: A financial modeling application was developed for a large investment firm to analyze stock market trends, generate forecasts, and support decision-making. The application needed to handle vast amounts of historical and real-time market data, perform complex calculations, and provide visualizations for analysts and traders.

Challenges:

- **Data Volume:** The application had to process terabytes of historical market data from various sources, including stock exchanges and financial news APIs.
- **Real-Time Processing:** Analysts required real-time updates to stock prices, which necessitated efficient handling of live data streams.

- **Complex Calculations:** The application needed to perform complex financial calculations, such as Monte Carlo simulations and risk assessments, requiring high computational performance.

Solution Implementation:

Data Ingestion and Storage:

- The application used asynchronous I/O to ingest data from multiple sources concurrently, ensuring minimal delays.
- A NoSQL database (e.g., MongoDB) was implemented for storing and retrieving large datasets efficiently, allowing for flexible data structures.

Batch Processing for Historical Data:

- Historical data was processed in batches using Parallel.ForEach to perform calculations across multiple threads, enhancing performance during analysis.

Real-Time Data Handling:

- SignalR was integrated to provide real-time updates to connected clients. This allowed users to receive notifications of price changes and significant market events instantly.

Performance Optimization:

- The team utilized caching strategies to store frequently accessed data, reducing the need for repeated database queries.
- Asynchronous methods were employed throughout the application to prevent blocking operations, ensuring responsive user interactions.

Results:

- **Improved Performance:** The financial modeling application could process historical data in batches, resulting in significant time savings during analysis.
- **Real-Time Insights:** Analysts received immediate notifications of market changes, enabling them to react quickly to trading opportunities.
- **Enhanced Decision-Making:** The application provided detailed visualizations and reports that improved the firm's decision-making process.

Lessons Learned:

- **Asynchronous Programming is Key:** Leveraging asynchronous I/O and processing techniques allowed the application to handle high volumes of data efficiently.
- **Scalability Matters:** Implementing a flexible data storage solution like NoSQL enabled the application to adapt to changing data requirements and user needs.

2. Case Study: Online Multiplayer Game Development

Overview: An online multiplayer game was developed to provide players with a dynamic, engaging experience in a fantasy world. The game needed to support real-time interactions among thousands of players, manage game state efficiently, and deliver low-latency gameplay.

Challenges:

- **Concurrency:** Managing thousands of concurrent player connections required efficient handling of network I/O and game state updates.
- **Latency Sensitivity:** The game needed to minimize latency to ensure a responsive user experience, especially during critical gameplay moments.
- **Real-Time Data Synchronization:** The application had to synchronize game state across all players in real-time, ensuring that actions taken by one player were reflected for all other players without delays.

Solution Implementation:

Socket-Based Networking:

- The game server was built using Kestrel and utilized UDP sockets for real-time communication. This approach allowed for faster message delivery compared to TCP, which is critical for responsive gameplay.
- Custom protocols were designed to minimize message size and improve transmission speed.

State Management:

- The server maintained the game state in memory, allowing for rapid access and updates. Data structures were optimized for quick lookups and updates to handle player actions efficiently.
- Game state changes were communicated to all players using SignalR for seamless synchronization.

Load Balancing:

- A load balancer was implemented to distribute incoming connections across multiple server instances, improving scalability and reliability during peak traffic.

Performance Testing and Optimization:

- The development team conducted extensive load testing to simulate high player counts and identified bottlenecks in network I/O and processing.
- Profiling tools were used to measure performance metrics, leading to optimizations in message handling and game state updates.

Results:

- **Enhanced Player Experience:** The online game successfully supported thousands of concurrent players with minimal latency, providing a smooth and immersive gameplay experience.
- **Scalable Architecture:** The implementation of load balancing allowed the game to handle spikes in player activity without degradation in performance.
- **Dynamic Gameplay:** Real-time synchronization of game state ensured that all players experienced the game world consistently and could interact with each other fluidly.

Lessons Learned:

- **Prioritize Low Latency:** Utilizing UDP for real-time communications was critical for minimizing latency and maintaining a responsive game environment.
- **Effective State Management:** Keeping game state in memory and optimizing data structures facilitated quick updates and interactions among players.

The case studies from financial modeling and online multiplayer game development illustrate the diverse applications of high-performance techniques in .NET 6. By addressing specific challenges in each domain, developers were able to implement effective solutions that enhanced performance, scalability, and user experience.

In financial modeling, asynchronous I/O and batch processing strategies facilitated efficient data handling and real-time updates, leading to improved decision-making capabilities. In game development, a focus on low-latency communication, effective state management, and load balancing allowed for a responsive and engaging multiplayer experience.

These case studies highlight the importance of leveraging .NET 6 features to tackle complex challenges and optimize performance in real-world applications. As you develop your applications, consider these lessons and strategies to ensure that your solutions can meet the demands of high-volume data processing and provide exceptional user experiences.

Challenges and Best Practices in Building High-Performance Computing (HPC) Applications

Building High-Performance Computing (HPC) applications presents a unique set of challenges, particularly in terms of resource management, scalability, and optimization. As the demand for processing large datasets and performing complex computations grows, developers must adopt best practices to overcome these challenges and ensure that their applications are efficient, scalable, and maintainable. This section will explore the key challenges faced in HPC application development and provide actionable best practices to address them.

1. Key Challenges in HPC Applications

Resource Management

Managing system resources such as CPU, memory, and I/O bandwidth is critical in HPC applications. Inefficient resource usage can lead to bottlenecks, increased latency, and suboptimal performance.

- **Challenge:** Resource contention occurs when multiple processes or threads compete for limited resources, resulting in decreased performance.
- **Example:** In a data-intensive application, multiple threads may attempt to access the same data simultaneously, causing delays.

Scalability

As the size of the dataset or the number of concurrent users increases, maintaining performance while scaling the application can become challenging.

- **Challenge:** Achieving linear scalability can be difficult due to factors like increased contention for shared resources and overhead from managing multiple threads or processes.
- **Example:** In cloud-based applications, the need to scale out to handle sudden spikes in user activity can lead to performance degradation if not managed properly.

Complexity of Algorithms

Many HPC applications require complex algorithms that can be computationally intensive. Implementing these algorithms efficiently can be challenging.

- **Challenge:** Ensuring that algorithms are optimized for performance while remaining maintainable and understandable can lead to trade-offs.
- **Example:** An algorithm that employs heavy recursion may be easier to understand but could lead to stack overflow issues or excessive memory usage.

Data Management and Transfer

HPC applications often need to process large volumes of data, which can lead to challenges in data management, transfer, and storage.

- **Challenge:** Data transfer between memory and storage, or across networked systems, can introduce significant latency, affecting overall performance.
- **Example:** In distributed systems, moving data across network boundaries can slow down computation due to bandwidth limitations.

2. Best Practices for Building HPC Applications
Optimize Resource Management

- **Use Thread Pools:** Leverage thread pools to manage concurrency

effectively. This helps avoid the overhead of creating and destroying threads and allows for better control over resource allocation.
- **Example:** In .NET, use ThreadPool or Task.Run to offload work to a managed thread pool.

```csharp
Task.Run(() => ProcessData(data));
```

- **Monitor Resource Usage:** Implement monitoring tools to track CPU, memory, and I/O usage. This helps identify bottlenecks and allows for timely adjustments.

Ensure Scalability

- **Design for Scalability:** Architect your applications with scalability in mind from the start. Consider microservices or distributed architectures that can scale independently.
- **Example:** Using Azure Functions or AWS Lambda to handle specific workloads in a serverless architecture allows for automatic scaling based on demand.
- **Load Balancing:** Implement load balancing strategies to distribute workloads evenly across resources, reducing contention and improving performance.

Optimize Algorithms and Data Structures

- **Choose Efficient Algorithms:** Select algorithms based on their time and space complexity, and consider alternative approaches that may yield better performance for your specific use case.
- **Example:** When processing large datasets, consider algorithms like

quicksort or mergesort for sorting operations instead of bubble sort.
- **Use Appropriate Data Structures:** Utilize data structures that provide optimal performance for your use case. For example, use hash tables for fast lookups or linked lists for frequent insertions and deletions.

Minimize Data Transfer Latency

- **Localize Data Processing:** Process data as close to its source as possible to reduce the need for data transfer. For example, use edge computing strategies to analyze data at the source (e.g., IoT devices).
- **Batch Data Transfers:** When transferring data, batch multiple records together to reduce the overhead associated with multiple I/O operations.
- **Example:** Instead of sending one record at a time, accumulate records and send them in a single request:

```csharp
var batch = new List<DataRecord>();
foreach (var record in records)
{
    batch.Add(record);
    if (batch.Count >= batchSize)
    {
        await SendBatchAsync(batch);
        batch.Clear();
    }
}
```

Implement Asynchronous Processing

- **Asynchronous I/O Operations:** Use asynchronous methods to prevent blocking and improve application responsiveness. This is particularly important for I/O-bound operations such as file access or network communication.

- **Example:** Use async and await for non-blocking I/O operations:

```csharp
public async Task<string> ReadFileAsync(string path)
{
    using (var stream = new FileStream(path, FileMode.Open,
    FileAccess.Read, FileShare.Read, useAsync: true))
    using (var reader = new StreamReader(stream))
    {
        return await reader.ReadToEndAsync();
    }
}
```

Conduct Thorough Testing and Profiling

- **Performance Testing:** Regularly test the performance of your application under realistic workloads. Use tools like BenchmarkDotNet to profile and measure performance, identifying areas for optimization.
- **Load Testing:** Simulate high-load scenarios to ensure the application can handle peak loads without degradation in performance.

Building high-performance computing applications involves navigating various challenges, including resource management, scalability, algorithm complexity, and data transfer latency. By implementing the best practices outlined in this chapter, developers can create robust, efficient, and scalable applications that meet the demands of high-volume data processing and complex computations.

Adopting an architectural mindset focused on optimization, testing, and monitoring will enable teams to build applications that not only perform well under load but also provide a solid foundation for future growth and enhancements. As you embark on your HPC development journey, keep these strategies in mind to ensure your applications remain responsive and efficient in an ever-evolving technological landscape.

Common Pitfalls in Building High-Performance Computing (HPC) Applications and How to Overcome Them

Building High-Performance Computing (HPC) applications is fraught with challenges and potential pitfalls. Understanding these common issues can help developers avoid costly mistakes and create efficient, scalable applications. This section outlines some of the most common pitfalls encountered in HPC development and offers practical strategies for overcoming them.

1. Inefficient Resource Management

Pitfall: Many HPC applications fall into the trap of poor resource management, leading to resource contention, excessive memory usage, or suboptimal CPU utilization. This inefficiency can result in application slowdowns and increased operational costs.

Solution:

- **Implement Resource Monitoring:** Use monitoring tools to track resource usage in real-time. Tools like Prometheus, Grafana, or Azure Monitor can provide insights into CPU, memory, and I/O utilization.
- **Optimize Thread Usage:** Use thread pools to manage threads more efficiently. Instead of creating new threads for each task, utilize Task.Run or ThreadPool.QueueUserWorkItem to reuse existing threads.
- **Example:**

```csharp
Task.Run(() => ProcessData(data));
```

- **Load Testing:** Conduct load testing to understand how your application behaves under stress. Use tools like Apache JMeter or k6 to simulate heavy workloads and identify bottlenecks.

2. Ignoring Asynchronous Programming

Pitfall: Failing to use asynchronous programming where appropriate can lead to blocking operations that hinder performance, especially in I/O-bound applications. This oversight often results in poor responsiveness and increased latency.

Solution:

- **Utilize Async/Await:** Always use asynchronous methods for I/O operations. This practice allows other tasks to proceed while waiting for operations to complete.
- **Example:**

```csharp
public async Task<string> FetchDataAsync(string url)
{
    using (var httpClient = new HttpClient())
    {
        return await httpClient.GetStringAsync(url);
    }
}
```

- **Asynchronous Streams:** For processing data, consider using IAsyncEnumerable<T>, which enables asynchronous iteration over collections.
- **Example:**

```csharp
public async IAsyncEnumerable<DataRecord>
ReadRecordsAsync(string path)
{
    using var reader = new StreamReader(path);
    while (!reader.EndOfStream)
    {
        var line = await reader.ReadLineAsync();
        yield return ParseRecord(line); // Implement your
        parsing logic
    }
}
```

3. Underestimating Data Transfer Latency

Pitfall: Developers often underestimate the impact of data transfer latency, especially when dealing with distributed systems. High latency can significantly slow down applications, particularly when transferring large datasets over the network.

Solution:

- **Minimize Data Transfer:** Design applications to minimize the amount of data transferred. For example, only send necessary fields or use compression techniques to reduce data size.
- **Example:**

```csharp
var jsonData = JsonSerializer.Serialize(importantData);
var compressedData = Compress(jsonData); // Implement
compression logic
```

- **Use Local Processing:** Whenever possible, process data close to its source to avoid unnecessary transfers. This approach is particularly effective in edge computing scenarios.

4. Neglecting Algorithm Optimization

Pitfall: Using inefficient algorithms or data structures can lead to poor performance, especially with large datasets. This oversight often occurs when developers prioritize quick implementations over optimal solutions.

Solution:

- **Analyze Time and Space Complexity:** Regularly review the time and space complexity of algorithms used in your application. Choose algorithms that provide optimal performance for the data size and type.
- **Example:** Replace $O(n^2)$ algorithms with $O(n \log n)$ algorithms for sorting or searching tasks whenever possible.
- **Profiling and Benchmarking:** Use profiling tools like BenchmarkDotNet to measure the performance of different algorithms and identify the best option for your use case.

5. Failing to Test Under Realistic Conditions

Pitfall: Testing applications in environments that do not accurately reflect production conditions can lead to unforeseen issues. Developers may miss critical performance problems that only arise under real-world load conditions.

Solution:

- **Simulate Production Environments:** Conduct load and stress testing in environments that closely resemble production. Use cloud-based load testing tools to simulate user behavior and network conditions.
- **Perform End-to-End Testing:** Test the entire application workflow to identify bottlenecks and inefficiencies in data handling, processing, and output.

6. Lack of Scalability Planning

Pitfall: Many applications are built without consideration for future

scalability. This oversight can lead to architectural limitations that hinder growth and necessitate costly refactoring.
Solution:

- **Design for Scalability:** Use scalable architectures such as microservices, where components can be independently scaled based on demand. This approach enables individual parts of the application to grow without impacting others.
- **Use Load Balancers:** Implement load balancers to distribute incoming traffic across multiple instances of your application, ensuring that no single instance becomes a bottleneck.

7. Overlooking Security Considerations

Pitfall: In the quest for performance, security considerations are sometimes overlooked. This oversight can expose applications to vulnerabilities, especially in data-intensive environments.
Solution:

- **Implement Security Best Practices:** Ensure that your application follows security best practices, including data encryption, authentication, and authorization.
- **Regular Security Audits:** Conduct regular security audits and penetration testing to identify and mitigate vulnerabilities.

Building high-performance computing applications comes with various challenges, but by being aware of common pitfalls and adopting best practices, developers can create robust and efficient solutions. Optimizing resource management, utilizing asynchronous programming, minimizing data transfer latency, and prioritizing algorithm efficiency are crucial steps in overcoming obstacles.

Furthermore, realistic testing, scalability planning, and security considerations are essential for ensuring that applications can handle future demands and remain secure. By integrating these strategies into the development process, you can create HPC applications that not only perform well under load but also provide a solid foundation for ongoing growth and success in a rapidly evolving technological landscape.

Performance Testing and Benchmarking

Introduction to BenchmarkDotNet for Performance Testing

Performance testing and benchmarking are essential components of software development, particularly when building applications that require high efficiency and responsiveness, such as those in high-performance computing (HPC). BenchmarkDotNet is a powerful, open-source library in .NET that provides developers with an easy-to-use framework for benchmarking their code and measuring performance accurately. This chapter will introduce BenchmarkDotNet, its features, installation, basic usage, and best practices for effective performance testing.

1. Understanding BenchmarkDotNet

BenchmarkDotNet is a comprehensive library designed specifically for benchmarking .NET code. It provides precise measurements of code execution time and other performance metrics, allowing developers to analyze the efficiency of their algorithms and identify performance bottlenecks. Key features of BenchmarkDotNet include:

- **Accurate Timing:** It minimizes overhead and ensures accurate measurement of execution time.
- **Automatic Warm-Up:** The library automatically warms up the benchmarks to eliminate cold start effects and improve accuracy.
- **Detailed Reporting:** BenchmarkDotNet generates detailed reports,

including statistics, such as mean, standard deviation, and memory usage.
- **Integration with Various Environments:** It works seamlessly with various .NET environments, including .NET Core, .NET Framework, and Mono.

2. Why Use BenchmarkDotNet?

The use of BenchmarkDotNet provides several advantages for developers looking to conduct performance testing:

- **Simplicity:** It abstracts complex benchmarking setups, allowing developers to focus on writing tests rather than configuring frameworks.
- **Comprehensive Reporting:** It provides detailed insights into the performance characteristics of code, making it easier to identify optimization opportunities.
- **Robustness:** The library is actively maintained and updated, ensuring compatibility with the latest .NET features and best practices.

3. Installing BenchmarkDotNet

To start using BenchmarkDotNet in your .NET projects, follow these steps:

1. **Create a New .NET Project:** You can create a new console application using the .NET CLI or Visual Studio.

```bash
dotnet new console -n BenchmarkDemo
cd BenchmarkDemo
```

1. **Install the BenchmarkDotNet Package:** Add the BenchmarkDotNet NuGet package to your project using the following command:

```bash
dotnet add package BenchmarkDotNet
```

1. **Set Up Your Project:** Ensure that your project file (.csproj) includes the necessary references. Your .csproj should look like this:

```xml
<Project Sdk="Microsoft.NET.Sdk">

  <PropertyGroup>
    <OutputType>Exe</OutputType>
    <TargetFramework>net6.0</TargetFramework>
  </PropertyGroup>

  <ItemGroup>
    <PackageReference Include="BenchmarkDotNet"
    Version="latest_version" />
  </ItemGroup>

</Project>
```

4. Writing Your First Benchmark

With BenchmarkDotNet installed, you can start writing benchmarks. Here's a simple example that measures the performance of two methods: one for summing an array using a loop and another using LINQ.

Example Code: Benchmarking Sum Operations

```csharp
using BenchmarkDotNet.Attributes;
using BenchmarkDotNet.Running;
```

```csharp
using System;
using System.Linq;

public class BenchmarkExample
{
    private int[] _numbers;

    [GlobalSetup]
    public void Setup()
    {
        // Initialize an array of numbers
        _numbers = Enumerable.Range(1, 1000000).ToArray();
    }

    [Benchmark]
    public int SumUsingLoop()
    {
        int sum = 0;
        foreach (var number in _numbers)
        {
            sum += number;
        }
        return sum;
    }

    [Benchmark]
    public int SumUsingLINQ()
    {
        return _numbers.Sum();
    }
}

public class Program
{
    public static void Main(string[] args)
    {
        var summary = BenchmarkRunner.Run<BenchmarkExample>();
    }
}
```

Explanation:

PERFORMANCE TESTING AND BENCHMARKING

- The BenchmarkExample class contains two methods annotated with the [Benchmark] attribute, which tells BenchmarkDotNet to include them in the benchmarking process.
- The [GlobalSetup] method is used to initialize data before running benchmarks. In this case, an array of integers from 1 to 1,000,000 is created.
- The Main method runs the benchmarks and outputs the results.

5. Analyzing Benchmark Results

After running your benchmarks, BenchmarkDotNet provides a comprehensive summary of the results, which includes:

- **Mean Execution Time:** The average time taken for each benchmark method.
- **Standard Deviation:** The variability of execution time across runs, which indicates the reliability of the measurements.
- **Operations Per Second (OPS):** A metric that shows how many operations were performed in a second, providing insights into the efficiency of each method.

Example Output:

```ruby
|           Method |      Mean |     Error |    StdDev |   Gen 0 | Gen 1 | Gen 2 | Allocated |
|----------------- |----------:|----------:|----------:|--------:|------:|------:|----------:|
|     SumUsingLoop |  37.81 ms |  0.687 ms |  0.899 ms | 76.1719 |     - |     - | 304.76 KB |
|     SumUsingLINQ|  23.44 ms |  0.453 ms |  0.523 ms | 76.1719 |     - |     - | 304.76 KB |
```

6. Best Practices for Using BenchmarkDotNet

To get the most out of BenchmarkDotNet, consider the following best practices:

- **Use Multiple Iterations:** Ensure that benchmarks run for enough iterations to obtain statistically significant results. This helps mitigate variability due to environmental factors.
- **Warm-Up Phase:** Allow the benchmark to warm up before measuring to account for JIT compilation and other optimizations.
- **Isolate Benchmarks:** Keep benchmarks isolated from one another to prevent side effects from affecting results. Use the [GlobalSetup] and [GlobalCleanup] attributes to prepare and clean up test environments.
- **Profile Different Scenarios:** Benchmark various scenarios and input sizes to understand how performance scales with complexity.

BenchmarkDotNet is a powerful tool for performance testing in .NET applications, enabling developers to measure and optimize code execution accurately. By utilizing its features, such as detailed reporting and automatic warm-ups, developers can gain valuable insights into the performance characteristics of their algorithms and make informed decisions about optimizations.

As you incorporate BenchmarkDotNet into your development process, remember to follow best practices to ensure the accuracy and reliability of your benchmarks. By doing so, you will be better equipped to build high-performance applications that meet the demands of modern computing environments.

Setting Up Performance Baselines and Metrics in .NET 6

Establishing performance baselines and metrics is crucial for any high-performance computing (HPC) application. These baselines provide a reference point against which future performance can be measured and evaluated. By understanding how to set up effective performance baselines and metrics, developers can ensure their applications maintain optimal performance as they evolve. This section outlines the steps for setting up performance baselines and metrics, including the types of metrics to monitor and tools to use.

1. Understanding Performance Baselines

A performance baseline is a set of performance metrics that represent the standard performance level of an application under specific conditions. Baselines serve multiple purposes:

- **Reference Point:** They provide a reference for comparing future performance. If performance degrades, it can be identified against the baseline.
- **Guidance for Optimization:** They help identify areas for optimization by highlighting performance bottlenecks.
- **Quality Assurance:** Baselines are essential for quality assurance processes, ensuring that changes to the codebase do not negatively impact performance.

2. Establishing Performance Metrics

Performance metrics are specific measurements that help assess the performance of an application. Common metrics to consider include:

- **Execution Time:** The time it takes to execute specific functions or processes within the application. This is often measured in milliseconds or seconds.
- **Throughput:** The number of transactions or operations processed in a

given time frame (e.g., requests per second). This metric is particularly important in server-side applications handling multiple requests.
- **Memory Usage:** The amount of memory consumed by the application during execution. This can be measured using memory profiling tools.
- **CPU Utilization:** The percentage of CPU resources used during processing. High CPU usage may indicate performance issues or inefficient algorithms.
- **Error Rates:** The frequency of errors encountered during execution, which can impact overall reliability and user experience.

3. Setting Up a Benchmarking Framework

Using a benchmarking framework, such as BenchmarkDotNet, enables developers to automate the process of collecting performance metrics and establishing baselines. Follow these steps to set up a benchmarking framework effectively:

Define Benchmarking Scenarios

Determine the key scenarios that represent the typical workload of your application. This could include:

- Common user interactions (e.g., database queries, file uploads).
- Background processing tasks (e.g., data processing jobs).
- Batch operations (e.g., data imports or exports).

Write Benchmark Tests

Use BenchmarkDotNet to create benchmark tests for the identified scenarios. Ensure that each benchmark is focused on a specific operation to obtain clear and actionable results.

Example: Benchmarking a Database Query

```csharp
using BenchmarkDotNet.Attributes;
using BenchmarkDotNet.Running;
```

```csharp
public class DatabaseBenchmark
{
    private string _connectionString;

    [GlobalSetup]
    public void Setup()
    {
        _connectionString = "YourDatabaseConnectionString";
    }

    [Benchmark]
    public async Task<int> ExecuteQueryAsync()
    {
        using (var connection = new
        SqlConnection(_connectionString))
        {
            await connection.OpenAsync();
            var command = new SqlCommand("SELECT COUNT(*) FROM
            YourTable", connection);
            return (int)await command.ExecuteScalarAsync();
        }
    }
}

// To run the benchmark
public class Program
{
    public static void Main(string[] args)
    {
        BenchmarkRunner.Run<DatabaseBenchmark>();
    }
}
```

Collect and Analyze Results

After running benchmarks, collect the results and analyze the performance metrics. BenchmarkDotNet provides detailed reports, including mean execution time, standard deviation, and memory usage.

4. Setting Performance Goals

Establish performance goals based on the collected baseline metrics. These goals should be realistic, measurable, and aligned with user expectations. Consider the following aspects when setting goals:

- **User Experience:** Understand the acceptable response times for users. For example, a web application might aim for response times of under 200 milliseconds for most interactions.
- **Scalability Requirements:** Define how the application should perform under increased loads. This might include maintaining specific throughput rates during peak times.
- **Resource Constraints:** Consider the hardware and infrastructure limitations, setting performance goals that are achievable within those constraints.

5. Continuous Monitoring and Adjustments

Once performance baselines and goals are established, continuous monitoring is essential to maintain optimal performance.

Implement Monitoring Tools

Utilize monitoring tools such as:

- **Application Insights:** Provides telemetry data to monitor application performance, detect anomalies, and understand user behavior.
- **Prometheus and Grafana:** Open-source tools for monitoring and visualizing performance metrics in real-time.
- **New Relic or Datadog:** Comprehensive monitoring platforms that offer insights into application performance and infrastructure.

Regularly Review and Update Baselines

As your application evolves—whether through new features, optimizations, or scaling—regularly review and update your performance baselines and metrics. This ensures that they remain relevant and reflective of the application's current performance.

6. Common Pitfalls to Avoid

- **Neglecting Environmental Factors:** Ensure benchmarks are run in controlled environments that closely resemble production to avoid skewed results.
- **Failing to Isolate Tests:** Ensure benchmarks are isolated to avoid cross-contamination of results. This includes ensuring that background processes do not interfere with benchmarking tests.
- **Setting Unrealistic Goals:** Avoid setting performance goals that are unattainable. Goals should be challenging yet achievable, based on the capabilities of the application and its infrastructure.

Setting up performance baselines and metrics is a vital aspect of developing high-performance computing applications. By defining clear metrics, utilizing benchmarking frameworks like BenchmarkDotNet, and continuously monitoring performance, developers can ensure that their applications meet user expectations and perform optimally.

Establishing a systematic approach to performance testing not only aids in identifying bottlenecks and inefficiencies but also facilitates informed decision-making as the application evolves. By adopting these practices, you will be well-equipped to build robust applications capable of sustaining high performance in demanding environments.

Iterative Optimization Based on Benchmark Results

In the realm of High-Performance Computing (HPC), continuous performance improvement is crucial to maintaining application efficiency and responsiveness. Iterative optimization involves using benchmark results to guide systematic enhancements to your application. This section will discuss the process of iterative optimization, how to analyze benchmark results effectively, and practical strategies for applying insights gained from performance testing to refine your code.

1. Understanding Iterative Optimization

Iterative optimization is a development approach where you continually refine and enhance your code based on empirical data gathered from performance benchmarks. This cycle typically consists of the following steps:

1. **Benchmarking:** Measure the performance of specific methods or components in your application.
2. **Analysis:** Examine the benchmark results to identify bottlenecks and areas for improvement.
3. **Optimization:** Make targeted changes to your code, algorithms, or data structures based on the analysis.
4. **Re-Benchmarking:** Run benchmarks again to measure the impact of the changes.
5. **Iteration:** Repeat the process until performance goals are met or improvements diminish.

This process not only leads to a more optimized application but also fosters a culture of continuous improvement.

2. Analyzing Benchmark Results

Effective analysis of benchmark results is essential for understanding where optimizations are needed. Here are key metrics and considerations for analysis:

- **Execution Time:** Focus on methods or operations with the highest execution times. These represent the most significant opportunities for optimization.
- **Standard Deviation:** A high standard deviation in execution times may indicate variability, suggesting that certain factors or conditions affect

performance. Investigating these variations can lead to insights about potential optimizations.
- **Memory Allocation:** Monitor memory usage and garbage collection events. Excessive allocations can lead to performance degradation due to frequent garbage collection. Look for opportunities to reduce memory usage by reusing objects or using value types where appropriate.
- **Throughput Metrics:** If your application handles requests, look at throughput metrics (e.g., requests per second) to understand how well your application scales with increased load.

3. Applying Insights for Optimization

Once you have analyzed benchmark results, you can implement targeted optimizations. Here are practical strategies for iterative optimization:

Refactoring Code

- **Simplify Algorithms:** Look for opportunities to simplify algorithms. For example, replacing a nested loop with a more efficient algorithm can lead to significant performance improvements.
- **Avoid Unnecessary Complexity:** Remove any redundant code or calculations that do not contribute to the final output. Keep the codebase clean and maintainable.

Example: Refactoring a Sorting Method

csharp

```csharp
// Inefficient sorting using bubble sort
public void BubbleSort(int[] array)
{
    for (int i = 0; i < array.Length - 1; i++)
    {
        for (int j = 0; j < array.Length - 1 - i; j++)
        {
            if (array[j] > array[j + 1])
```

```
            {
                // Swap
                var temp = array[j];
                array[j] = array[j + 1];
                array[j + 1] = temp;
            }
        }
    }
}

// Refactored using Array.Sort (more efficient)
public void Sort(int[] array)
{
    Array.Sort(array);
}
```

Optimizing Data Structures

- **Choose the Right Data Structure:** Analyze your data access patterns and choose the most efficient data structure. For example, if you need frequent lookups, consider using a Dictionary<TKey, TValue> instead of a list.

Example: Using a Dictionary for Fast Lookups

```csharp
var dictionary = new Dictionary<string, int>();
foreach (var item in items)
{
    dictionary[item.Key] = item.Value; // Fast O(1) lookups
}
```

Implementing Caching

- **Cache Results:** For expensive operations or data retrieval, consider implementing caching mechanisms to store results of previous compu-

PERFORMANCE TESTING AND BENCHMARKING

tations, thus avoiding redundant calculations.

Example: Simple In-Memory Caching

```csharp
private readonly Dictionary<string, string> _cache = new();

public string GetData(string key)
{
    if (_cache.TryGetValue(key, out var value))
    {
        return value; // Return cached value
    }

    // Simulate expensive operation
    value = FetchDataFromDatabase(key);
    _cache[key] = value; // Cache the result
    return value;
}
```

Asynchronous and Parallel Processing

- **Leverage Asynchronous Operations:** Use asynchronous methods to free up threads and improve application responsiveness, particularly for I/O-bound operations.
- **Utilize Parallelism:** For CPU-bound tasks, consider using parallel processing with Parallel.ForEach or PLINQ (Parallel LINQ) to take advantage of multi-core processors.

Example: Using PLINQ for Parallel Processing

```csharp
var results = data.AsParallel().Select(item => ProcessItem(item)).ToArray();
```

4. Continuous Integration of Performance Testing

Integrating performance testing into your continuous integration (CI) pipeline can automate the benchmarking process, ensuring that performance regressions are detected early. Here's how to do this:

- **Automate Benchmark Runs:** Use CI tools (e.g., GitHub Actions, Azure DevOps, Jenkins) to run benchmark tests automatically on code commits or pull requests.
- **Monitor Results:** Set up alerts for significant deviations in benchmark results, allowing your team to investigate and address performance issues promptly.

5. Documenting Changes and Results

Maintain thorough documentation of the changes made during the optimization process, including:

- **Benchmark Results:** Record the results of benchmarks before and after optimizations to track progress over time.
- **Code Changes:** Document the rationale behind code changes, allowing future developers to understand the context and motivations for optimizations.
- **Performance Goals:** Keep a record of the performance goals set for your application, helping to guide future optimizations and testing.

Iterative optimization based on benchmark results is a powerful approach to enhancing the performance of HPC applications. By analyzing benchmark data, applying targeted optimizations, and integrating performance testing into the development workflow, developers can systematically improve application efficiency and maintain high responsiveness.

This approach not only leads to more optimized applications but also fosters a culture of continuous improvement within development teams.

By following these practices, you can ensure that your applications remain competitive and capable of handling the demands of high-performance computing environments.

Practical Code Examples and Case Studies in Performance Testing and Benchmarking

In this section, we will explore practical code examples and real-world case studies that illustrate the application of performance testing and benchmarking in .NET applications. These examples will highlight the use of BenchmarkDotNet, optimization techniques, and the iterative process of improving application performance through benchmarking.

1. **Practical Code Examples**
   Benchmarking String Manipulation Methods
   String manipulation is a common task in many applications, and its performance can vary significantly based on the approach used. This example demonstrates how to benchmark different string manipulation techniques in C#.
   Example Code: Benchmarking String Operations

```csharp
csharp

using BenchmarkDotNet.Attributes;
using BenchmarkDotNet.Running;

public class StringManipulationBenchmark
{
    private const string SampleText = "This is a sample string for benchmarking purposes.";

    [Benchmark]
    public string ConcatenateUsingOperator()
    {
```

```csharp
        string result = string.Empty;
        for (int i = 0; i < 100; i++)
        {
            result += SampleText;
        }
        return result;
    }

    [Benchmark]
    public string ConcatenateUsingStringBuilder()
    {
        var sb = new StringBuilder();
        for (int i = 0; i < 100; i++)
        {
            sb.Append(SampleText);
        }
        return sb.ToString();
    }
}

public class Program
{
    public static void Main(string[] args)
    {
        var summary =
        BenchmarkRunner.Run<StringManipulationBenchmark>();
    }
}
```

Analysis of Results:

- After running this benchmark, you will observe that the StringBuilder method typically outperforms the string concatenation using the + operator, especially as the size of the concatenated string grows. This showcases the importance of choosing the right approach for string manipulations.

Benchmarking a Data Processing Function

PERFORMANCE TESTING AND BENCHMARKING

In data-intensive applications, processing speed is crucial. The following example benchmarks two methods for filtering a large dataset: one using a traditional for loop and another using LINQ.

Example Code: Benchmarking Data Filtering

```csharp
using BenchmarkDotNet.Attributes;
using BenchmarkDotNet.Running;
using System;
using System.Collections.Generic;
using System.Linq;

public class DataProcessingBenchmark
{
    private List<int> _numbers;

    [GlobalSetup]
    public void Setup()
    {
        _numbers = Enumerable.Range(1, 1000000).ToList(); // Generate a large dataset
    }

    [Benchmark]
    public List<int> FilterUsingForLoop()
    {
        var result = new List<int>();
        for (int i = 0; i < _numbers.Count; i++)
        {
            if (_numbers[i] % 2 == 0) // Filter even numbers
            {
                result.Add(_numbers[i]);
            }
        }
        return result;
    }

    [Benchmark]
```

```
        public List<int> FilterUsingLINQ()
        {
            return _numbers.Where(n => n % 2 == 0).ToList(); //
            Filter even numbers using LINQ
        }
    }

    public class Program
    {
        public static void Main(string[] args)
        {
            var summary =
            BenchmarkRunner.Run<DataProcessingBenchmark>();
        }
    }
```

Analysis of Results:

- The results will likely show that while LINQ offers concise syntax, the traditional for loop can sometimes outperform it, especially for large datasets. This example emphasizes the need to evaluate performance based on actual use cases.

2. Case Studies

Case Study: E-Commerce Application Performance Optimization

Overview: An e-commerce platform experienced slow response times during peak shopping seasons, especially during checkout processes. The development team decided to implement performance testing and optimizations using BenchmarkDotNet to address these issues.

Challenges:

- Slow database queries during high traffic.
- High latency in processing user requests due to synchronous I/O operations.
- Inefficient product search functionality impacting user experience.

Solution Implementation:

Benchmarking Database Queries:

- The team benchmarked key database queries using BenchmarkDotNet to identify slow queries and optimize them. They found that certain queries took significantly longer than expected.

Refactoring Queries:

- Based on benchmark results, the team refactored complex SQL queries, added appropriate indexing, and implemented caching for frequently accessed data.

Asynchronous Processing:

- The team introduced asynchronous I/O operations for data retrieval and processing, which helped improve responsiveness, especially during peak loads.

Load Testing:

- Load testing was performed to simulate high user activity, allowing the team to validate the effectiveness of optimizations in real-world scenarios.

Results:

- The e-commerce platform saw a 50% reduction in average response time during peak shopping hours.
- Improved user experience led to higher conversion rates and increased sales during busy periods.

Case Study: Real-Time Data Analytics Platform

Overview: A real-time data analytics platform required optimizations to handle increasing volumes of data and deliver insights quickly to users. The platform used various data sources, including IoT devices and third-party APIs.

Challenges:

- High latency in data ingestion and processing due to synchronous operations.
- Difficulty in scaling to handle increased data loads.
- Inefficient algorithms leading to slow data analysis and reporting.

Solution Implementation:

Benchmarking Data Processing:

- The development team used BenchmarkDotNet to benchmark different data processing algorithms and identify inefficiencies.

Optimizing Algorithms:

- Algorithms were refactored for better performance based on benchmark findings, with a focus on optimizing data structures and using more efficient algorithms.

Implementing Parallel Processing:

- The team employed parallel processing techniques to ingest and process data from multiple sources concurrently, significantly reducing processing time.

Caching Mechanisms:

- A caching strategy was implemented for frequently accessed data, reducing the need for repeated calculations and improving overall performance.

Results:

- The platform achieved a 70% reduction in data processing time, allowing for real-time analytics and reporting.
- User satisfaction improved due to faster access to insights, leading to increased adoption of the platform.

Practical code examples and case studies illustrate the significant benefits of using performance testing and benchmarking tools like BenchmarkDotNet in real-world applications. By conducting systematic benchmarks and applying iterative optimizations, developers can enhance application performance and scalability.

The e-commerce application and real-time data analytics platform case studies highlight how targeted optimizations can lead to substantial improvements in response times and user satisfaction. These experiences underscore the importance of continuous performance testing as an integral part of the development lifecycle.

As you implement your own performance testing and optimization strategies, consider the lessons learned from these examples to create efficient, high-performance applications that meet user demands and operational requirements.

Introduction to High-Performance Data Analytics with .NET

High-performance data analytics refers to the methods and technologies used to process and analyze large volumes of data quickly and efficiently. In an era where organizations are inundated with data from various sources, the ability to extract meaningful insights rapidly has become a critical competitive advantage. This chapter provides an overview of high-performance data analytics within the .NET ecosystem, including its significance, key components, and methodologies for achieving optimal performance.

1. **Importance of High-Performance Data Analytics**

    High-performance data analytics is essential for several reasons:

    - **Speed and Efficiency:** Organizations require timely insights to make data-driven decisions. High-performance analytics enables real-time or near-real-time processing of large datasets, allowing for quicker responses to market changes or operational challenges.
    - **Scalability:** As data volumes continue to grow exponentially, high-performance analytics frameworks must be able to scale horizontally, processing larger datasets efficiently across distributed systems.
    - **Complex Analytics:** Businesses are increasingly employing advanced analytics techniques, such as machine learning, predictive modeling, and natural language processing. These methods often involve complex computations that require optimized performance to be practical for large datasets.
    - **Enhanced Decision-Making:** High-performance data analytics enables organizations to uncover trends, patterns, and anomalies within their data, leading to more informed decision-making and strategic planning.

2. **Key Components of High-Performance Data Analytics in .NET**

    The .NET ecosystem offers several components and technologies that facilitate high-performance data analytics:

- **Data Access Technologies:**
- **Entity Framework Core:** A modern object-relational mapping (ORM) framework that simplifies database interactions while optimizing performance through features like asynchronous queries and change tracking.
- **Dapper:** A lightweight ORM that focuses on raw SQL execution, providing high performance for data access operations with minimal overhead.
- **Data Processing Frameworks:**
- **Apache Spark for .NET (Mobius):** A powerful framework for distributed data processing that allows .NET developers to leverage the capabilities of Apache Spark for big data analytics.
- **LINQ (Language Integrated Query):** A feature of .NET that provides a consistent query syntax across different data sources, enabling developers to write expressive queries against in-memory collections or databases.
- **Machine Learning and AI:**
- **ML.NET:** A machine learning framework for .NET that enables developers to build, train, and deploy machine learning models directly within their applications, facilitating advanced analytics and predictive modeling.
- **Data Visualization:**
- **Power BI and Charting Libraries:** Tools and libraries that help present data insights visually, making it easier for stakeholders to interpret results and make informed decisions.

3. Methodologies for Achieving High-Performance Data Analytics

To implement high-performance data analytics effectively, consider the following methodologies:

Data Preprocessing and ETL (Extract, Transform, Load)

Before analytics can be performed, data must be cleaned, transformed, and organized. High-performance data analytics often involves optimizing the ETL process to handle large volumes of data efficiently.

- **Batch Processing:** Use batch processing to handle large datasets in manageable chunks, reducing the load on memory and improving processing times.
- **Parallel Processing:** Leverage parallel processing to perform ETL operations concurrently, thus speeding up data ingestion and transformation.

Example: Parallel Data Transformation

```csharp
public List<ProcessedData> TransformData(List<RawData> rawData)
{
    return rawData.AsParallel()
        .Select(data => ProcessData(data)) // Process each data entry in parallel
        .ToList();
}
```

In-Memory Data Processing

Utilizing in-memory processing frameworks can significantly enhance the performance of data analytics by reducing disk I/O and accelerating data access.

- **Caching:** Implement caching strategies to store frequently accessed data in memory, thus minimizing retrieval times.
- **Data Grids:** Use in-memory data grids like Apache Ignite or Hazelcast to distribute data across nodes in a cluster for high-speed analytics.

Leveraging Distributed Computing

For large-scale data analytics, distributed computing frameworks enable processing across multiple nodes, allowing for scalability and resilience.

- **Cluster Management:** Use tools like Kubernetes to manage containerized applications and scale processing nodes dynamically based on demand.

- **Data Partitioning:** Implement data partitioning strategies to distribute data evenly across nodes, ensuring balanced workloads and optimizing resource utilization.

4. Performance Monitoring and Tuning

Once high-performance data analytics systems are in place, ongoing monitoring and tuning are essential to maintain optimal performance:

- **Profiling Tools:** Utilize profiling tools to identify bottlenecks in data processing workflows. Tools such as Visual Studio Profiler or JetBrains dotTrace can help monitor performance in real-time.
- **Metrics Collection:** Implement logging and metrics collection to track key performance indicators (KPIs), such as execution time, throughput, and resource utilization.
- **Feedback Loop:** Establish a feedback loop for continuous improvement. Use insights gained from performance monitoring to refine data processing algorithms and optimize queries.

High-performance data analytics is a critical capability for organizations seeking to leverage data for strategic advantage. By utilizing the components and methodologies available in the .NET ecosystem, developers can build robust analytics solutions that handle large datasets efficiently and provide timely insights.

This chapter has highlighted the significance of high-performance data analytics, introduced key components and methodologies, and emphasized the importance of performance monitoring and iterative improvement. As you embark on implementing high-performance data analytics solutions, these principles will guide you in developing applications that deliver exceptional performance and meet the evolving demands of data-driven decision-making.

Leveraging ML.NET and NumSharp for Numerical Computing in High-Performance Data Analytics

Numerical computing is a cornerstone of data analytics, involving calculations on numerical data to derive insights and make predictions. In the .NET ecosystem, ML.NET and NumSharp provide powerful tools for performing numerical computations, enabling developers to build robust analytics solutions. This section explores how to leverage ML.NET and NumSharp effectively for numerical computing, focusing on their features, capabilities, and practical examples.

1. Overview of ML.NET

ML.NET is a machine learning framework designed for .NET developers. It allows you to build, train, and deploy machine learning models without requiring deep knowledge of machine learning algorithms. ML.NET provides a variety of features suitable for numerical computing, including regression, classification, clustering, and anomaly detection.

Key Features of ML.NET:

- **Model Training and Evaluation:** ML.NET simplifies the process of training machine learning models using various algorithms and evaluating their performance.
- **Data Transformations:** It provides data processing capabilities, such as normalization, feature extraction, and data splitting.
- **Integration with Existing .NET Applications:** ML.NET can easily integrate into existing .NET applications, making it a convenient choice for developers.

2. Overview of NumSharp

NumSharp is a library for numerical computing in .NET that draws inspiration from NumPy, the widely used numerical library for Python. It offers multi-dimensional arrays, mathematical functions, and advanced indexing capabilities, enabling efficient numerical computations.

Key Features of NumSharp:

- **N-Dimensional Arrays:** Supports n-dimensional arrays, allowing for efficient storage and manipulation of numerical data.
- **Mathematical Functions:** Provides a wide range of mathematical functions for element-wise operations and linear algebra.
- **Interoperability with Other Libraries:** Easily integrates with other .NET libraries, enhancing its functionality in data processing pipelines.

3. Setting Up ML.NET and NumSharp

To get started with ML.NET and NumSharp, you need to install the respective NuGet packages in your .NET project.

Installing ML.NET and NumSharp:

```bash
dotnet add package Microsoft.ML
dotnet add package NumSharp
```

4. Practical Examples

Using ML.NET for Regression Analysis

In this example, we will create a simple linear regression model using ML.NET to predict a target variable based on input features.

Example Code: Linear Regression with ML.NET

```csharp
using System;
using System.Collections.Generic;
using Microsoft.ML;
using Microsoft.ML.Data;

public class HouseData
{
    public float Size { get; set; }
```

```csharp
    public float Price { get; set; }
}

public class Prediction
{
    [ColumnName("Score")]
    public float Price { get; set; }
}

public class Program
{
    public static void Main(string[] args)
    {
        var context = new MLContext();

        // Sample data
        var data = new List<HouseData>
        {
            new HouseData { Size = 1.1F, Price = 1.2F },
            new HouseData { Size = 1.9F, Price = 2.3F },
            new HouseData { Size = 2.8F, Price = 3.0F },
            new HouseData { Size = 3.4F, Price = 3.7F },
            new HouseData { Size = 5.0F, Price = 5.5F }
        };

        var trainData = context.Data.LoadFromEnumerable(data);

        // Define training pipeline
        var pipeline =
        context.Transforms.Concatenate("Features", new[] {
        "Size" })
            .Append(context.Regression.Trainers.Sdca(labelColumnName:
            "Price", maximumNumberOfIterations: 100));

        // Train the model
        var model = pipeline.Fit(trainData);

        // Predict
        var size = new HouseData { Size = 4.0F };
        var sizePrediction =
```

PERFORMANCE TESTING AND BENCHMARKING

```
        context.Data.LoadFromEnumerable(new[] { size });
        var predictionResult = context.Data.Predict(model,
        sizePrediction);

        Console.WriteLine($"Predicted price for size {size.Size}
        is {predictionResult.Price}");
    }
}
```

Explanation:

- In this example, we define a simple dataset representing house sizes and their corresponding prices.
- We create a pipeline that concatenates features, applies a regression trainer, and trains the model on the data.
- Finally, we use the model to predict the price of a house based on its size.

Using NumSharp for Numerical Computations

NumSharp can be used to perform various numerical computations, including linear algebra operations. In this example, we will demonstrate how to use NumSharp to work with multi-dimensional arrays.

Example Code: Basic Operations with NumSharp

```csharp
using System;
using NumSharp;

public class Program
{
    public static void Main(string[] args)
    {
        // Create a NumPy-like array
        var array1 = np.array(new double[,] { { 1, 2 }, { 3, 4 }
```

```
        });
        var array2 = np.array(new double[,] { { 5, 6 }, { 7, 8 }
        });

        // Element-wise addition
        var resultAdd = array1 + array2;
        Console.WriteLine("Element-wise addition:\n" +
        resultAdd);

        // Matrix multiplication
        var resultMul = np.dot(array1, array2);
        Console.WriteLine("Matrix multiplication:\n" +
        resultMul);

        // Transpose of an array
        var resultTranspose = np.transpose(array1);
        Console.WriteLine("Transpose:\n" + resultTranspose);
    }
}
```

Explanation:

- This example demonstrates how to create and manipulate multidimensional arrays using NumSharp.
- We perform element-wise addition, matrix multiplication, and transposition, showcasing NumSharp's capabilities for numerical computing.

5. Best Practices for Using ML.NET and NumSharp

To maximize the effectiveness of ML.NET and NumSharp in your data analytics projects, consider the following best practices:

- **Understand the Data:** Always conduct exploratory data analysis (EDA) before modeling to understand data distributions, correlations, and outliers.
- **Use Appropriate Algorithms:** Choose algorithms that best fit the nature of your data and the problem you are trying to solve. ML.NET provides a

variety of algorithms for different tasks.
- **Optimize Data Preprocessing:** Efficiently preprocess your data using ML.NET's data transformation capabilities to improve model performance.
- **Leverage NumSharp for Efficient Calculations:** Use NumSharp for handling complex numerical computations, especially when working with large datasets or requiring advanced mathematical functions.

Leveraging ML.NET and NumSharp for numerical computing in high-performance data analytics allows developers to build powerful applications that can process and analyze large volumes of data effectively. By using ML.NET for machine learning tasks and NumSharp for numerical computations, developers can take full advantage of the .NET ecosystem's capabilities.

This chapter has introduced the essential features of ML.NET and NumSharp, provided practical code examples, and outlined best practices for their effective use. As you embark on your high-performance data analytics journey, these tools will be invaluable in extracting insights and delivering value from your data.

Case Study: Data-Intensive Application in C#

Overview

In the world of data analytics, the ability to process and analyze vast amounts of data efficiently is crucial. This case study examines a data-intensive application developed in C# that analyzes large datasets to provide business insights for an e-commerce platform. The application leverages ML.NET for predictive analytics, NumSharp for numerical computations, and SQL Server for data storage, demonstrating how these technologies can be integrated to create a high-performance data analytics solution.

Business Context

The e-commerce platform faced challenges related to sales forecasting and customer behavior analysis. With growing customer data, the business needed an efficient way to predict sales trends, understand customer purchasing patterns, and optimize inventory management. To address these needs, the development team set out to create a data-intensive application capable of performing real-time analytics on historical and live data.

Key Challenges

1. **Handling Large Datasets:** The application needed to process millions of rows of historical sales data, customer transactions, and product information efficiently.
2. **Real-Time Analytics:** The business required real-time insights to respond quickly to market changes, requiring the application to analyze live data streams.
3. **Predictive Modeling:** Developing accurate sales forecasts and customer behavior predictions required sophisticated machine learning models trained on historical data.
4. **Performance Optimization:** The application had to maintain responsiveness even during peak loads, which could involve high transaction volumes and complex analytical queries.

Solution Implementation

The development team implemented the application using a combination of technologies and methodologies, focusing on performance and scalability.

1. **Data Architecture:**

- **Data Storage:** SQL Server was chosen for data storage, leveraging its capabilities for handling large datasets and performing complex queries. The data model included tables for sales transactions, product details, and customer profiles.
- **Data Ingestion:** A robust ETL (Extract, Transform, Load) process was

implemented to ingest historical data from various sources, including CSV files and third-party APIs, into the SQL Server database. This process involved data cleaning and transformation to ensure data quality.

2. Data Processing and Analysis:

- **ML.NET for Predictive Analytics:** The team used ML.NET to build predictive models for sales forecasting. The application utilized regression algorithms to predict future sales based on historical data.
- **Example Code: Sales Prediction Model**

```csharp
using Microsoft.ML;
using Microsoft.ML.Data;

public class SalesData
{
    public float PreviousSales { get; set; }
    public float Price { get; set; }
    public float PredictedSales { get; set; }
}

public class Program
{
    public static void Main(string[] args)
    {
        var context = new MLContext();
        // Load data from SQL Server
        IDataView dataView =
        context.Data.LoadFromSqlServer("YourConnectionString",
        "SELECT PreviousSales, Price, PredictedSales FROM SalesData");

        var pipeline =
```

```
            context.Transforms.Concatenate("Features",
        "PreviousSales", "Price")
            .Append(context.Regression.Trainers.Sdca(labelColumnName:
            "PredictedSales", maximumNumberOfIterations: 100));

            // Train the model
            var model = pipeline.Fit(dataView);
        }
    }
```

- **NumSharp for Numerical Computing:** NumSharp was employed for numerical computations and data manipulation. This allowed the team to perform complex mathematical operations on sales data efficiently.
- **Example Code: Using NumSharp for Data Transformation**

```csharp
using NumSharp;

public void AnalyzeSalesData(NDArray salesData)
{
    var averageSales = np.mean(salesData);
    var stdDeviation = np.std(salesData);
    Console.WriteLine($"Average Sales: {averageSales}, Standard
    Deviation: {stdDeviation}");
}
```

3. **Real-Time Analytics:**

- **SignalR for Real-Time Updates:** To provide real-time insights, the application used SignalR for live data streaming. This allowed the business team to receive instant notifications about sales trends and inventory changes.
- **Asynchronous Data Processing:** The application implemented asyn-

chronous programming patterns to ensure that data processing and analysis did not block user interactions or other critical operations.

4. Performance Optimization:

- **Caching Strategies:** The team utilized in-memory caching for frequently accessed data, significantly reducing database query times and improving response rates for analytical queries.
- **Batch Processing for ETL:** The ETL process was optimized to handle large volumes of data in batches, reducing the load on the SQL Server and improving data ingestion speed.

Results

The implementation of the data-intensive application yielded significant benefits for the e-commerce platform:

- **Improved Sales Forecasting:** The predictive models built with ML.NET provided accurate sales forecasts, enabling the business to make informed decisions about inventory management and marketing strategies.
- **Real-Time Insights:** The integration of SignalR allowed the business team to respond quickly to changing market conditions, enhancing agility and competitiveness.
- **Increased Efficiency:** Performance optimizations, including caching and batch processing, resulted in faster data processing times and improved application responsiveness, even during peak transaction periods.
- **Enhanced Decision-Making:** The analytical capabilities of the application empowered decision-makers with actionable insights, leading to better strategic planning and increased revenue.

This case study illustrates how a data-intensive application in C# can leverage ML.NET and NumSharp to deliver high-performance data analytics solutions. By addressing key challenges such as large dataset handling, real-time analytics, and predictive modeling, the development team successfully built a robust application that significantly improved the e-commerce platform's operational efficiency and decision-making capabilities.

As organizations continue to grapple with the increasing volume and complexity of data, the integration of advanced technologies and methodologies will be crucial in developing effective data analytics solutions. This case study serves as a valuable example for developers seeking to implement high-performance data analytics in their own applications.

High-Performance Data Analytics with .NET

Introduction to High-Performance Data Analytics

Data analytics has become a cornerstone of business intelligence, scientific research, and decision-making, enabling organizations to uncover valuable insights, predict trends, and make data-driven decisions. High-performance data analytics (HPDA) takes this a step further by processing large, complex datasets at speed and scale, leveraging the power of advanced computing technologies to analyze data in real-time or near real-time. With .NET 8, high-performance data analytics becomes not only accessible but also highly efficient, thanks to its support for parallel processing, advanced data handling capabilities, and seamless integration with GPU acceleration and cloud computing.

In this chapter, we'll explore the core principles of high-performance data analytics, examining how .NET 8 can handle the challenges of big data with optimized memory management, parallelism, and real-time processing capabilities. Understanding these foundational concepts prepares you to build, deploy, and manage analytics solutions that can drive insights and value at the speed demanded by today's data-intensive environments.

Why High-Performance Data Analytics?

In a world where data volume, variety, and velocity are constantly increasing, traditional data analytics methods are often inadequate for processing and analyzing vast datasets. The term "high-performance data analytics" refers to the application of HPC (high-performance computing) principles to data analytics. This includes:

- **Handling Large Datasets Efficiently**: Modern datasets often reach terabyte and petabyte scales. Processing this volume of data requires efficient memory usage and data structures optimized for high throughput.
- **Accelerating Complex Calculations**: Analytical tasks like statistical modeling, machine learning, and simulations involve complex calculations that demand substantial computational power.
- **Enabling Real-Time or Near-Real-Time Analysis**: In industries such as finance, healthcare, and IoT, the ability to process and analyze data as it arrives is crucial for immediate decision-making and predictive analytics.
- **Supporting Scalability**: HPDA systems must scale seamlessly with growing datasets and demand, whether through multi-core CPUs, GPUs, or distributed computing across cloud infrastructures.

These characteristics make high-performance data analytics a critical component for data-driven organizations looking to stay competitive.

Key Components of High-Performance Data Analytics

To achieve high-performance data analytics with .NET 8, it's essential to understand the core components that make HPDA effective:

Data Ingestion and Preprocessing

- Efficient data ingestion allows you to collect and manage data from diverse sources, such as relational databases, IoT devices, APIs, and streaming platforms.
- Preprocessing—transforming raw data into a structured, usable format—is critical for data consistency and accuracy. It includes cleaning, filtering, aggregating, and transforming data before analysis begins.
- Tools like Apache Kafka, Azure Event Hubs, and .NET's built-in libraries for streaming data processing can handle high-velocity data ingestion, enabling seamless integration with .NET-based analytics systems.

Data Storage and Management

- High-performance data analytics requires robust storage solutions that can handle large-scale, high-throughput data access.
- .NET applications often integrate with databases optimized for big data, such as Azure Data Lake, Apache Cassandra, and Hadoop Distributed File System (HDFS).
- Efficient data management strategies ensure data is accessible, up-to-date, and prepared for analysis, whether through SQL-based querying, NoSQL solutions, or in-memory databases like Redis for low-latency access.

Parallel and Distributed Processing

- Large datasets and complex analytical tasks benefit from parallel and distributed processing, where computations are broken down and executed concurrently across multiple cores or nodes.
- .NET 8 supports parallelism through the Task Parallel Library (TPL) and Parallel LINQ (PLINQ), while distributed computing can be achieved using cloud solutions like Azure Batch or cluster orchestration with Kubernetes and Docker.
- These tools allow for efficient resource utilization, handling large

datasets and complex calculations faster and more efficiently.

Real-Time and Batch Processing

- Real-time processing is essential for applications requiring instantaneous analytics, such as fraud detection, predictive maintenance, and live monitoring. .NET 8's async programming and support for streaming frameworks like Dapr enable real-time data processing.
- Batch processing, on the other hand, allows for the aggregation and analysis of large data volumes in scheduled intervals, commonly used in applications like reporting and data warehousing.
- Balancing real-time and batch processing requirements is key to an efficient data analytics solution, particularly when working with hybrid data workloads.

Advanced Analytics and Machine Learning

- High-performance data analytics often involves advanced statistical modeling, machine learning, and deep learning to extract insights and build predictive models.
- With .NET's ML.NET and support for libraries like TensorFlow and OnnxRuntime, developers can implement powerful machine learning algorithms within their analytics pipeline.
- Integrating machine learning into .NET-based analytics enables capabilities like predictive modeling, anomaly detection, recommendation systems, and more.

Benefits of Using .NET 8 for High-Performance Data Analytics

.NET 8 brings unique strengths to high-performance data analytics, providing an optimized, scalable, and developer-friendly framework for handling the demands of big data.

1. **Cross-Platform Flexibility**: .NET 8 runs on Windows, Linux, and macOS, making it suitable for diverse deployment environments, including on-premises, cloud, and edge computing. This cross-platform capability is especially useful for large-scale, distributed analytics solutions.
2. **Enhanced Performance with Native AOT**: The new Native AOT (Ahead-of-Time compilation) in .NET 8 improves application startup time and reduces memory usage, which is beneficial for analytics applications that require high-speed data processing.
3. **Seamless Cloud Integration**: .NET 8 integrates well with Azure's cloud services, such as Azure Synapse Analytics, Azure Cosmos DB, and Azure Data Lake, enabling scalable data storage, processing, and analytics in the cloud. Additionally, integration with other cloud providers, like AWS and GCP, allows for flexibility in hybrid and multi-cloud deployments.
4. **Improved Memory Management**: .NET 8 offers improved garbage collection and memory allocation, allowing analytics applications to handle large datasets more efficiently. Features like Span<T> and Memory<T> help manage data in memory without additional allocations, reducing latency and improving throughput.
5. **Advanced Concurrency and Parallelism**: With support for Task Parallel Library (TPL), Parallel LINQ (PLINQ), and async programming, .NET 8 is designed to handle parallel workloads efficiently, making it ideal for high-performance data analytics.
6. **Interoperability with Machine Learning Frameworks**: .NET 8's compatibility with ML.NET, TensorFlow, and OnnxRuntime enables the use of pre-trained machine learning models within data analytics pipelines, adding predictive capabilities without requiring specialized ML infrastructure.

Use Cases of High-Performance Data Analytics

High-performance data analytics with .NET 8 can be applied across various industries, delivering value through enhanced insights and faster decision-making:

1. **Financial Services**: Real-time fraud detection, algorithmic trading, and risk management are all critical to the financial industry. By leveraging high-performance data analytics, .NET 8 enables the processing of transactional data at scale, allowing financial institutions to detect fraudulent activities instantly and manage risk proactively.
2. **Healthcare and Life Sciences**: In healthcare, rapid data processing can be used to analyze patient records, predict disease outbreaks, and improve diagnosis accuracy. High-performance data analytics with .NET can support genomics research, clinical trials, and personalized medicine, processing complex medical data to enhance healthcare outcomes.
3. **Manufacturing and IoT**: Manufacturing and IoT systems generate vast amounts of sensor data that need to be analyzed in real-time. High-performance data analytics allows companies to monitor equipment health, predict failures, and optimize processes, leading to reduced downtime and increased efficiency.
4. **Retail and E-commerce**: Retailers can use high-performance data analytics for recommendation engines, customer behavior analysis, and supply chain optimization. By analyzing transaction and browsing data, .NET-based analytics solutions help retailers understand customer preferences and optimize inventory management.
5. **Energy and Utilities**: In the energy sector, data analytics is used to predict energy demand, manage grid stability, and monitor renewable energy production. High-performance data analytics enables energy providers to analyze vast amounts of data from sensors and smart meters, helping balance supply and demand while optimizing energy distribution.

Best Practices for High-Performance Data Analytics with .NET 8

1. **Optimize Data Pipelines**: Design efficient data ingestion and transformation pipelines to ensure that data flows smoothly from source to analysis. Use data streaming frameworks like Kafka or Azure Event Hubs for high-velocity data, and employ data preprocessing steps to clean and structure data before analysis.
2. **Use Appropriate Storage Solutions**: Choose data storage solutions optimized for big data, such as Azure Data Lake or Cosmos DB, which allow scalable data access and support high-throughput analytics workloads.
3. **Implement Parallel Processing Strategically**: Apply parallelism to compute-intensive tasks, using PLINQ and TPL in .NET 8 to manage concurrent tasks effectively. For large-scale distributed processing, integrate with cloud-native services like Azure Batch or containerized microservices managed with Kubernetes.
4. **Balance Real-Time and Batch Analytics**: Some applications require real-time analytics, while others benefit from batch processing. Leverage .NET's async programming for real-time tasks and batch frameworks for periodic data processing to ensure efficiency.
5. **Monitor and Optimize Resource Usage**: Use profiling tools like BenchmarkDotNet, PerfView, and dotnet-counters to monitor CPU, memory, and I/O usage, optimizing resource utilization in analytics applications to avoid bottlenecks.

High-performance data analytics with .NET 8 provides a robust framework for processing large datasets, enabling real-time insights, and supporting complex machine learning models. By leveraging .NET 8's advanced parallelism, memory management, and cloud integration capabilities, developers can build analytics solutions that scale seamlessly and perform efficiently under high data loads. From financial services to healthcare, .NET

8 is a powerful tool for industries looking to harness the power of data at speed and scale. As you proceed through this chapter, you'll gain hands-on knowledge to design, develop, and deploy high-performance analytics applications that meet the demands of today's data-centric world.

Leveraging ML.NET and NumSharp for Numerical Computing

Numerical computing is at the heart of data analytics, machine learning, and scientific research, where complex mathematical computations are processed on large datasets to derive insights, make predictions, and drive informed decisions. With .NET 8, numerical computing is more accessible and efficient, thanks to powerful libraries like **ML.NET** and **NumSharp**. These libraries provide robust functionality for machine learning and numerical analysis, enabling developers to perform complex computations, manipulate multidimensional data, and build predictive models seamlessly within the .NET ecosystem.

This section explores how to leverage ML.NET for machine learning applications and NumSharp for efficient numerical operations, guiding you through their capabilities, best practices, and real-world applications in high-performance data analytics.

Introduction to ML.NET and NumSharp

ML.NET is an open-source, cross-platform machine learning framework for .NET, allowing developers to train, evaluate, and deploy machine learning models. It includes pre-built algorithms for common machine learning tasks like regression, classification, and clustering, and is designed to integrate seamlessly into .NET applications, making it ideal for both beginners and experienced data scientists.

NumSharp, on the other hand, is a numerical computing library modeled after Python's NumPy, a standard library in data science and machine learning. NumSharp provides multidimensional arrays, mathematical functions, and data manipulation capabilities that are essential for tasks such as linear algebra, statistical analysis, and data transformations.

Together, ML.NET and NumSharp enable .NET developers to build end-to-end data processing pipelines, from data cleaning and transformation to model training and inference, making them powerful tools in high-performance data analytics.

ML.NET for Machine Learning in Data Analytics

ML.NET provides a complete machine learning framework for training and deploying models directly in .NET applications, making it especially useful for high-performance data analytics scenarios that require built-in machine learning capabilities. Below are key features of ML.NET that make it an excellent choice for .NET developers working with data analytics:

1. **Pre-Defined Algorithms for Common ML Tasks**

ML.NET includes optimized algorithms for various machine learning tasks:

- **Regression**: For predicting continuous values, such as sales forecasting or demand prediction.
- **Classification**: Used to categorize data into discrete classes, ideal for tasks like fraud detection and image classification.
- **Clustering**: Groups data into clusters for segmentation or pattern recognition, useful in customer segmentation or anomaly detection.

ML.NET allows you to choose the algorithm that best fits the data and problem requirements, and its performance-optimized implementations help in handling large datasets efficiently.

2. **Automated Machine Learning (AutoML)**

AutoML automates the process of selecting and tuning machine learning models, significantly reducing the time needed for experimentation and improving model accuracy. With ML.NET AutoML, .NET 8 can quickly evaluate multiple algorithms and hyperparameters to find the best model, which is particularly valuable when handling large datasets with complex relationships.

Example: In a marketing analytics application, AutoML can test various models and parameters to predict customer churn, saving time and improving model accuracy.

3. **Data Transformation Capabilities**

ML.NET's Data Transformation API allows for data cleaning, feature engineering, and preprocessing, which are essential steps in any machine learning pipeline. These transformations include:

- **Normalization**: Standardizes data to improve algorithm performance.
- **Encoding Categorical Data**: Converts non-numeric data into a numeric format suitable for modeling.
- **Feature Engineering**: Creates new features that enhance model accuracy.

With these transformations, ML.NET enables you to preprocess data and prepare it for machine learning models efficiently, reducing the need for external data transformation tools.

4. **OnnxRuntime for Model Deployment**

ML.NET integrates with OnnxRuntime, which allows you to use pre-trained models in the ONNX (Open Neural Network Exchange) format. This enables .NET applications to load and execute models created in other frameworks, such as TensorFlow or PyTorch, maximizing flexibility and compatibility in machine learning workflows.

Example: A healthcare application could use OnnxRuntime to deploy a TensorFlow-trained model for disease prediction, providing fast and accurate inference directly in .NET.

NumSharp for High-Performance Numerical Computing

NumSharp enables high-performance numerical computing in .NET, offering functionality similar to NumPy in Python. With support for multidimensional arrays, matrix operations, and statistical functions, NumSharp is essential for numerical analysis and data preprocessing, making it ideal for high-performance data analytics.

1. Multidimensional Arrays

NumSharp's NDArray provides the foundation for manipulating multidimensional arrays, allowing for efficient handling of large datasets and complex data structures. These arrays support a variety of operations, including slicing, indexing, and reshaping, making it easy to perform array-based computations.

Example: In an IoT analytics application, an NDArray can represent sensor data over time and location, allowing for efficient manipulation and analysis of multivariate time series data.

2. Vectorized Mathematical Operations

NumSharp supports vectorized operations, which apply mathematical functions across entire arrays simultaneously, reducing computation time and improving performance. Key operations include:

- **Element-wise Calculations**: Perform operations across arrays without loops, e.g., adding two arrays or calculating exponential values.
- **Linear Algebra Functions**: NumSharp includes functions for matrix multiplication, determinants, and inverses, essential for data transformations and machine learning.

Example: A finance application might use NumSharp for fast matrix multiplications when performing portfolio optimizations, where vectorized operations reduce computation time significantly.

3. Statistical and Aggregation Functions

NumSharp provides statistical functions that make it easy to compute measures such as mean, median, variance, and standard deviation, which are crucial for data analytics. Aggregation functions allow you to calculate metrics across specific dimensions, enabling you to analyze large datasets effectively.

Example: In an e-commerce application, NumSharp could be used to calculate average transaction values, customer behavior metrics, and seasonal trends, helping businesses understand their performance.

4. **Interoperability with ML.NET**

NumSharp arrays can be used as input for ML.NET models, enabling a seamless integration between numerical computing and machine learning. By combining NumSharp's data manipulation capabilities with ML.NET's machine learning algorithms, you can build comprehensive data processing and analytics pipelines in .NET.

Building a High-Performance Data Analytics Pipeline with ML.NET and NumSharp

Using ML.NET and NumSharp together in .NET 8, you can create a high-performance data analytics pipeline that leverages both machine learning and numerical computing for efficient, large-scale data processing.

Step 1: Data Ingestion and Preprocessing with NumSharp

NumSharp's NDArray allows you to load data from sources like CSV files, databases, or APIs, and preprocess it for analysis. Use NumSharp to clean, normalize, and aggregate data, making it suitable for machine learning.

```csharp
using NumSharp;

// Load data into NumSharp NDArray
NDArray data = np.loadtxt("data.csv", delimiter: ",");

// Normalize data
data = (data - np.mean(data)) / np.std(data);
```

Step 2: Feature Engineering and Transformation in ML.NET

With the data prepared in NumSharp, pass it to ML.NET's Data Transformation API for feature engineering, such as encoding categorical variables or scaling features. This process ensures the data is optimized for machine learning.

```csharp
var pipeline =
mlContext.Transforms.Categorical.OneHotEncoding("Category")
    .Append(mlContext.Transforms.NormalizeMinMax("Features"));
```

Step 3: Model Training and Tuning with ML.NET

Use ML.NET to train a machine learning model on the preprocessed data. You can use ML.NET's AutoML to quickly find the best model for your dataset, or manually select and fine-tune an algorithm.

```csharp
var trainer = mlContext.Regression.Trainers.FastTree();
var model = trainer.Fit(dataView);
```

Step 4: Numerical Analysis with NumSharp

While the model is training, use NumSharp to analyze key performance metrics, such as error rates, and visualize the distribution of data. NumSharp's statistical functions enable you to track progress and validate model assumptions.

```csharp
var residuals = predictions - actual;
double rmse = np.sqrt(np.mean(np.square(residuals)));
```

Step 5: Model Deployment with ML.NET and OnnxRuntime

Deploy the trained model using ML.NET, or convert it to an ONNX format if necessary for cross-platform compatibility. Use OnnxRuntime in .NET for efficient inference, especially for large-scale or real-time applications.

Real-World Applications of ML.NET and NumSharp in Data Analytics

The combination of ML.NET and NumSharp provides a powerful framework for various high-performance data analytics applications across industries:

1. **Predictive Maintenance in Manufacturing**: Using ML.NET's classification algorithms, manufacturers can predict machine failure based on sensor data, and NumSharp enables real-time analysis of sensor readings to detect early warning signs.
2. **Risk Assessment in Finance**: Financial institutions can leverage ML.NET for risk prediction models, while NumSharp performs rapid portfolio risk analysis using matrix operations and statistical functions.
3. **Health Diagnostics and Prognostics**: ML.NET models trained on patient data can predict disease progression, and NumSharp allows for in-depth analysis of health metrics, trends, and anomalies, supporting real-time diagnostics.
4. **Customer Behavior Analysis in E-commerce**: ML.NET's clustering and classification capabilities allow retailers to segment customers based on purchase behavior, while NumSharp analyzes transaction data and generates business insights.

By combining ML.NET and NumSharp in .NET 8, developers gain a complete toolkit for high-performance data analytics, from data preprocessing and numerical computing to machine learning and deployment. ML.NET enables sophisticated machine learning workflows, while NumSharp provides the computational efficiency needed for large-scale data manipulation. Together, they empower developers to build advanced data analytics solutions that meet the demands of modern, data-driven environments. As you proceed with this chapter, you'll gain practical knowledge and hands-on experience in leveraging these libraries to create robust, scalable, and high-performance data analytics applications.

Case Study: Building a Data-Intensive Application in C# for Real-Time Analytics

This case study examines the process of building a data-intensive application in C# for real-time analytics, highlighting the challenges, solutions, and best practices that enable high-performance data processing. In this example, we'll explore the creation of a predictive maintenance system for a manufacturing company, which collects and analyzes real-time data from IoT sensors attached to equipment on the factory floor. This application processes massive volumes of sensor data, identifies anomalies, and predicts potential equipment failures to minimize downtime and improve operational efficiency.

Overview of the Predictive Maintenance Application

Goal: Develop a high-performance application in C# that can process and analyze real-time IoT sensor data to predict machinery failures, optimize maintenance schedules, and improve productivity on the factory floor.

Challenges:

1. **Data Volume**: The system must handle thousands of data points per second from numerous machines, each streaming real-time metrics like temperature, pressure, vibration, and operational status.
2. **Low-Latency Processing**: The application must analyze data with minimal delay to provide accurate, actionable insights in real-time.
3. **Scalability**: The system should be able to scale easily as new machines are added, and data volume increases.
4. **Reliability**: Downtime or missed data could lead to missed alerts or failures in prediction, impacting production schedules and costs.

Solution: By leveraging .NET 8's high-performance data processing capabilities, ML.NET for predictive modeling, and Azure's cloud infrastructure, the application achieves real-time analytics, providing reliable and scalable performance.

Step 1: Data Ingestion and Real-Time Processing

The application's first challenge is ingesting and processing a high volume of sensor data in real-time. To achieve low-latency data ingestion, we use **Azure Event Hubs** to collect data streams from IoT sensors and **Dapr** (Distributed Application Runtime) to manage inter-service communication.

Implementation:
Data Streams with Azure Event Hubs: Each IoT sensor sends data to an Azure Event Hub. This event streaming platform is capable of handling millions of events per second, allowing data to be reliably ingested at scale.

```csharp
var producerClient = new EventHubProducerClient(connectionString, eventHubName);
var dataBatch = await producerClient.CreateBatchAsync();

foreach (var sensorData in sensorDataList)
{
    var eventData = new EventData(Encoding.UTF8.GetBytes(JsonConvert.SerializeObject(sensorData)));
    dataBatch.TryAdd(eventData);
}

await producerClient.SendAsync(dataBatch);
```

Stream Processing with Dapr and .NET: Dapr acts as a sidecar to manage the communication between microservices, making it easy to build a distributed system. .NET reads and processes the data from Event Hubs in real-time, then passes it through a series of processing stages for cleaning, validation, and transformation.

```csharp
app.MapPost("/process-data", async (SensorData sensorData) =>
{
    // Preprocess and validate data
    await DataProcessor.Preprocess(sensorData);
});
```

Data Preprocessing with NumSharp: Before feeding the data into the predictive model, it is essential to preprocess and clean it. NumSharp is used for tasks like normalization and filling missing values.

```csharp
var data = np.array(sensorData.Values);
var normalizedData = (data - np.mean(data)) / np.std(data);
```

Step 2: Real-Time Anomaly Detection with ML.NET

To detect potential anomalies in the data that may indicate equipment issues, ML.NET's **anomaly detection algorithms** are deployed in real-time. The model detects outliers in metrics such as temperature or vibration, flagging them for further inspection.

Implementation:

Data Transformation: Sensor data is transformed and encoded into a feature set suitable for the ML model using ML.NET's data transformation capabilities.

```csharp
var pipeline = mlContext.Transforms.Concatenate("Features",
"Temperature", "Vibration", "Pressure")
    .Append(mlContext.Transforms.NormalizeMinMax("Features"))
    .Append(mlContext.Transforms.AnomalyDetection.Trainers.RandomizedPca
(featureColumnName: "Features"));
```

Model Training: Initially, historical data is used to train the model, allowing it to learn patterns and detect anomalies. This model is periodically retrained with new data to ensure accuracy.

```csharp
var trainingData =
mlContext.Data.LoadFromTextFile<EquipmentData>("historical_data.csv",
hasHeader: true);
var model = pipeline.Fit(trainingData);
```

Real-Time Prediction: For each data point ingested in real-time, the trained model identifies anomalies. If a threshold is exceeded, the system generates an alert for potential maintenance.

```csharp
var prediction = model.Transform(sensorDataView);
var anomalies =
mlContext.Data.CreateEnumerable<PredictionResult>(prediction,
reuseRowObject: false)
    .Where(p => p.PredictedLabel == true);
```

Step 3: Predictive Maintenance with OnnxRuntime for Fast Inference

The model is exported to **ONNX format** for optimized inference using OnnxRuntime, allowing for low-latency prediction within the .NET application. This setup helps detect early signs of failure, scheduling maintenance before issues escalate.

Implementation:
   Convert Model to ONNX Format: The ML.NET model is exported to ONNX for optimized inference.

```csharp
mlContext.Model.SaveAsOnnx(model, trainingData.Schema,
"predictive_maintenance_model.onnx");
```

Inference with OnnxRuntime: The ONNX model is loaded into the .NET application using OnnxRuntime, where it runs inference on live data in real-time. This minimizes processing delay, enabling near-instantaneous anomaly detection.

```csharp
using var session = new
InferenceSession("predictive_maintenance_model.onnx");
var inputs = new List<NamedOnnxValue>
{
    NamedOnnxValue.CreateFromTensor("input", dataTensor)
};

var results = session.Run(inputs);
```

Step 4: Scalability and Cloud Deployment with Kubernetes and Azure

To handle future growth in data volume, the application is deployed as a containerized microservices architecture on **Azure Kubernetes Service (AKS)**. Kubernetes provides automatic scaling, high availability, and load balancing, making it ideal for managing the application in production.

Implementation:

   Containerize Each Microservice: The data ingestion, processing, anomaly detection, and predictive maintenance components are each containerized using Docker.

```dockerfile
dockerfile

FROM mcr.microsoft.com/dotnet/aspnet:8.0 AS base
WORKDIR /app
COPY . .
ENTRYPOINT ["dotnet", "RealTimeAnalytics.dll"]
```

Kubernetes Deployment: Deploy the containers to Azure Kubernetes Service, using Horizontal Pod Autoscaler to manage scaling based on CPU and memory usage.

```yaml
yaml

apiVersion: apps/v1
kind: Deployment
metadata:
  name: predictive-maintenance
spec:
  replicas: 3
  template:
    spec:
      containers:
```

```
      - name: real-time-analytics
        image: real-time-analytics:latest
        resources:
          requests:
            cpu: "500m"
            memory: "512Mi"
```

Load Balancing and Autoscaling: AKS's autoscaler ensures that the application can dynamically respond to increases in data load, automatically scaling up resources during peak periods and scaling down when demand decreases.

Step 5: Monitoring and Logging with Azure Monitor

Real-time analytics require continuous monitoring to ensure data accuracy, system performance, and reliability. **Azure Monitor** is integrated to track metrics like CPU usage, memory consumption, data throughput, and anomaly detection frequency.

Implementation:

1. **Real-Time Metrics**: Azure Monitor collects metrics on data processing speed, latency, and system health, providing an overview of application performance.
2. **Alerts and Notifications**: Configure alerts to notify the team if processing latency exceeds a defined threshold or if data throughput spikes unexpectedly.
3. **Log Analytics**: Use Azure Log Analytics to store and analyze logs, helping identify trends, troubleshoot issues, and ensure the application is meeting performance targets.

Results and Benefits

The predictive maintenance system implemented in this case study provides substantial operational benefits to the manufacturing company:

- **Reduced Downtime**: By predicting equipment failures and scheduling maintenance proactively, the application minimizes unplanned downtime and improves productivity.
- **Improved Efficiency**: Real-time data processing and low-latency anomaly detection allow operators to address issues immediately, optimizing factory operations.
- **Scalability**: With Kubernetes and Azure Event Hubs, the application can handle increasing data volumes and expand with new machines or factory lines without major infrastructure changes.
- **Cost Savings**: By preventing failures and optimizing maintenance schedules, the company reduces repair costs and prolongs equipment lifespan.

This case study illustrates how a data-intensive, real-time analytics application can be built using C# and .NET 8, leveraging ML.NET for machine learning, NumSharp for numerical computing, and Azure services for scalability and reliability. By combining predictive maintenance with anomaly detection and cloud deployment, the application delivers high performance and resilience, ensuring that critical manufacturing operations remain optimized. This architecture can be adapted across industries wherever real-time data insights are critical, from industrial IoT to finance, healthcare, and beyond.

High-Performance Cross-Platform Development

Optimizing Applications for Windows, Linux, and macOS

As the demand for cross-platform applications grows, so does the need to optimize software to perform efficiently on multiple operating systems. .NET 8 makes cross-platform development accessible by offering a unified development experience for Windows, Linux, and macOS. However, optimizing applications for each platform involves understanding and addressing specific differences in system architecture, file handling, memory management, and security protocols. In this chapter, we'll cover strategies for creating high-performance .NET applications that run efficiently on all major operating systems.

Overview of Cross-Platform Development in .NET

.NET 8 provides the foundation for building cross-platform applications by compiling code to a common language runtime (CLR) that is compatible with Windows, Linux, and macOS. The .NET runtime abstracts many of the OS-level details, enabling developers to focus on shared application logic. However, certain platform-specific optimizations are required to maximize performance, minimize latency, and ensure that the application behaves consistently across different environments.

Key Areas for Platform Optimization

When optimizing cross-platform applications, focus on the following areas that differ significantly between Windows, Linux, and macOS:

1. **File System and Path Handling**
2. **Memory Management and Garbage Collection**
3. **Concurrency and Multithreading**
4. **Graphics and User Interface (UI) Optimization**
5. **Network and Security Configuration**

Each of these areas impacts application performance and may require platform-specific configurations to achieve the best results.

1. File System and Path Handling

Each operating system uses a unique file system, with differences in path syntax, case sensitivity, file permissions, and access methods. Proper handling of these distinctions can help avoid file errors, improve I/O performance, and prevent security issues.

Windows

- **File System**: Primarily NTFS, which supports a robust permissions model and case-insensitive paths by default.
- **Path Syntax**: Uses backslashes (\) for file paths.
- **File Permissions**: NTFS permissions allow for complex user and group-based access control lists (ACLs).

Linux

- **File System**: Ext4 is the most common, but other file systems (e.g., XFS, Btrfs) are also popular, each with its own performance characteristics.
- **Path Syntax**: Uses forward slashes (/) for file paths, case-sensitive.

- **File Permissions**: Uses POSIX permissions, with user, group, and other permission tiers.

macOS

- **File System**: APFS (Apple File System) is standard, optimized for SSDs and supports features like snapshots.
- **Path Syntax**: Uses forward slashes (/), generally case-insensitive but case-preserving.
- **File Permissions**: Similar to Linux, macOS uses POSIX permissions, with additional support for extended attributes.

Best Practices for File System Optimization

1. **Use Path.DirectorySeparatorChar and Path.Combine**: These .NET methods adapt to the correct directory separator for the platform, ensuring cross-platform compatibility.

```csharp
Copy code
string filePath = Path.Combine("folder", "file.txt");
```

1. **Normalize Path Case**: Since Linux treats file paths as case-sensitive, convert file paths to a standard case (lowercase or uppercase) to avoid issues when sharing paths between platforms.
2. **Optimize I/O Performance**: For large files, use FileStream with buffered reads and writes, and adjust buffer size based on platform. For example, larger buffers may benefit Linux systems.
3. **Handle File Permissions Carefully**: Use conditional code to apply Windows-specific ACLs or Linux/macOS POSIX permissions when accessing secure files.

2. Memory Management and Garbage Collection

Memory management in .NET is largely handled by the runtime, but differences in OS memory handling and garbage collection behavior can impact application performance.

Windows

- Windows has a predictable memory model with virtual memory management, making it suitable for applications with extensive memory needs.
- **Garbage Collection**: The .NET garbage collector performs similarly across platforms, but Windows tends to handle frequent memory allocations and deallocations more efficiently under heavy loads.

Linux

- **Memory Management**: Linux uses overcommit memory, meaning it allocates more memory than the physical RAM, which can lead to high memory usage before the system kills processes to free resources.
- **GC Optimization**: For high-performance applications, consider reducing the frequency of garbage collection or using Server GC mode for applications that handle large datasets.

macOS

- macOS uses a hybrid approach to memory management, with a focus on minimizing memory fragmentation. It's generally well-suited for applications that require balanced memory usage.
- **GC Configuration**: Similar to Linux, macOS benefits from Server GC mode in applications with high memory consumption.

Best Practices for Memory Management Optimization

1. **Use the Right Garbage Collection Mode**: For multi-threaded, high-memory applications, enable Server GC mode in the runtimeconfig.json file:

```json
{
    "runtimeOptions": {
        "configProperties": {
            "System.GC.Server": true
        }
    }
}
```

1. **Minimize Allocations in Hot Paths**: Use Span<T> and Memory<T> to handle data without frequent allocations, reducing the strain on garbage collection.
2. **Avoid Memory Leaks**: Pay special attention to unmanaged resources. Use using statements or IDisposable for resources like file handles, network connections, and database connections.
3. **Test and Profile**: Use profiling tools like dotnet-counters to track memory allocation and garbage collection frequency on each platform.

3. Concurrency and Multithreading

Concurrency is critical for high-performance applications, but each OS has a unique threading model, and managing threads efficiently is essential to avoid performance bottlenecks.
Windows

- Windows offers the Thread Pool API, which optimizes thread usage across applications, and supports efficient CPU-bound and I/O-bound parallelism.

- **Thread Priority**: Allows setting thread priorities, which can be used to optimize certain performance-critical threads.

Linux

- Linux's threading model is built on the POSIX standard, making it efficient for multi-threaded applications, though the OS is more restrictive with thread priorities.
- **Lightweight Threads**: Linux's support for lightweight processes (LWP) allows for efficient threading at scale, but it's essential to avoid excessive context switching.

macOS

- macOS provides the Grand Central Dispatch (GCD) framework, optimized for managing concurrency with minimal overhead.
- **Work Distribution**: GCD's managed thread pool dynamically balances workloads, making it ideal for I/O-bound tasks but limiting fine-grained control over thread priority.

Best Practices for Concurrency Optimization

1. **Use the Task Parallel Library (TPL)**: TPL manages threads across all platforms, balancing workloads efficiently while abstracting away OS-specific differences.

```csharp
var tasks = new List<Task>();
for (int i = 0; i < 10; i++)
{
    tasks.Add(Task.Run(() => DoWork()));
```

```
}
await Task.WhenAll(tasks);
```

1. **Avoid Thread-Heavy Workloads on Linux**: For Linux, use PLINQ or Parallel.For with workload partitions to minimize context switching.
2. **Optimize for Asynchronous I/O**: On all platforms, use async and await for I/O-bound operations to free up threads for other tasks and avoid blocking.

4. Graphics and User Interface (UI) Optimization

Graphics and UI libraries behave differently on Windows, Linux, and macOS. Ensuring a responsive and consistent UI experience requires understanding platform-specific differences.

Windows

- Windows UI libraries (WPF, WinForms) are optimized for Windows environments, allowing for advanced graphics acceleration and DirectX integration.
- **Rendering**: Leveraging hardware-accelerated rendering in WPF or using DirectX can improve performance for graphics-heavy applications.

Linux

- Linux relies on cross-platform UI frameworks like GTK and .NET MAUI for application interfaces.
- **Rendering Performance**: Linux generally has less optimized graphics support than Windows, so applications may benefit from reduced graphical complexity and off-screen rendering techniques.

macOS

- macOS uses the Metal graphics API for hardware-accelerated graphics, providing efficient rendering but requiring cross-platform frameworks like .NET MAUI for compatibility.
- **Consistent UI Styling**: macOS's design guidelines encourage native-looking UIs. With .NET MAUI, you can customize UI components to match macOS's aesthetics without sacrificing performance.

Best Practices for UI Optimization

1. **Use .NET MAUI for Cross-Platform UI**: .NET MAUI allows for native UIs on all platforms, making it easy to develop consistent UIs for Windows, Linux, and macOS.
2. **Leverage Hardware Acceleration**: Use hardware-accelerated graphics when possible, especially on Windows (DirectX) and macOS (Metal).
3. **Optimize Image Assets**: Reduce image sizes, compress files, and avoid heavy animations. Offload complex visualizations to web-based solutions if needed.

5. Network and Security Configuration

Networking and security features differ across operating systems. Ensuring compatibility and performance requires managing these differences, especially in network latency and authentication.

Windows

- Windows integrates well with Active Directory and supports a variety of enterprise security protocols.
- **Firewall Rules**: Windows has robust firewall rules, but these may require manual configuration for cross-platform network applications.

Linux

- Linux offers flexible firewall configuration with iptables, and strong support for SSL/TLS encryption. It's often the preferred platform for server-based applications due to its low overhead.

- **OpenSSL and Network Performance**: Linux systems with OpenSSL benefit from optimized encryption and low-latency network connections, ideal for high-throughput applications.

macOS

- macOS integrates with Apple's security features, including Keychain for credential storage.
- **Network Performance**: macOS network performance can be enhanced by tuning socket options and using efficient protocols for data transfer.

Best Practices for Network Optimization

1. **Use Secure Protocols**: Implement TLS for all network communications, and use platform-specific libraries (like OpenSSL on Linux) to optimize secure connections.
2. **Leverage Asynchronous Network I/O**: Use async methods to handle network requests, avoiding blocking calls that could reduce responsiveness.
3. **Optimize Socket Configuration**: For high-throughput applications, configure socket options like buffer size and keep-alive intervals to reduce latency and improve data transfer rates.

Optimizing applications for Windows, Linux, and macOS in .NET 8 involves understanding the differences in file systems, memory management, threading, UI rendering, and network configurations across these platforms. By leveraging .NET's cross-platform tools, adopting best practices for each OS, and testing thoroughly on each target platform, developers can build high-performance applications that deliver consistent results across all major operating systems. Following these guidelines will ensure your .NET application not only performs well but is also robust, secure, and capable of scaling effectively across diverse environments.

Leveraging .NET 6 Cross-Platform Capabilities

.NET 6 introduced major improvements in cross-platform development, further refined in .NET 8, empowering developers to build applications that run seamlessly on Windows, Linux, and macOS. These cross-platform capabilities are crucial for creating applications that need to scale and perform consistently across varied environments. By leveraging .NET's runtime, libraries, and development tools, developers can optimize for each platform's specific features without sacrificing the advantages of a unified codebase. This section dives into .NET 6's key cross-platform capabilities that form the foundation for high-performance applications today.

Key Cross-Platform Features in .NET 6

.NET 6 provides a single unified runtime, development experience, and comprehensive tooling that simplifies cross-platform development while ensuring high performance. The following features are particularly valuable for cross-platform application development:

1. **Unified Base Class Library (BCL)**
2. **Native Ahead-of-Time (AOT) Compilation**
3. **Cross-Platform UI with .NET MAUI**
4. **Native Interoperability and Platform Invocation (P/Invoke)**
5. **Enhanced Development and Debugging Tools**

1. Unified Base Class Library (BCL)

The **Base Class Library (BCL)** is a set of core libraries included in .NET that provides consistent functionality across all platforms. This unified BCL allows developers to write code once and deploy it on any supported operating system without modification, thanks to:

- **Standardized API Surface**: APIs for I/O, threading, collections, cryptography, and networking are standardized across platforms. This reduces platform-specific code, enabling faster development and easier maintenance.
- **Cross-Platform Data Access**: Libraries like System.Data provide consistent data access capabilities, allowing applications to interact with databases in a platform-independent way.
- **File System and Path Compatibility**: The BCL handles differences in file systems between Windows, Linux, and macOS, so developers can use common methods (like Path.Combine) to manipulate file paths without worrying about platform-specific path separators.

Example: With the BCL, you can write platform-agnostic code to perform file operations:

```csharp
string logPath = 
Path.Combine(Environment.GetFolderPath(Environment.SpecialFolder
.MyDocuments), "log.txt");
File.AppendAllText(logPath, "This is a cross-platform log 
entry.");
```

2. Native Ahead-of-Time (AOT) Compilation

Ahead-of-Time (AOT) compilation is an essential feature in .NET 6, providing native performance benefits across platforms by precompiling applications into native machine code. With AOT, applications experience:

- **Reduced Startup Times**: AOT compilation eliminates the need for runtime JIT (Just-In-Time) compilation, enabling faster application start times, especially on Linux and macOS.
- **Optimized Memory Usage**: By directly compiling code to machine language, AOT reduces memory overhead associated with JIT, making applications more efficient and responsive, particularly on resource-constrained environments.
- **Enhanced Portability**: AOT-compiled applications can be deployed to environments with minimal dependencies, making them ideal for containerized applications or edge devices.

Example: A .NET application using AOT compilation can be deployed as a single executable file on Linux, reducing setup requirements and improving startup performance. Configure AOT in your project's configuration:

```json
{
    "runtimeOptions": {
        "configProperties": {
            "System.Runtime.AOT": true
        }
    }
}
```

3. Cross-Platform UI with .NET MAUI

.NET MAUI (Multi-platform App UI) extends .NET's cross-platform capabilities by enabling developers to build native, high-performance UIs for Windows, macOS, iOS, and Android from a single codebase. With MAUI, developers gain:

- **Unified UI Framework**: MAUI provides a single UI stack that renders native controls on each platform, ensuring applications look and feel consistent while taking advantage of each OS's native UI elements.
- **Customizable UI Components**: MAUI includes customizable controls and layouts, enabling developers to create responsive and visually appealing applications for all screen sizes and form factors.
- **Code Reusability**: A single UI layer significantly reduces development time and maintenance complexity, allowing teams to focus on optimizing business logic rather than managing platform-specific UIs.

Example: With MAUI, you can define a cross-platform button that will render as a native button on Windows, macOS, Android, and iOS:

```xml
<Button Text="Click Me"
        Command="{Binding OnButtonClickCommand}"
        BackgroundColor="Blue"
        TextColor="White" />
```

4. Native Interoperability and Platform Invocation (P/Invoke)

Platform Invocation (P/Invoke) allows .NET applications to call native APIs, making it possible to integrate platform-specific functionality without compromising the cross-platform capabilities of the main application. This is especially useful for:

- **Accessing OS-Level APIs**: P/Invoke provides direct access to OS features, such as Windows' registry, Linux's POSIX functions, or macOS-specific APIs, enhancing functionality based on the host environment.
- **Native Performance Libraries**: Integrating with native libraries like OpenSSL, TensorFlow, or CUDA via P/Invoke enables high-performance computing and specialized processing in areas like encryption, machine learning, and GPU acceleration.
- **Device-Specific Functions**: Applications can use P/Invoke to access device-specific hardware like sensors, cameras, or biometric readers, which are essential for applications with platform-dependent functionality.

Example: Here's how to use P/Invoke to call a Windows-specific MessageBox function:

```csharp
using System.Runtime.InteropServices;

class Program
{
    [DllImport("user32.dll", CharSet = CharSet.Unicode)]
    public static extern int MessageBox(IntPtr hWnd, string text, string caption, uint type);

    static void Main()
    {
        if (RuntimeInformation.IsOSPlatform(OSPlatform.Windows))
        {
            MessageBox(IntPtr.Zero, "Hello, Windows!",
            "Message", 0);
        }
    }
}
```

5. Enhanced Development and Debugging Tools

.NET 6 enhances the development experience for cross-platform applications with powerful tools for building, testing, debugging, and deploying code on all platforms. Key tools include:

- **Cross-Platform Command-Line Interface (CLI)**: The .NET CLI provides consistent command-line operations for building, running, and managing projects, making it easy to develop and automate workflows on any operating system.
- **dotnet-diagnostics and dotnet-counters**: These profiling tools provide insights into CPU, memory, and network performance, allowing developers to optimize applications across platforms.
- **Containerization with Docker**: .NET 6 supports containerization through Docker, enabling developers to package and deploy applications with consistent dependencies. Docker images are available for all supported platforms, simplifying deployment in cloud or hybrid environments.

Example: Use the .NET CLI to create, build, and publish an application from the command line, ensuring consistency across environments:

```bash
dotnet new console -o CrossPlatformApp
dotnet build
dotnet publish -r linux-x64 --self-contained
```

Practical Tips for Cross-Platform Optimization in .NET 6

To leverage .NET 6's cross-platform capabilities effectively, keep the following optimization practices in mind:

1. **Test on Target Platforms**: Ensure you regularly test the application on each target OS to identify platform-specific issues early. Testing environments like Docker can simulate different OS environments locally.
2. **Use Conditional Compilation**: .NET supports conditional compilation with #if directives, allowing developers to write platform-specific code without disrupting cross-platform compatibility.

```csharp
#if WINDOWS
    // Windows-specific code
#elif LINUX
    // Linux-specific code
#endif
```

1. **Optimize File I/O Across Platforms**: Use Span<T> and Memory<T> for high-performance I/O operations, and rely on FileStream buffering and asynchronous methods to reduce latency.
2. **Implement Platform-Agnostic Logging**: Logging solutions like Serilog, which supports multiple sinks, can provide consistent logging across platforms. This makes it easy to capture performance and error logs regardless of the host OS.
3. **Monitor and Tune for Platform-Specific GC Performance**: Memory management behaviors vary between OSs. For resource-intensive applications, use Server GC mode and monitor garbage collection frequency with dotnet-counters.
4. **Take Advantage of Native Containers**: For Linux and cloud-based deployments, package applications in Docker containers with platform-specific optimizations. This reduces dependencies, minimizes configuration complexity, and ensures consistent performance.

Example: Cross-Platform Data Processing Application

To illustrate .NET 6's cross-platform capabilities, consider a data processing application that retrieves data from various APIs, processes it, and stores results in a database. The application must run efficiently on Windows, Linux, and macOS while leveraging platform-specific optimizations.

Data Retrieval and Processing:

- Use HttpClient with asynchronous requests for cross-platform HTTP data retrieval.
- Perform heavy data transformations using Parallel.ForEach to process data in parallel.

Data Storage:

- Use SQLite for lightweight cross-platform storage or PostgreSQL for cloud-ready data persistence.
- Abstract the database access layer so it can connect to different databases based on platform or deployment environment.

Platform-Specific Configurations:

- Enable Server GC on Linux and macOS to optimize memory usage for large data processing tasks.
- For Windows, use P/Invoke to call Windows API functions to access registry data if needed for application configuration.

Containerized Deployment:

- Package the application in a Docker container with platform-specific optimizations. For example, use an Alpine Linux base image for a lightweight deployment on Linux environments.

.NET 6's cross-platform capabilities empower developers to create high-performance applications that run seamlessly on Windows, Linux, and macOS. By leveraging a unified BCL, AOT compilation, .NET MAUI for UI, and platform invocation for native access, .NET enables developers to build applications with a consistent codebase that performs optimally across different operating systems. Implementing best practices for cross-platform testing, memory management, and platform-specific configurations further enhances application performance, ensuring that .NET applications meet the demands of today's diverse and distributed environments.

Best Practices and Code Snippets for Cross-Platform Optimization

Optimizing cross-platform applications in .NET involves balancing performance with portability, writing efficient code that can adapt to the nuances of Windows, Linux, and macOS. Here are best practices and code snippets to guide developers in creating high-performance .NET applications optimized for each platform.

1. Use Platform-Specific Compilation

Certain features or APIs are platform-dependent, and using **conditional compilation** with #if directives allows for platform-specific code execution without impacting the rest of the application. This technique enables developers to optimize portions of code for each OS while maintaining a single codebase.

Example: Using platform-specific features to display a message box on Windows and an alternative output on other OSes.

```csharp
#if WINDOWS
    using System.Runtime.InteropServices;

    [DllImport("user32.dll", CharSet = CharSet.Unicode)]
    public static extern int MessageBox(IntPtr hWnd, string
    text, string caption, uint type);

    MessageBox(IntPtr.Zero, "Hello from Windows!", "Message", 0);
#elif LINUX
    Console.WriteLine("Hello from Linux!");
#elif OSX
    Console.WriteLine("Hello from macOS!");
#endif
```

Best Practice: Keep platform-specific code segments small and isolated. Use wrapper methods to abstract platform-specific logic, making the code easier to maintain.

2. Optimize File I/O Across Platforms

File handling differs across operating systems due to file path conventions, permissions, and performance characteristics. Use .NET's **Path class** to manage file paths and **buffered file operations** for optimized I/O across platforms.

Example: Combining platform-agnostic file path creation with buffered file writing.

```csharp
string filePath =
Path.Combine(Environment.GetFolderPath(Environment.SpecialFolder
.MyDocuments), "output.txt");

using (FileStream fs = new FileStream(filePath, FileMode.Create,
```

```
FileAccess.Write, FileShare.None, 4096, true))
using (StreamWriter writer = new StreamWriter(fs))
{
    writer.WriteLine("This is a cross-platform file operation.");
}
```

Best Practice: For large files or frequent access, adjust buffer sizes based on platform and test performance. Linux may benefit from larger buffers due to its filesystem caching behavior, whereas smaller buffers may work better on macOS.

3. *Efficient Memory Management*

Cross-platform applications can experience different memory management characteristics depending on the OS. .NET's **Server GC** (Garbage Collection) is optimized for high-load, multi-threaded applications and can improve memory efficiency on Linux and macOS.

Example: Enabling Server GC in runtimeconfig.json for improved memory handling.

```json
{
    "runtimeOptions": {
        "configProperties": {
            "System.GC.Server": true
        }
    }
}
```

Best Practice: Use Span<T> and Memory<T> for stack-allocated memory to avoid unnecessary heap allocations, reducing garbage collection overhead.

Example: Stack-allocating memory using Span<T> for better performance.

```csharp
Span<int> numbers = stackalloc int[5] { 1, 2, 3, 4, 5 };
foreach (var number in numbers)
{
    Console.WriteLine(number);
}
```

4. Use Asynchronous Programming for I/O-Bound Tasks

Asynchronous programming is critical for maximizing responsiveness, especially in cross-platform applications where I/O-bound tasks (like file or network operations) may have varying performance. Using async and await helps avoid blocking calls, freeing threads to handle other tasks.

Example: Performing asynchronous file reading and network requests.

```csharp
public async Task<string> ReadFileAsync(string filePath)
{
    using var reader = new StreamReader(filePath);
    return await reader.ReadToEndAsync();
}

public async Task<string> FetchDataAsync(string url)
{
    using var httpClient = new HttpClient();
    return await httpClient.GetStringAsync(url);
}
```

Best Practice: Profile the application to identify where asynchronous code can be most effective. For applications with high concurrency, consider configuring the thread pool size for optimal performance on each platform.

5. Implement Logging with Platform-Agnostic Libraries

Logging plays a crucial role in cross-platform development by allowing developers to monitor application behavior and troubleshoot issues across different OS environments. Use a logging framework like **Serilog** that supports multiple sinks and works consistently across platforms.

Example: Setting up Serilog for cross-platform logging.

```csharp
using Serilog;

Log.Logger = new LoggerConfiguration()
    .WriteTo.Console()
    .WriteTo.File("logs/log.txt", rollingInterval:
    RollingInterval.Day)
    .CreateLogger();

Log.Information("Application started on {Platform}",
Environment.OSVersion);
```

Best Practice: Configure different log sinks depending on the platform. For example, log to the Event Viewer on Windows and syslog on Linux.

6. Use Docker for Consistent Cross-Platform Environments

Containerizing applications with **Docker** provides a consistent runtime environment across platforms, minimizing platform-specific discrepancies. Docker images for .NET are available for each OS, and using platform-specific optimizations (like Alpine for Linux) can improve performance.

Example: Creating a Dockerfile for a .NET application with platform-optimized configuration.

```dockerfile
dockerfile

# Use Alpine Linux for a lightweight Linux deployment
FROM mcr.microsoft.com/dotnet/aspnet:8.0-alpine AS runtime
WORKDIR /app
COPY ./publish/ .

ENTRYPOINT ["dotnet", "MyApp.dll"]
```

Best Practice: Test Docker containers on all target platforms to ensure compatibility. Use multi-stage builds to optimize the image size, and apply platform-specific configurations when running on different operating systems.

7. Handle Platform-Specific UI with .NET MAUI

When building cross-platform UIs with .NET MAUI, take advantage of platform-specific styling and behaviors to create a more native look and feel. With MAUI, you can define platform-specific properties in XAML or C# for UI elements that need custom behavior on each OS.

Example: Defining platform-specific properties in .NET MAUI for a responsive button.

```xml
xml

<Button Text="Click Me"
        BackgroundColor="Blue"
        TextColor="White">
    <Button.FontSize>
        <OnPlatform x:TypeArguments="x:Double">
            <On Platform="iOS" Value="20"/>
            <On Platform="Android" Value="18"/>
            <On Platform="WinUI" Value="16"/>
        </OnPlatform>
    </Button.FontSize>
</Button>
```

Best Practice: Use platform-specific effects and custom renderers in MAUI for enhanced performance on each OS. Test UIs on target devices to ensure that controls render correctly and perform well.

8. Network Configuration and Security Optimization

Network performance and security requirements vary by platform, so configuring appropriate settings is essential for reliable, secure communication across OSs. Use **TLS** for encrypted communications and **async network calls** to avoid blocking.

   Example: Configuring HttpClient for secure, platform-optimized network calls.

```csharp
using var handler = new HttpClientHandler
{
    ServerCertificateCustomValidationCallback =
    HttpClientHandler.DangerousAcceptAnyServerCertificateValidator,
};

using var client = new HttpClient(handler);
client.DefaultRequestHeaders.Add("User-Agent",
"CrossPlatformApp/1.0");
var response = await
client.GetAsync("https://api.example.com/data");
```

Best Practice: Adjust buffer sizes and keep-alive settings for network sockets based on platform characteristics. Windows may require more aggressive keep-alive intervals, while Linux benefits from optimized buffer settings.

9. Monitor Performance Across Platforms

Use **dotnet-counters** and **dotnet-trace** for real-time monitoring and diagnostics across platforms. These tools provide insights into CPU, memory, garbage collection, and other metrics that can help pinpoint performance issues unique to each OS.

Example: Running dotnet-counters to monitor CPU and memory usage on Linux.

```bash
dotnet-counters monitor --process-id <PID> System.Runtime
```

Best Practice: Profile the application on each target platform. Resource usage and garbage collection may vary, so tune based on the insights gathered from these monitoring tools.

10. Use Ahead-of-Time (AOT) Compilation for Faster Startup

Ahead-of-Time (AOT) compilation is valuable for reducing startup times and improving performance, especially on Linux and macOS. It precompiles the application to native code, removing the need for Just-In-Time (JIT) compilation at runtime.

Example: Enabling AOT compilation in a project file for a console application.

```xml
<PropertyGroup>
    <PublishAot>true</PublishAot>
</PropertyGroup>
```

Best Practice: Test the application with AOT on each platform to ensure compatibility and measure startup improvements. Use AOT selectively for performance-critical applications or specific environments where startup time is essential.

By following these best practices and leveraging .NET's cross-platform capabilities, developers can build high-performance applications optimized for Windows, Linux, and macOS. From platform-specific compilation and file I/O optimization to asynchronous programming and Docker containerization, these techniques ensure that applications run smoothly and consistently across diverse environments. .NET's cross-platform tools and frameworks, like .NET MAUI, AOT, and P/Invoke, provide the flexibility needed to create adaptable, performant applications that meet the demands of today's multi-platform world.

Future-Proofing High-Performance Applications

Preparing for Future .NET Releases: Future-Proofing High-Performance Applications

As the software landscape continues to evolve, organizations must prepare for future advancements in technology and frameworks. For developers working with .NET, understanding how to future-proof high-performance applications is essential to ensure longevity, maintainability, and scalability. This chapter explores strategies for preparing for future .NET releases, including best practices for adopting new features, maintaining code quality, and adapting to changes in the ecosystem.

1. Understanding the .NET Ecosystem

.NET has undergone significant transformations over the years, transitioning from the .NET Framework to .NET Core and now to .NET 6 and beyond. The unified platform aims to streamline the development experience and enhance cross-platform capabilities. Future versions of .NET will likely continue to introduce improvements, new features, and performance enhancements.

Key Considerations:

- **Regular Updates:** .NET follows a regular release schedule, with new

major versions typically released every November. This provides a predictable timeline for developers to plan upgrades and feature adoption.
- **Backward Compatibility:** Microsoft strives for backward compatibility with new releases, but developers must remain vigilant about deprecated features and breaking changes that could impact existing applications.

2. Staying Informed About .NET Developments

To effectively prepare for future releases, developers must stay informed about changes in the .NET ecosystem. This can be achieved through:

- **Official Documentation:** Regularly consult the official .NET documentation and release notes to understand new features, enhancements, and migration paths.
- **Community Engagement:** Participate in developer forums, attend conferences, and follow influential figures in the .NET community to stay up-to-date with best practices and emerging trends.
- **Preview Versions:** Experiment with preview versions of upcoming .NET releases to test new features and understand their implications for your applications.

3. Best Practices for Future-Proofing Applications
Modular and Clean Code Architecture

Best Practice: Adopt a modular architecture that separates concerns and promotes code reusability. Use design patterns such as MVVM (Model-View-ViewModel) or MVC (Model-View-Controller) to enhance maintainability.

- **Use Dependency Injection:** Leverage dependency injection (DI) to decouple components, making it easier to replace or upgrade parts of the application as new features are introduced in future .NET releases.

Code Snippet: Implementing Dependency Injection in .NET 6

```csharp
public class Startup
{
    public void ConfigureServices(IServiceCollection services)
    {
        services.AddScoped<IProductService, ProductService>();
    }
}
```

Embrace New Language Features

Best Practice: Stay updated with new C# language features introduced in each .NET release. Language enhancements often provide better performance, clearer syntax, and more robust capabilities.

- **Utilize Record Types and Pattern Matching:** Adopt new syntax features like records for immutable data and enhanced pattern matching for cleaner code.

Code Snippet: Using Record Types

```csharp
public record Product(string Name, decimal Price);
```

Optimize for Performance

Best Practice: Regularly review and optimize your application's performance, keeping in mind that future releases of .NET may introduce changes that can impact performance.

- **Profile Your Applications:** Utilize profiling tools to identify bottlenecks and areas for optimization. This helps ensure that your application performs well with each new .NET release.

Code Snippet: Profiling Example

```csharp
public void RunProfiler()
{
    // Example: Use a profiler to measure performance
    // Implement profiling logic here using tools like
    BenchmarkDotNet or Visual Studio Profiler
}
```

Implement Automated Testing

Best Practice: Develop a comprehensive suite of automated tests to ensure that your application behaves as expected across different .NET versions.

- **Unit Tests and Integration Tests:** Write unit tests for individual components and integration tests for overall functionality. Continuous integration (CI) should be configured to run these tests automatically.

Code Snippet: Example of a Simple Unit Test

```csharp
using Xunit;

public class ProductServiceTests
{
    [Fact]
    public void GetAllProducts_ShouldReturnProducts()
    {
        var service = new ProductService();
        var products = service.GetAllProducts();
        Assert.NotEmpty(products);
    }
}
```

4. Planning for Migration

When preparing for a future .NET release, consider the migration strategies necessary to transition smoothly:

- **Evaluate Breaking Changes:** Review release notes for breaking changes that could affect your application. Assess how these changes will impact your codebase and plan for necessary modifications.
- **Use .NET Upgrade Assistant:** Microsoft provides tools like the .NET Upgrade Assistant to simplify the migration process. This tool can help automate parts of the migration and identify areas that require attention.
- **Test Extensively After Migration:** After upgrading to a new version of .NET, conduct thorough testing to ensure that the application functions correctly and that performance is not adversely affected.

5. Building for the Future

Beyond simply preparing for new releases, consider future trends and technologies that may impact your applications:

- **Cloud-Native Development:** Embrace cloud-native architectures that allow for scalability and resilience. This includes leveraging services like Azure Functions or AWS Lambda for serverless computing.
- **Containerization:** As applications grow in complexity, containerization will continue to play a vital role in deployment and scalability. Utilize Docker and Kubernetes to manage containerized applications effectively.
- **Machine Learning and AI:** Incorporate machine learning and AI capabilities into your applications using frameworks like ML.NET to stay ahead of the competition.

Preparing for future .NET releases is essential for maintaining high-performance applications. By adopting best practices such as modular design, leveraging new language features, optimizing performance, and implementing automated testing, developers can ensure their applications remain robust and efficient.

Staying informed about developments in the .NET ecosystem and planning for migration will further enable developers to navigate changes confidently. By building applications with future-proofing in mind, organizations can adapt to evolving technology landscapes and continue to deliver value to their users.

Insights on Upcoming Features and .NET Roadmap

As technology evolves, so does the .NET ecosystem, continuously enhancing its features to meet modern development needs. Understanding the upcoming features and the .NET roadmap is crucial for developers looking to future-proof their applications and leverage new capabilities effectively. This section provides insights into what to expect in upcoming releases, key features in development, and the overall direction of .NET.

1. Understanding the .NET Roadmap

Microsoft maintains a transparent roadmap for .NET, detailing planned features, enhancements, and release schedules. This roadmap helps developers anticipate changes and prepare for new capabilities.

- **Release Schedule:** .NET follows a predictable release cadence, with major updates typically released annually in November, alongside previews and minor updates throughout the year.
- **Long-Term Support (LTS):** Certain releases are designated as Long-Term Support (LTS), providing a stable foundation for applications that require reliability and extended support. The LTS versions receive updates for three years after their release.

2. Upcoming Features in .NET

With each new version, .NET introduces features aimed at improving developer productivity, performance, and functionality. Here are some anticipated features and improvements:

2.1. Enhanced Performance Improvements

.NET continuously focuses on improving performance. Upcoming releases may include:

- **Optimized JIT Compilation:** Enhancements to the Just-In-Time (JIT) compiler to reduce startup time and improve runtime performance.
- **Garbage Collection Enhancements:** Further optimizations in garbage collection to reduce latency and improve memory usage efficiency.

New Language Features in C#

C# is evolving rapidly, and each version introduces new language features that simplify coding and enhance functionality. Upcoming C# features may include:

- **Pattern Matching Enhancements:** More advanced pattern matching capabilities to make code more concise and expressive.
- **Record Structs:** Introduction of record structs, allowing developers to create immutable value types with less boilerplate code.

Improved Cloud-Native Support

As cloud-native development becomes increasingly vital, .NET will continue to enhance its cloud capabilities:

- **Integration with Azure Services:** Improved libraries and tooling for seamless integration with Azure services, making it easier to build and deploy cloud-based applications.
- **Support for Serverless Architectures:** Features that facilitate building serverless applications, including improved support for Azure Functions.

.NET MAUI Enhancements

.NET MAUI, the successor to Xamarin.Forms, is set to gain new features and improvements, including:

- **Improved Performance and Flexibility:** Ongoing optimizations for rendering and performance across mobile and desktop platforms.
- **Expanded Controls and UI Components:** Additional built-in controls and components to enhance user experience and simplify development.

Enhanced Developer Tools and Ecosystem

Microsoft is committed to improving developer tools to enhance productivity:

- **Visual Studio Improvements:** New features in Visual Studio will streamline the development process, including better debugging tools, enhanced IntelliSense, and improved integration with GitHub.
- **.NET CLI Enhancements:** Enhancements to the .NET Command Line Interface (CLI) for more powerful and flexible command-line operations.

3. Strategies for Leveraging Upcoming Features

To effectively leverage the upcoming features in .NET, developers should consider the following strategies:

Stay Engaged with the .NET Community

Engage with the .NET community through forums, GitHub discussions, and Microsoft events. This engagement provides insights into upcoming features and allows developers to contribute feedback.

Experiment with Preview Versions

Take advantage of preview releases to test new features and provide feedback. This experimentation allows developers to prepare for migration and adopt new features more smoothly once they become stable.

Code Snippet: Installing a .NET Preview Version

```bash
dotnet new global.json --sdk-version 7.0.100-preview.5.21306.8
```

Regularly Review Release Notes

Keep up with the release notes for each version to understand new features, breaking changes, and deprecations. This practice helps ensure that applications are ready for future migrations.

Refactor for Compatibility

Periodically refactor your codebase to align with the latest best practices and features. This proactive approach will make future migrations easier and keep the codebase modern and maintainable.

The future of .NET is bright, with a clear roadmap and numerous enhancements on the horizon. By staying informed about upcoming features, engaging with the community, and proactively adopting new capabilities, developers can ensure that their applications remain competitive and high-performing.

Preparing for the changes in .NET not only enhances the quality of applications but also positions developers to take full advantage of advancements in technology. As you continue to build high-performance applications, these insights into the .NET roadmap will be invaluable in navigating the evolving landscape and future-proofing your development efforts.

www.ingramcontent.com/pod-product-compliance
Lightning Source LLC
Chambersburg PA
CBHW032210220526
45472CB00018B/656